WHEN KINGS RODE TO DELHI

WHEN
KINGS R[illegible]DE TO DELHI

GAB[illegible]TING

GYAN

Published by

GYAN

Gyan Publishing House
5, Ansari Road
Daryaganj, New Delhi-110002
Phone: 011-47034999, 9811692060
E-mail: books@gyanbooks.com

Distribution Network
gyanbooks.com
India, USA, Canada, UK, Australia, France

ISBN : 978-81-212-4217-2 (PB)
First Published, London, 1912

2nd Impression 2020

Printed at: Gyan Press, Delhi.

When Kings Rode to Delhi
Author: Gabrielle Festing

When Kings Rode to Delhi

BY

GABRIELLE FESTING

AUTHOR OF
'FROM THE LAND OF PRINCES,' 'JOHN HOOKHAM FRERE AND HIS FRIENDS,' 'ON THE DISTAFF SIDE,' ETC.

WITH ILLUSTRATIONS

William Blackwood and Sons
Edinburgh and London
1912

The House of Timur;
Timur, Babar, Humayun, Akbar, and Jahangir.

TO

G. S.,

F. M. F.,

AND

N. F.

PREFACE.

THIS book is an attempt to treat the history of Delhi as I had already treated the history of some of the states of Rajputana in a former book, 'From the Land of Princes.'

The principal sources from which it has been taken are, first and foremost, the eight volumes of the 'History of India as Told by its Own Historians' (edited by Elliot and Dowson); Ferishta's 'History of Hindustan'; the Memoirs of Babar; the Memoirs of Gul-badan Begam; the Ain-i-Akbari, and Akbarnameh; Manucci's 'Storia do Mogor'; Hawkins' Voyages; Sir T. Roe's Embassy; and Bernier's Travels. Among modern writers, Todd's 'Annals and Antiquities of Rajast'han'; Elphinstone's History of India; Keene's 'Turks in India,' and History of India; Erskine's 'Babar and Humayun'; Grant Duff's

'History of the Marathas'; S. Lane Poole's 'Mediaeval India'; J. B. Cunningham's 'The Sikhs'; W. L. Macgregor's 'Sikhs'; Forrest's 'Cities of India'; and Fanshawe's 'Delhi.'

The book is intended only for the general reader, or the traveller in India, and was written in the hope of making some of these realise a little of the fascination of the history of India in what a Rajput, speaking to the author, called "old-king-time." It is not intended for the scholar, but, should such a one take it up, he is entreated to remember that consistency in spelling is almost unattainable in a work of this kind. Certain names, such as "Meerut," have been left in an incorrect form because it was possible that the reader might have some association with them written thus; others, probably unfamiliar in any spelling appear in one of the forms approved by scholars and historians.

The illustrations are reproduced by permission from drawings and miniatures in the India Office. The portraits of Timur are merely conventional, since no genuine likeness of him was known to his descendant, the Emperor Jahangir. Though Manucci does not give her name, it seemed allowable to suppose that the beautiful drawing catalogued as "Gul Saffa, the mistress of Dara Shekoh," represents the dancing-girl whose story he tells.

My thanks are due to Sir Theodore Morison for his great kindness in reading and revising the proofs of the book; to Sir W. Lee-Warner; to Mr Foster, the Superintendent of Records at the India Office; to Dr Thomas, the Librarian at the India Office, for his kindness in facilitating and directing my search for drawings; and to the officials of the London Library.

September 1912.

CONTENTS.

ILLUSTRATIONS.

PROLOGUE

ON THE ROAD TO DELHI

PROLOGUE.

ON THE ROAD TO DELHI.

FROM Delhi, past Panipat to Karnal and Thanesar, stretches the great plain,—a dreary yellow waste, the dead level of its surface sometimes heaving into slight undulations, sometimes broken by tufts of coarse grass and low scrubby bushes showing where a little moisture has struggled through the burning sand—but everywhere weighing upon the beholder with the same sense of desolation and flatness.

"Everywhere a silent void, as if the plain were intended by Nature to be the battlefield of nations."

If this were the intent with which the great plain of Delhi was created, it has been fulfilled, over and over again, through nearly three thousand years. Long ago, in times when myth and history had not been separated, a great battle was fought near Thanesar, between two rival clans, the Kauravas and the Pandavas, about

1000 B.C. Two thousand years passed, and when the fierce Muslim, Mohammad Ghori, swept down from the north to destroy the Hindu temples and to slay the idolaters with the sword, it was upon this plain at Narain, beyond Karnal, that the last Rajput king of Delhi met him, and drove him back in 1191. Upon the same place, a year later, the Rajput host again waited the invader, and were defeated and mowed down by thousands. It was the death-blow to the Rajput dominion in Hindustan; never again has one of the fire-born races ruled in Delhi.

More than three hundred years later, Zahir-ad-din Babar, the Moghul, broke the undisciplined host of the Sultan Ibrahim Lodi near Panipat, and won Delhi for himself and his descendants. On the self-same spot his grandson, Akbar, overthrew the army of Bengal that would have driven him and his Khans back to the northern hills whence their fathers came. Nearly two hundred years more, and Nadir Shah the Persian was met on the plain by a feeble army and an unready king, who had not the spirit to die well, though they stood upon ground made holy with the blood of heroes. Three-and-twenty years after his coming, the leader of the great Maratha Confederacy sent round the word · "The cup is full to the brim and cannot hold another drop;" and led his host out of their fortified camp at Panipat to be cut to pieces by the Afghans of Ahmad Shah Daurani.

There is no wonder that the plain is haunted ground, and that the benighted wayfarer may still hear the shouts of phantom armies, the clash of their weapons and the neighing of their steeds, as he wanders over the darkling plain. For it is a far cry to Delhi, and many have found it farther than they could reach.

In the following pages are the stories of some of those who took the road to Delhi. Some came there only for the sake of spoil and plunder, others came because it had been proved many a time that who was master of Delhi could be master of all Hindustan.[1]

The story of the first battle upon the great plain belongs to the far-off ages when the gods came down from heaven and loved the daughters of men. Few English readers have ever persevered from the first to the last of the 220,000 long lines of the Mahabharata, which tells of the deadly feud between the five Pandavas, the sons of Pandu, and their cousins, the hundred Kauravas, the sons of the blind king Dhritarashtra. Dhritarashtra divided his kingdom be-

[1] Hindustan—the part of the Indian peninsula to the north of the Vindhya Mountains.

tween his sons and his nephews, giving the city of Hastinapura (fifty-nine miles to the north-east of Delhi) to the Kauravas, and the city of Indraprastha to the Pandavas. Not two miles out of the Delhi gate, where the massive walls and stately mosque of Sher Shah look across the plain, the name of "Indrapat" preserves the tradition that here, more than two thousand years before the time of Sher Shah, the five brothers made their fortress.

But the cousins could not be at peace with one another, and at length each clan gathered its hosts and encamped at Kurukshetra, "the field of the Kurus," near Thanesar.

For eighteen days they fought, each singling out his man and striving with him hand to hand, while arrows fell about them, "sparkling like the rays of the sun," and when the sudden Indian darkness covered the plain, they lighted torches and went on with the work. At length all the Kauravas were slain, and the Pandavas became lords of the realm.

For some time they ruled in such splendour as no king in India knew, before or after them, and then a curse fell upon them from the high gods. There were signs in heaven and on earth, everywhere portents of ill; a great earthquake slew many of their kin, others perished in a forest fire; the nymphs of Indra's heaven cried from the skies to the terrified people, "Arise, get you hence!"; a mighty wave of the sea swept inland, destroying one of the chief cities of Hindustan. Then the five brothers took the fire from their palace hearth and flung it into the bosom of Mother Ganges, in token that they had done with the things of this world; they left their kingdoms and their state, and wandered forth towards the rising sun, followed by their wife, Draupadi, fairest of women, and their faithful dog. On, on they journeyed till they reached the everlasting snow of the Himalayas, and there, first Draupadi, then the four younger brothers, one by one, fell and perished by the wayside. Only the eldest brother, with the dog, climbed upwards till he reached the cloud-peak of Mount Meru, where Indra, lord of the firmament, drinks the *amrita*—the water of life—in his paradise, the Swerga, with the lesser gods and with the souls of those who have attained to everlasting happiness. The gate opened wide to the Pandava, who would not enter without his dog, and through his love and loyalty, Draupadi and the four brothers were released from the torments wherewith they were expiating their sins in the flesh, and brought to dwell with him, blessed for evermore.

So, into the snows of Himalaya, or into the dazzling radiancy of the Swerga, vanish the forms of the brother kings who won their kingdom on the great plain. After them, no other figure is clearly revealed upon the road to Delhi for over two thousand years.

I.

MAHMUD OF GHAZNI—1000-1030

"The standards of the Sultan Mahmud then returned happy and victorious to Ghazni, the face of Islam was made resplendent by his exertions, the teeth of the true faith displayed themselves in their laughter, the breasts of religion expanded, and the back of idolatry was broken."

—Tarikh Yamini of Al' Utbi.

I.

MAHMUD OF GHAZNI—1000-1030.

THE real history of India begins with the Muslim conquest.

Strictly speaking, as has often been pointed out, there is no such thing as the history of India; there are the histories of the different races who from time to time have entered the country, for good or for ill. Some have swept over the land like a flight of locusts, blighting, wasting, destroying, but leaving no other trace to recall their presence when time had covered the desolation that they wrought. Others remained in the land, took to themselves wives from its daughters, and left the heritage that they had won with the sword to children in whose veins flowed the blood of two races. Then India conquered her conquerors; as the northern blood grew thin and feeble, they lost their grip upon the sword-hilt, and when a fresh flood of invasion swept down from beyond the Himalayas, it engulfed them beneath its tide, or washed them away to some backwater, unheeded and forgotten.

For nearly two thousand years after the Pandavas and Kauravas fought upon the great plain beyond Delhi, the mists hang round about Hindustan. Here and there a legend, a tradition, an inscription on rock or pillar, may give a glimpse of kings and princes. Alexander shows clearly, for a moment, pouring libations to the three great rivers, Indus, Jhelum, and Chenab, before he turns his back upon his farthest conquest. Chinese pilgrims between 300 and 600 A.D. have something to tell of their experiences. But all is broken and fragmentary, unsatisfactory as a puzzle of which half the pieces are lost.

The mists do not roll back and leave the stage clear until two years after Roderic, "the last of the Goths," and the chivalry of Spain had been overwhelmed in the eight days' battle on the banks of the Guadalete. Then, in the year 712, the Arabs occupied Sind. So far and no farther they advanced, for other than they were destined to reap the harvest of Hindustan "in the name of the Prophet."

It was the Turks who were to tread the road to Delhi, and it may be that the whole course of Indian history might have been changed if the son of a Turkish slave had not caught small-pox in his boyhood, and, being ugly, resolved to be terrible.

Sabuktagin, the slave, had been bought from a merchant of Turkestan by Alptagin, governor of Khorasan, who set up an independent little kingdom for himself in the heart of the Afghan mountains, at Ghazni.

It once befell that the slave had gone out hunting, and rode down a tiny fawn. He lifted it to his saddle, and was riding on, when he saw that the mother had followed him, crying in her distress. Her piteous eyes went to his heart, so that he gave her back her child. Fawn and doe sped away to the herd, yet as she went the mother turned back, again and again, to look at Sabuktagin.

That night, in a dream, the Prophet appeared to the slave, and told him that, since he had had compassion upon helpless creatures over which he had the mastery, God would give him the mastery over a kingdom in reward; let him not forget to be merciful unto men in the hour of his dominion.

On Alptagin's death, the dream was fulfilled; Sabuktagin became ruler of Ghazni in his place, and soon found his master's shoes too strait for him. Round him were the wild Afghan tribes—masterless men, thieves and murderers, continually at war among themselves, but capable of being united for conquest and plunder. Down into the

Kabul valley they followed Sabuktagin, under the green banner of the Prophet—the first Muslim to enter India through those gates of the North-West which have opened since then to many flood-tides of invasion—and returned, laden with spoil, to tell the reivers of the hills what unimaginable wealth lay beyond the mountain barriers.

For India was to the hungry Turk and Tatar what "the Indies" were to be to the poverty-stricken gentlemen of Spain. There was wealth in the teeming soil of Bengal, yielding two or three crops every year; there was wealth of wheat and palm in the upper provinces—sugar-cane, oil-seeds, flax, cotton, ginger, spices, and so forth. Even the jungles had their harvests of lac and silk cocoons. There was wealth of ivory, wealth of gold and silver and precious stones, stored in the palaces of the kings, or in those idol temples which it was the duty of every true believer to plunder and destroy. And all this was poorly defended; once beyond the gates of the hills, the plains lay open to the invader, divided up into petty kingdoms, ruled by petty kings, who were too much at odds with one another to combine against any foe.

The easiest method, in those times, to win both spiritual and material advantage, was to wage war against the infidel. Every Muslim who fell in the strife was sure of attaining Paradise; every Muslim who survived—if the place of campaign were judiciously chosen—had a good chance of making his fortune. So, when Sabuktagin died, King Mahmud his son vowed by God and his Prophet that every year he would lead a foray into Hindustan.

How that vow was kept during the years from 1000 to 1026, the Hindus knew to their cost. Raja Jaipal of Lahore, whom Sabuktagin had once defeated, could tell how he and his forces and his three hundred elephants were routed near Peshawar, and he and fifteen of his kindred brought prisoners before the conqueror, their necklaces of pearls and rubies, worth 90,000 guineas apiece, torn from them, and themselves set free, in clemency or contempt. The rajas of the Punjab could tell how Mahmud sent them in headlong rout, and slew and spoiled for two days upon end. The booty sent to Ghazni from the virgin fortress of Nagarkot could tell how the men of the hills fell upon the golden ingots and cups of silver, gold and silver pillars, "jewels and unbored pearls and rubies shining like sparks or iced wine, emeralds as it were sprigs of young myrtle, diamonds as big as pomegranates." Kanauj, then the chief city of Hindustan, girt with walls thirty miles round, could tell how her seven forts yielded in a single day, and how the neighbouring princes and chiefs were swept down by "the devilish Afghan spearmen, until the slave-markets of Persia were glutted, and a servant could be bought for a couple of shillings."

Every new victory brought fresh volunteers from beyond the Oxus, to swell the Muslim host. No hill was too steep, no snow too heavy, no river too swift, to stay the conqueror's march, and the terror-stricken Hindus whispered that "the Image-breaker" and the armies who followed him were not men of middle earth. United, the Hindu rajas might have defeated them over and over again; but then, as ever, they were divided by feuds and jealousies, and could make no stand against a host welded together by the two mightiest passions that can sway the soul of man—religious zeal, and greed of gain.

The crowning hour came in the winter of 1026, when Mahmud led his army across a desert three hundred and fifty miles broad, where there was little water, and still less forage for the horses, to attack the great temple of Somnath—then the richest and most famous shrine in India. Here was the holy place of Siva, and the stone that had fallen from Heaven. More than ten thousand villages had been bestowed upon the temple. A thousand Brahmins daily served its shrines, fi e hundred dancing-girls sang and postured at its gates. Three hundred barbers were kept to shave the pilgrims who came from all parts of India to the sacred place where the souls of men met after separation from the body, where the very waters of the Arabian Sea rose and fell in unending adoration of the Moon-God, the Lord of Birth and Death.

The long desert march was ended; the rajas who opposed Mahmud's progress were put to flight; travel-stained and toil-worn, the army gazed on the line of fortifications that linked the mainland with the peninsula upon which the temple stood. The battlements were crowded with armed warriors, and with priests who hurled curses at the invaders in the name of the god. For three days the battle raged round the walls; each day the Muslim were driven back, pierced with arrows, flung headlong from scaling-ladders. On the third day, fresh reinforcements came to the besieged, and the besiegers turned to flee. Then Mahmud flung himself from his horse upon the ground, and called upon the One True God, the God of battles, to come to the help of His own—as Elijah might have called before smiting the priests of Baal. Then once more he led his men to the assault. With wild shouts of "Allahu

Akbar," "God is great," they broke the enemy's lines; five thousand Hindus lay dead upon the field at the close of day, and the garrison, to the number of four thousand, took to their boats and escaped by sea.

Over the dead and the dying, amongst a swarm of fanatic priests who spat defiance at him, humming like angry bees, but not daring to resist further, and weeping votaries who called in vain upon the Great God, with hands clasped round their necks, Mahmud and his captains forced their way into the shrine. All within was dark, mysterious; no ray of sunlight was ever suffered to rest upon the fifty-six pillars, adorned with precious stones, that supported the roof; in the centre hung a single lamp, its light flickering over veils covered with gems, over the great gold chain, fifteen hundred pounds in weight, the pride and glory of the shrine, that supported the bronze bell sounded by worshippers when they came to pray, and over the rough men, with the reek of battle still upon them, who came stamping where never any feet save those of the priests had trod. Right before them was the idol itself.

"Hew the accursed thing in pieces," commanded Mahmud; "let one piece be set in the threshold of my mosque at Ghazni, and another in the threshold of my own palace, where true believers may trample upon them."

Then the priests fell upon their faces and entreated the conqueror; they alone knew where all the treasures of the temple were hidden—treasures far exceeding those which he saw around him. Let him take the last pearl, the last grain of gold-dust, and spare the sacred image.

The captains were ready to hear the prayer; idol-breaking was good sport, besides being a religious duty, but there was more solid satisfaction in acquiring riches. Mahmud whirled his mace about his head. "On the day of Resurrection, let me hear the call, 'Where is that Mahmud who broke the greatest of the heathen idols?'" he cried, "not 'Where is that Mahmud who sold it to the infidels for gold?'"—and he cleft the image asunder. As his followers pressed round, eager to smite in their turn, from a hollow within it there poured forth diamonds, pearls, rubies—a secret store, which the Brahmans had hoped to keep for themselves when all else was lost.

So runs the story, which has been a joy and an example to true Muslims of countless generations; and it is unkind, with modern commentators, to point out that there was no image in the central shrine at Somnath—only a rude stone cylinder (which being solid could not contain treasure), such as may be seen all over India to this day.

More than a year passed in plunder and conquest, in putting down one king and setting up another, before Mahmud turned from Gujarat, and set his face once more to the northern hills. The road by which he had come was blocked by two hostile armies, and his forces were so thinned by the sword and the climate that even he durst not offer battle to the enemies of the faith. Certain Hindus undertook to guide him, by way of the salt deserts to the east of Sind, and he set forth when the hot season was already far advanced—that hot season which no words can describe to those who have not experienced it, when the blind white glare of the sky is as brass overhead, and the ground is as iron underfoot, when there is no rest by day or by night, even for those in dwellings built to exclude the sun's rays. For three days and nights Mahmud and his army wandered among the sands, without water, tortured by the mirage, or the saline encrustations that mocked them with visions of distant pools and lakes, their throats dry, their tongues lolling out of their mouths with thirst. Many of the troops went raving mad, and perished miserably among the wastes and ridges of sand.

Then Mahmud turned upon the Hindu guides, and ordered that they should be put to the torture. In the extremity of torment, one of them laughed aloud. "We are Brahmans, and priests of Somnath! We have led the spoilers of temples, the slayers of cows, astray in the wilderness, and here shall their bones whiten, to tell how the Great God was avenged."

The army was distracted; some rushed to and fro, cursing the day when they came into India; some lay down in dumb despair and died. As was his wont upon the battlefield, Mahmud prostrated himself, and called upon the One True God to preserve his warriors. When a quarter of the night had been spent in prayer, a light shone to the north of the camp. "Lo, a sign from Allah!" Mahmud rose and led his army thither, and after a long night march they found water. Not yet, however, were their distresses over, for the wild Jats of the Salt Ranges fell upon them as they emerged from the desert, and it was a wearied and forlorn remnant that came back to Ghazni.

A retaliatory campaign against the Jats in the following year was Mahmud's last expedition into India. For the next four years he enjoyed the fruits of his labours, enriching Ghazni with cisterns, aqueducts, and a mosque which was the wonder of the East, founding and endowing a university, conversing with philosophers, divines and astronomers, and poets whom he compelled to his court, and in leisure moments copying out the Koran "for the good of his soul."

In the year 1030 he died—on the whole, the finest example of a Muslim conqueror that we shall meet until we come to Babar five hundred years later. Severe to his enemies, he was not vindictive or wantonly cruel; he was inflexibly just; though he slew the idolaters by thousands in fair fight, he never massacred them in cold blood for the sake of religion. In his family relations he was a striking contrast to Eastern potentates of all times, who habitually poisoned, blinded, or imprisoned inconvenient relations, for the better security of their thrones. Unfortunately for his reputation, he affronted the Persian Homer, Firdausi, who fastened upon him the reproach of avarice, which his lavish gifts to art and learning would disprove. Yet a picturesque tradition is stronger than fact, and amid the splendours of Ghazni men told how their founder, on his deathbed, loved his treasure so much that he would have it all brought before him, and then wept bitterly because he must leave it. And in Sa'adi's "Rose-Garden," we are told that in a vision a king of Khorasan saw Mahmud "dead for a hundred years," his body turned to dust, but his restless eyes still rolling in their sockets, looking for the gold that had passed into the keeping of another.

The vision was true, in another way from that which the poet intended: the gold was all that remained of Mahmud's conquests. He was a great soldier, a man of infinite courage and exhaustless energy in body and mind, but he was no builder of empires. He could make conquests, but he had no power to retain more of them than the spoil that he bore away to the mountains. All that he won in Persia was lost to his descendants within ten years of his death, and though they kept the Punjab, it was taken by a stronger power, with the other possessions of the Ghaznawid kings, in the following century.

In the Fort at Agra may yet be seen a pair of sandal-wood gates, brought from Mahmud's tomb at Ghazni by order of Lord Ellenborough, who imagined them to be part of the spoil that the Idol-breaker carried away from Somnath. There was to have been a formal restitution to the Brahmans, but before that could be arranged it was proved that the gates could have had no connection with Somnath or with Mahmud, as they dated from a period considerably later than his. They are almost the only relics left in Hindustan to recall the name of one who pointed the way upon the Delhi road to succeeding generations, though he himself never reached the city.

II.

THE TRIUMPH OF THE CRESCENT—1191-1206

"Surely never was a tragedy, not even of the house of Atreus, of deeper and more moving woe. It is the story of Juliet and her Romeo, but involving in the pathetic fate of these Rajput lovers the doom of a great mediæval Aryan empire."—Sir G. BIRDWOOD.

II.

THE TRIUMPH OF THE CRESCENT—1191-1206.

In Delhi, long ago, there was a great raja, named Anangpal. At the entrance of his palace he had placed two stone lions, and by their side he had fixed a bell in order that those who sought justice might strike it, whereupon he would summon them before him, hear their complaints, and render justice.

One day, a crow came and sat on the bell and struck it, and the raja asked who it was that made complaint. "It is a fact, not unknown, that bold crows will pick meat from between the teeth of lions; as stone lions cannot hunt for their prey, whence could the crow obtain food?" So the raja ordered that as the crow had thus complained of hunger, some goats and sheep should be killed, upon which it might feed for several days.

This tradition of Old Delhi has come down to us through a Muslim poet of the early fourteenth century, whose high-spirited indifference to dates leaves it uncertain whether the raja were Anangpal I., the Tuar, who refounded Delhi in 730 A.D., and left the Arrangpur Band near Old Delhi as his memorial, or his namesake, Anangpal II., who repeopled the city in 1052, as an inscription on the Iron Pillar testifies, six-and-twenty years after Mahmud of Ghazni had led his last expedition into India.

Delhi is supposed to have been colonised from Kanauj, one of the oldest and greatest states in India, during the sixth century, and it was then that they set up the Iron Pillar which stands to this day in the court of the Kutb Mosque. The Hindus say that it rested upon the head of the great World-Serpent, who upheld Mount Meru and the seven divisions of the earth upon his great coils. There came a foolish King of Delhi of the Tuar race, who, not content to take the story upon trust, must needs move the pillar, in the hope of seeing the snake. Wherefore the curse fell upon him that his kingdom also should be removed.

If there be any foundation for this story, the hero is probably the last King of Delhi, defeated in battle by one of the Tomara race, whose line became Kings of Delhi in their turn. Tuar and Tomara alike were Rajputs, and Rajputs ruled what were the three other greatest kingdoms of

India at that time—the Chauhans at Ajmir, the Rathors at Kanauj, the Baghilas at Gujarat.

The Rajputs were all sprung of the Kshatriya or warrior caste—that caste which grew so powerful in the mythical ages of Hindu history that the god Vishnu became incarnate as Parasu Rama in order to destroy them, and restore the authority of the Brahmans. In these days, though Rajput communities are to be found all over India, they are the ruling race only in the deserts and sand wastes and rugged hills of the country that is called after them, Rajputana, whither they fled when the Muslim conquerors drove them from cities and plains. Chief of all is the Maharana of Udaipur or Mewar, whom men call "the Sun of the Hindus," descended from a prince who expelled the Arabs from Sind when they had been established there for just one hundred years.

In many ways the Rajputs bear such a strong resemblance to the Highlanders of Scotland that one might seem to be reading some of Walter Scott's stories, with trifling differences of names and costumes. They had the same reckless daring, the same devoted loyalty to the chief to whom they were bound by the ties of their clan, the same love of sport, the same readiness to take offence and quarrel among themselves when they could find no other enemy to give them employment,—a weakness which ruined them as it ruined the Highlanders. Their women held a very different position from other women in India; queens and princesses went in and out freely among the men, sharing their sports and exercises, and even riding with them to battle, until they learned from the Muslims the custom of shutting up the women behind the curtain.

After all these centuries, the Rajput bearing remains what it was in their heroic age, something that marks them out from all other races of India; the poorest is by birth a gentleman, and therefore the equal of the greatest. To see a Rajput on horseback, clattering through the streets that his ancestors cleared with the sword, or on foot, swaggering through the press in a market-place, is to realise a scene from the legends that tell how Prithwi Raj or Goman Sing went forth "at the time of the year when kings go to battle."

The last Tomara King of Delhi had no sons, and when he came to die, he left his kingdom to his grandson, Rai Pithora of Ajmir, thereby uniting Chauhans and Tomaras under one head. Fiercely raged Jaya Chandra, Raja of Kanauj, the son of another daughter of the Tomara, who had looked to join Delhi to Kanauj and be over-lord of all the Hindus.

There was a solemn rite called the Aswamedha or Horse Sacrifice that only great kings might celebrate. The horse was consecrated and set loose to stray at its will, followed by the owner or his champion. If any man ventured to stop or turn it aside, the champion must give battle, and if it went unchecked till the period of its wandering was over, that was a sign that all men over whose territories it had passed acknowledged the supremacy of its owner. To these material difficulties were added religious ones; as the celebrant of a hundred Aswamedhas became equal to Indra, lord of the firmament, "the golden god" was always on the watch against a rival, and usually carried off the sacred horse by fraud or by violence, before it could be sacrificed with solemn rites on its return.

In spite of all these obstacles, Rai Pithora succeeded in performing the Aswamedha, the last king, it is said, who was ever to celebrate it, and was acknowledged as "Prithwi Raj" or sovereign lord. By way of retaliation, Jaya Chandra issued invitations to the wedding of his daughter, who, according to ancient usage, was to choose a husband from among the assembled princes. A solemn feast was to be made, and every one who took part in it, down to the scullions in the kitchen, must be of royal blood. Like the Aswamedha, this feast is a claim to supremacy on the part of the holder.

Rajas, princes, chieftains came from every part of the land, for not one but had heard of the beauty and wisdom of the Princess Sangagota. Some say that Prithwi Raj was not invited, others that he refused to appear as the vassal of Kanauj. However it was, he came not, and so Jaya Chandra had his image modelled in clay and set up as doorkeeper—the lowest office of all.

The princes were gathered in the great hall at Kanauj, and the Princess entered, bearing the garland that she was to fling round the bridegroom whom she chose. One glance round the assembly, and she had turned quickly to the right and thrown the wreath about the neck of the clay image. An armed figure rose in her path, strong hands swung her to the back of the horse that pawed at the gate, and Prithwi Raj himself was carrying off his bride. Through five days they rode, while he and his companions kept up a running fight with their pursuers, and in the end he brought her safely to Delhi.

Some miles beyond modern Delhi stands "Kila Rai Pithora," the massive fort that he built to defend his city, and within the circuit of its walls remain many of the pillars of the twenty-seven Hindu and Buddhist places of worship that it contained in his time. He had need to strengthen his defences. Jaya Chandra, though he sent his daughter's wedding clothes after her, had not forgiven his son-in-law, and would give him no help against the enemy that advanced upon Delhi in the year 1191,—nay, some would have it that he actually invited Mohammad Ghori to chastise the prince who had robbed him of a kingdom and a daughter.

The Ghaznawid kings, the successors of the Idol-breaker, had continued to count the Punjab among their dominions, and one of its governors, who had been Mahmud's treasurer, made a raid upon Benares, farther east than any Muslim army had dared to go before his time. He only held it for a few hours, and was then obliged to retreat, but he and his men used those few hours to the best advantage, and returned with plunder that recalled the days of Mahmud. In the hundred years that followed, the kings of Ghazni dwelt among their hills, with little or no influence upon the history of India, until they were defeated and driven out by another hill clan, the Afghans of Ghor, who took Ghazni by storm, leaving scarcely one stone upon another. Only the marble tomb of the Idol-breaker and two tall minarets remain to show where stood the palaces, libraries, museums, and mosques that he and his successors founded.

The Ghaznawids took refuge in the Punjab, and made Lahore their capital. In 1186 the last of them was imprisoned by Mu'izz-ad-din, commonly known as Mohammad Ghori, who with his brother had succeeded to the chieftaincy of the Afghans of Ghor. The brothers were descended from Zohak, "the Snake," the first of kings to order offending subjects to be crucified or flayed alive, who was condemned to all eternity to be devoured by the two serpents that sprang from the place where Eblis had kissed his shoulders.

The elder brother, Ghiyas-ad-din, remained at Ghor, while Mohammad followed in the path of the Image-breaker. "Thirty years had Mahmud ravaged Hindustan from the Indus to the Ganges; and for thirty years Mohammad Ghori harried the same country in the same way."[1] Beginning with the Arab colony in Sind, he worked systematically down to Lahore, and then advanced upon Sirhind.

With such an enemy on their borders it was time that all the Rajput powers forgot their differences and united to expel him. Over and over again in their history had all their bravery bene-

[1] S. Lane Poole.

fited them nothing, because they would not lay aside some trivial quarrel for the common good. Jaya Chandra wished to see his son-in-law humbled, careless of what that humbling might bring to the other Rajput states. Gujarat was jealous of Delhi, and held aloof. Prithwi Raj went forth alone to meet the invader at Narain, north of Kurnal, on the great plain outside Delhi.

Mohammad's men had had no experience of a Rajput charge, and at the first onset his right and left wings fell back. A breathless messenger rushed to him where he stood in the centre, and advised him to look to his own safety, since the day was lost. "Enraged at this counsel, he cut down the messenger, and rushing on towards the enemy with a few followers, committed terrible slaughter." He charged the elephant of Prithwi Raj's brother, the Viceroy of Delhi, and delivered his lance full into the prince's mouth, knocking out many of his teeth. Prithwi Raj, seeing his brother's danger, sent an arrow through Mohammad's right arm, and the Afghan, faint with loss of blood, would have fallen from his horse if a faithful servant had not leapt up behind him and carried him off the field. Some say that he actually fell, and lay unconscious among a heap of dead, until rescued by some of his bodyguard, who had returned under cover of night to search for his corpse. His army fled headlong, and was pursued by the exulting Rajputs for nearly forty miles.

Mohammad went back to Ghor, aching with the sense of defeat. The first thing that he did on his return was to disgrace every officer who had not followed him in his last desperate charge to the Rajput's elephant, parading them round the city like a string of horses or mules, with their noses thrust into bags filled with barley, "which he forced them to eat like brutes," and then throwing them into prison.

A year was spent "in pleasure and festivity"; then he gathered an army of 120,000 chosen horse, strong-limbed muscular Afghans and Turks, their helmets encrusted with jewels, their armour inlaid with gold and silver, and set off from Ghazni without deigning to tell any man whither he led them.

When he reached Peshawar, a wise old man of Ghor prostrated himself before him and cried, "O King, we trust in thy conduct and wisdom, but as yet we know not thy design."

Mohammad answered him: "Old man, know that since the time of my defeat in Hindustan, notwithstanding what appeared to the eye, I have never slumbered in ease, or waked but in sorrow and anxiety. I have therefore determined with this army to recover my lost honour from those idolaters, or die in the attempt."

Then the old man, kissing the ground, spake once more: "Victory and triumph be thine attendants, and fortune be the guide of thy paths! But, O King, let the petition of thy slave find favour in thy ears, and let those whom thou hast justly disgraced be suffered with thee to wipe out the stain upon their reputation."

So word was sent back to Ghazni that the disgraced officers should be set at liberty, and that any who wished to retrieve lost fame might join his army. One and all flocked to the camp, and Mohammad, who had learned wisdom from the old man, gave each a robe of honour according to his rank. King and army athirst to cleanse their tarnished honour in Hindu blood, they moved down to Lahore, whence Mohammad sent an ambassador to Prithwi Raj, summoning him to accept Islam, or to meet the true believers in battle.

Now the sense of impending evil hung heavily over the Chauhan Raja, and by night the shadows of doom fell across his spirit. He dreamed that a woman, fairer than all the daughters of men, seized him and bore him from Sangagota; then she disappeared, and he thought that a great war elephant bore down upon him and crushed him, and he woke with panting heart and quivering lips muttering the Rajput war-cry.

He told his dream to Sangagota in the morning, and she knew well that it portended death and disaster; but she answered him in the words handed down to us by the minstrel Chand Bardai, who had ridden with his master when Prithwi Raj brought the princess on his saddle-bow from Kanauj to Delhi.

"Victory and fame to my lord! O Sun of the Chauhans, in glory and in pleasure who has tasted so deeply as thou? To die is the destiny, not only of man but of the gods. All desire to throw off the old garment; to die well is to live for ever. Think not of self, but of immortality; let the sword divide the foe, and I will be one with thee[1] hereafter."

Then the Raja went forth and performed sacrifice to the gods: but neither prayers nor offerings could reverse the doom.

When Mohammad's ambassador reached him, Prithwi Raj saw that here was the danger which his soul had foreboded. He was not one to change his creed at an enemy's bidding, but he had seen enough of his enemy to fear that he would not easily be driven back again without

[1] *Lit.*: "I will be your *ardhanga*"—your half-body.

the help that Kanauj and Gujarat refused to give. While his council deliberated, he went to the women's rooms and asked counsel of Sangagota.

"Who asks women for advice?" she began, as if in mockery; and then cast self on one side and rose to his need. "We are at once thieves and sanctuaries, we are vessels of virtue and of vice, of knowledge and of ignorance. . . . They say: 'In woman there is no wisdom.' Yet woman shares your joys and your sorrows. Even when you depart for the mansion of the sun, we part not. . . . We are as the lake, and you are the swans; what are you when absent from our bosoms?"

Then the Raja understood that even though he went to death, his wife would follow him, and he mustered his hosts. When the day of parting came, Sangagota armed him for battle. "In vain she sought the rings of his corslet; her eyes were fixed on the face of the Chauhan, as those of the famished wretch who finds a piece of gold. The sound of the drum reached the ear of the Chauhan; it was as a death-knell to her; and as he left her to head Delhi's heroes, she vowed that henceforth only water should sustain her. 'I shall see him again in the mansion of the sun; but never more in Delhi!'"

Only the Gehelot Raja of Chitor waited with Prithwi Raj upon the same field of Narain where he had vanquished Mohammad in the previous year. Yet it was a goodly host that confronted the Afghans on the opposite bank of the river Sarasvati, with long miles of tents that covered the plain, and standards and pennons streaming against the eastern sky. So strong were they in their own eyes that they wrote to Mohammad Ghori pointing out their superiority in numbers, and offering to allow him to retreat in safety if he repented of his rashness in coming against them.

Mohammad returned a courteous answer; he was only the general of his brother, and could not retreat without leave. He would report their offer to the king, and until an answer should arrive, he should be glad if there might be truce between the hosts.

The Rajputs assented, and passed the interval in sports and revelling, till one night Mohammad crossed the Sarasvati ere break of dawn, and fell upon their camp.

Thrown into confusion at first, the Rajput cavalry rallied, and held the Afghans in play till the main body of the army had formed up. All day the fight raged, and it was sunset when Mohammad, who had learned something of Rajput tactics from his disaster, lured them out of their lines by a feigned retreat. As they thundered headlong in pursuit, forgetting all else in the delight of riding down a flying enemy, Mohammad led his reserves—twelve thousand men in steel armour—upon the scattered host. Panic and confusion spread through the ranks of the Rajputs, and "this prodigious army, once shaken, like a great building tottered to its fall and was lost in its own ruins." "For miles the stricken field was bestrewn with castaway flags and spears and shields, and heaped bows, and jewelled swords, and plumed casques, and exquisitely chiselled and damascened gauntlets, greaves, and breastplates, and gaily dyed scarves, intermingled with the countless dead."

The Viceroy of Delhi, the Raja of Chitor, and nearly a hundred and fifty princes and chieftains, the flower of Rajast'han, lay dead upon the field. Mohammad identified the Viceroy's body by the mark of his own lance-blow, given in the former battle. Of Prithwi Raj's fate many stories are told. One says that he was surrounded and taken prisoner, sword in hand, and murdered in cold blood when the fight was over; another, that sent in chains to Ghazni, to be exhibited to the populace when his conqueror should return in triumph, he died on the way by his own hand. Another story makes him dismount from his elephant when the day was lost, and flee on horseback towards Delhi, being cut down by his pursuers before he could reach Sangagota. A sadder legend still—probably without foundation —tells of a day when, grown old and blind in prison, he was brought forth, like Samson, to make sport for his enemies. However and wherever he died, Sangagota saw him no more on earth. Decked in her bridal jewels, she mounted the pyre, and went to meet him through the flames.

Ajmir was taken by assault, and its inhabitants put to the sword, or reserved for slavery. Mohammad's favourite slave, Kutb-ad-din Aybek, took Delhi, and was left as Viceroy of Hindustan while Mohammad went back to Ghazni for a while.

In the following year, when Mohammad returned to India, Jaya Chandra of Kanauj led an army against him. It was too late to save daughter and son-in-law, too late to save the Rajput dominion in Hindustan,—nothing was left to the miserable old man whose selfish resentment had opened the way to the invader, except to make a good end—and he made it, upon the banks of the Jumna, between Chandwar and Etawa, fighting to his last breath. His body was identified among the heaps of slain by his case of false teeth, held together by gold wire.

Benares fell; the idols in more than a thousand

temples were broken to pieces, the temples were purified and consecrated to Muslim worship before Mohammad's army, lāden with treasure, took the road to Ghazni. The Rathors of Kanauj fled into the deserts of Marwar ("the region of death"), where they have remained ever since.

Ghiyas-ad-din's death, a few years later, made his brother king in name as well as in fact. By this time the greater part of northern India had fallen to him or to his lieutenants, and if Mohammad had been satisfied to enjoy it, he might have founded a great Muslim kingdom in Hindustan. But it was to the north, not to the south, that his ambition pointed, and in an expedition against the modern Khiva he met total defeat. Scarcely a hundred men of his army were left with him to cut their way through their enemies, and retire to Ghazni.

At the news of this disaster, the chief cities of his dominions promptly set up new rulers. The Ghakkars—a race of mountaineers living at the foot of the Sivalik range "without either religion or morality"—overran the Punjab and seized Lahore. Kutb-ad-din Aybek, faithful to his salt, came to his master's help. The Ghakkars, caught between two armies, were defeated and dispersed, Lahore was recovered, Multan and the other rebellious cities were reduced to order.

Gathering a fresh army, Mohammad was on his way to conquer Turkestan, when he was murdered in his tent upon the banks of the Indus, in 1206, by a band of twenty Ghakkars, sworn to avenge the death of their king. "His spirit flew above the eight Paradises and the battlements of the inner heavens, and found those of the ten Evangelists." "The treasure he left behind him," we are told, "is almost incredible; he had in diamonds alone, of various sizes, four hundred pounds' weight."

Cut short in the middle of his career, he had yet achieved something. He had left a Muslim ruler at Delhi, and from that hour, until the proclamation of the White Queen, a Muslim has been king there.

Prithwi Raj, too, has left his mark, not only in the massive lines of the fortifications he built to keep out the invader, but in the hearts of his countrymen, to whom he was "the personification of every Rajput virtue, the pattern of all Rajput manhood." To his story—so it is said—half the men and women in India still listen on winter nights.

It was afternoon on May 11, 1857—more than six hundred and sixty years since Prithwi Raj had fled from the stricken field at Narain. The companies of the 38th Native Infantry, set to guard the powder magazine, broke from all control. They would not kill their officers, like other native regiments, but they would not wait inactive, when the Great Mutiny had woke the city at early morning. As they hurried to join the comrades who were looting and burning in all directions, their cry was the battle-cry never heard in Delhi since the days of the last Chauhan raja—"Prithwi Raj ki jai!"[1]

[1] "Victory to the kingdom of Prithwi!" or "Hail to the kingdom of Prithwi!"

III.

THE SLAVE KINGS OF DELHI

Kutb-ad-din Aybek . .	1206-1210
Shams-ad-din Altamish .	1211-1236
Raziya-ad-din . . .	1236-1240
Ghiyas-ad-din Balban .	1266-1287

"The whole country of India is full of gold and jewels, and of the plants which grow there are those fit for making wearing apparel, and aromatic plants and the sugar-cane, and the whole aspect of the country is pleasant and delightful. Now since the inhabitants are chiefly infidels and idolaters, by the order of God and his Prophet, it is right for us to conquer them." —*Malfuzat-i-Timuri.*

III.

THE SLAVE KINGS OF DELHI.

I.

A WELL-MEANING friend once ventured to condole with Mohammad Ghori because he had no sons to come after him.

"What matters that?" answered the Sultan. "Have I not thousands of sons in my Turkish slaves?"

To Western minds it seems impossible that slaves could ever take the place of sons, whereas it was a matter of common experience in the East. Too often does the son of a great man fall as much below the common level as his father rises above it: the slave was selected for some special quality, owed his advancement to his wits, and knowing that he was liable to be cast down in an instant if he failed his lord, took care not to disappoint him.

The slave whom Mohammad sent as his representative to Delhi was a Turkoman, Aybek ("Moon lord"). Sold in childhood to a rich merchant of Naishapur, his talents were soon discovered by his master, who sent him to school; sold, with the rest of the estate, after the merchant's sudden death, he passed into the hands of Mohammad Ghori.

On a night of festivity, Mohammad distributed rich gifts among all his slaves; Aybek received his share with the rest, but gave it away to his fellows as soon as they were dismissed from the presence.

This came to the ears of Mohammad, who sent for Aybek and asked why he had not chosen to keep his master's gifts.

"All that this poor slave can need is already supplied by your Majesty's bounty," answered Aybek, kissing the ground; "he has no desire to burden himself with superfluities, so long as he retains your Majesty's favour."

This reply pleased the Sultan, who gave Aybek an office near his person, and shortly afterwards appointed him Master of the Horse. On Mohammad's disastrous expedition against Khiva, Aybek was made prisoner, and loaded with irons; a few days later, the King of Khiva having been defeated, Aybek was discovered sitting on a camel on the field, and welcomed with great joy by his master.

When Mohammad Ghori returned to Ghazni after overcoming Prithwi Raj, he left Aybek, now known as Kutb-ad-din ("Polestar of the Faith"), as his viceroy in India, to carry on the work of conquest. When he came back in the following year, Aybek met him at Peshawar, with a present of horses and elephants. It was an arrow from the bow of Aybek that slew the Raja of Benares in the great battle on the banks of the Jumna. The Sultan rewarded him with the present of a white elephant taken from the Raja, which he ever afterwards rode, and which is said to have pined away with grief at his death.

Ajmir, Gwalior, and Gujarat yielded in turn to Mohammad's viceroy, and one of his fellow slaves took possession of Bengal in Mohammad's name.

There is a story that seeing Aybek grow in power every day, jealous rivals began to hint to Mohammad that the slave was aiming at nothing less than the kingdom for himself. Some friend at Court sent information to Aybek, who immediately left India and travelled at topmost speed to Ghazni. One morning, when the Court was all assembled, the Sultan asked whether it were true that Aybek had revolted.

"Too true, alas!" replied Aybek's rivals. "He

has thrown off his allegiance—we know for certain that he designs to make himself king."

Then the Sultan kicked the foot of the throne upon which he sat and clapped his hands together, calling "Aybek!"

"Here I am," answered the viceroy, as he came forth from the place beneath the throne where his master had hidden him.

In shame and terror, the accusers prostrated themselves and kissed the ground. "I pardon you this time," proclaimed the Sultan: "beware how you speak against Aybek again."

"My son," Mohammad called the slave, and Aybek was more faithful to him than many sons in Oriental history to their fathers.

In 1206 came the reward. After Mohammad Ghori had fallen under the daggers of the Ghakkars, his nephew and successor at Ghazni sent throne, canopy, standards, drums, and other tokens of royalty to Aybek, "desirous of securing his interest, and being by no means able to oppose his power if he refused to acknowledge him."

It needed no ordinary man to hold the sceptre of Delhi, where the Muslim soldiers and officials were a garrison in an alien land. The upper classes lay dead upon the battlefields where the Crescent had borne them down, or had fled beyond the reach of the invaders, but the middle classes — merchants and tradesfolk — and the peasants were many millions, while their conquerors, though continually recruited from the north, were few in number in comparison. The Muslims, however, had a powerful ally in their religion, while the Hindus were hampered at every turn by the laws of caste. With the Muslims, every man who could wield a sword might strike a blow for God and His Prophet; with the Hindus, the warriors formed a caste by themselves. With the Muslims, every man who was not of Islam was bound to go, to quote the words of one of their own historians, "into that fire which God has lighted for infidels and those who deny a resurrection, for those who say no prayers, hold no fasts, and tell no beads. Amen"; every one who accepted Islam was free to rise to any rank or distinction in this world, and was tolerably certain of a good place in the next. The Hindus were equally convinced of the future of those who differed from them in religion; but with them each man must remain in the caste to which he was born. This in itself kept them divided, while the faith of the Prophet united men of every race and class against them.

Delhi prospered under Aybek's rule, if we may believe the Muslim historians; "he continued to exercise justice, temperance, and morality; his kingdom was governed by the best laws,"—which naturally means that preference was given to Muslims, though we are told by another writer that in Aybek's reign "the people were happy," and "the wolf and the sheep drank together out of the same pond." His reign was a short one; only four years after having been proclaimed King of Delhi, in 1210 he was thrown against the pommel of his saddle while playing polo at Lahore, and received an injury which caused his death.

He left an everlasting memorial of himself within what had been the Fort of Prithwi Raj: there he built the innermost court of the Kutb Mosque in 1191, and six years later, added the screen of arches in front of the west end of the court. All his materials were taken from the Jain and Hindu temples in the Fort, and the curious may still discover Jain figures, half effaced, upon the beautifully carven pillars, among flowers, leopards' heads, bells, and tassels, or trace the birth of Krishna above the window on the outer side of the north wall.

> "The Mosque is the depository of the grace of God,
> The music of the prayer of it reaches to the moon,"

says Amir Khusru, "the Parrot of Hind," who

saw it less than a hundred years after the time of Aybek. At the south-east angle of the court, like the campanile of some Italian cathedral, rises the tallest minaret in the world, the Kutb Minar; begun by Aybek and completed by his successors, it preserves the name of the Turkoman slave who founded the Muslim kingdom of Delhi.

Four hundred years after his death men in Hindustan had found no higher praise for generosity than to say, "Such a one is as liberal as Kutb-ad-din-Aybek."

II.

In the days when Mohammad Ghori was making his way gradually towards Hindustan, there was a certain Khan of Turkistan whose youngest son was remarkable for such grace, intelligence, and beauty as excited jealousy in the hearts of his elder brothers. One day, under pretext of taking the child to see a drove of horses, they enticed him from father and mother, and sold him to the horse-dealers, who carried him to Bokhara, where he was bought by "a great and noble family," who nourished and educated him like a son.

In after years, he was wont to tell how once

he was given a piece of money and sent to the bazaar to buy grapes. On the way he lost the money, and "being of tender age, began to cry for fear": while he wept, a faquir came up to him, and hearing his trouble, took him by the hand, bought grapes, and gave them to him with the words, "When you obtain wealth and dominion, take care that you show respect to faquirs and pious men, and maintain their rights." The child promised, and did not forget to keep his word: "It is firmly believed that no king so benevolent, so sympathetic, and so respectful to the learned and to the old as he was, ever rose by his native energy to the cradle of empire."

From the great and noble family he passed to a merchant, who brought him to Ghazni, and offered him to the Sultan Mohammad. "No Turk equal to him in beauty, virtue, intelligence, and nobleness had at that time been brought to that city," and when the Sultan offered a thousand dinars in refined gold, the merchant refused to sell him for so low a price. Thereupon the Sultan gave orders that no one else should buy him, and the merchant, after staying for a year in Ghazni, in the hope of doing business, went back disconsolate to Bokhara, taking his property with him.

After three years he again brought the boy to Ghazni, and found that no one dared to purchase him in defiance of the Sultan. Another year of waiting had passed when Aybek, who had just conquered Gujarat, came to Ghazni, heard of the slave, and asked his master's leave to buy him.

"I said that no man should buy him in Ghazni, and no man shall," returned the Sultan; "if you want him, take him to Delhi and buy him there."

So the slave was brought to Delhi, and became the property of Aybek. The meaning and correct pronunciation of the Turkoman name he had borne up to that time are both unknown. The usual form is "Altamish," which has no meaning, but may be a corruption of a Turki word—Il-tutmish, "Hand-grasper."

The Viceroy of Hindustan, who had begun life as a slave, loved the gracious youth, whom he made chief of the guards and kept near his person, calling him his son. When Aybek brought his army from Hindustan to crush the Ghakkars, the gallantry of Altamish attracted the attention of Sultan Mohammad, who saw him ride into the bed of the Jhelum to pursue the enemy, "sending them from the tops of the waves through the depths of hell." On learning that this was the lad whom he had forbidden his subjects of Ghazni to purchase, he called him into his presence and bade Aybek "treat him well, since he was destined to great works." Aybek then formally set Altamish free, and made him indeed a son by marrying him to one of his daughters.

Aybek's own son proved so unfit to take his father's place that the principal men of Delhi invited Altamish to rule in his stead. As Shams-ad-din Altamish, the new king reigned in Delhi, and had to fight for his throne with rivals in various parts of Hindustan; "but as he was assisted by divine favour, every one who resisted him or rebelled was subdued."

It was in his reign that Chingiz Khan, the Mongol, swept across Asia, sending kings and armies to right and left of him in desperate fear. Jalal-ad-din, the Shah of what is now Khiva—successor to him who had been too many for Mohammad Ghori—was driven towards Lahore, whither Altamish came to meet him with an army. Beaten back, the Shah retreated towards Sind: thither Chingiz Khan followed him, marching with such haste that "there was no difference between night and day, and no time for cooking food," and cut his army to pieces. The Mongol army wintered in the plains of Hindustan (1221-2), in order to keep watch on Jalal-ad-din's movements, and the unhappy Turkish governor of the province in which they cantoned themselves, perforce "bound the girdle of obedience round his waist, and provided all the supplies he could for the use of the army." In the spring they returned to Central Asia by the way they came.

After their departure Altamish gradually extended his authority, until nearly the whole of Hindustan was more or less subject to him, and in 1229 he was recognised as sovereign of India by the "Commander of the Faithful," the Caliph of Baghdad, who sent an embassy to Delhi.

Among all his conquests, he found time to continue some of Aybek's other work. He completed the Kutb and added another courtyard to the mosque, at the north-west corner of which his tomb may be seen. "One of the richest examples of Hindu art applied to Mohammadan purposes that old Delhi affords," the Slave King's last resting-place was probably built by the daughter whose story is one of the saddest memories that cling about the city.

III.

Altamish could conquer an empire and rule it; but, successful in all else, he was as unsuccessful as King Solomon in training his sons. The eldest died before him, and is buried at the village of Malakpur, beyond Delhi; of the others, each was more incompetent, foolish, and idle than his brother.

As is often seen in the children of great men, the daughter had all the talents and abilities which the son lacked. Raziyat-ad-din[1] Begam was her father's favourite, "although she was a girl and lived in retirement." She could read the Koran with correct pronunciation, and was so capable in other ways that while he was at the siege of Gwalior, he appointed her regent in his absence. So well did she fulfil her trust that on his return he ordered his ministers to prepare a firman appointing her heir to the kingdom and successor to the throne.

The scandalised ministers remonstrated; it was a thing without precedent to make a mere woman rule over true believers, and could not be tolerated. True, the Princess Raziya was the child of his Majesty's chief wife, Aybek's daughter, while the heir-apparent was the child of a slave, but a double strain of royal blood could not atone for the disability of sex.

"My sons are devoted to the pleasures of youth," answered Altamish; "not one of them is fit to be king. They are not able to rule the country. After my death, you will find no one more qualified to rule the state than my daughter."

[1] "Devoted to the Faith."

It was afterwards agreed by common consent that the "king had judged wisely," confesses a Delhi historian; but when Altamish died, custom and religious prejudice were too strong for the nobles of Delhi, who took Rukn-ad-din Firoz Shah, Raziya's half-brother, and proclaimed him king.

"He was very generous; no king in any reign had ever scattered gifts, robes of honour, and grants in the way that he did." Singers, dancing-girls, and buffoons grew wealthy by his favour; and even the common people shared in his largesse when he rode out upon an elephant through streets and bazaars, in his drunken jollity "flinging *tankas* of red gold around him, for people to pick up and rejoice over." He was handsome, which makes for popularity with the crowd, and his neglect of the affairs of state might have done him no harm if he had found some competent minister to rule while he reigned.

"Kings should possess all virtues that their people may live at ease," says the chronicler already quoted. "They should be generous, that the army may live satisfied; but sensuality, gaiety, and the society of the base and unworthy, bring an empire to ruin."

The moral is excellent, though it has little or no application to Rukn-ad-din Firoz, who perished by reason not of his own vices, but the vices of his mother.

This woman, Shah Turkan, had been a Turki slave-girl, promoted to be the wife of the king, flouted and scorned by the ladies of the harem for her low birth. In her husband's lifetime she could only console herself with a parade of devotion, lavishing offerings upon shrines and holy men; now that her son's weakness gave her an opportunity, she avenged past slights by putting to a cruel death the rivals who had mocked her. Her next victim was Kutb-ad-din, Raziya's brother, whom she caused to be blinded, and afterwards to be slain.

Raziya, careless of her own danger, attacked mother and son with vehement reproaches. Rebellion broke out in Hindustan, and while the king led an army to repress it, Shah Turkan plotted to seize Raziya and slay her as her brother had been slain.

Now Altamish had made an edict that any one coming to demand justice at his hands should put on a coloured dress, so as to be distinguished at a glance among the white-robed crowd. On a Friday morning, as devout Muslims thronged to the chief mosque of Delhi, they saw Raziya standing upon the terrace of the old palace, looking down upon them. She was clad in the garments of the wronged, and made an appeal not to the king but to the people, reminding them of the long reign of her father, and the many benefits he had conferred upon them. Now the wise old king was dead, and his daughter must ask justice from those to whom he had rendered it many a time. "My brother has killed his brother, and now he would slay me also."

As she pleaded before them, eloquent as the wisest, helpless as the poorest, all Delhi rose in revolt. The wicked queen-mother was thrown into the prison she had prepared for her step-daughter, and Rukn-ad-din Firoz, hurrying back at the news of his mother's imprisonment, was met by "an army of Turks and nobles," who seized him and brought him before Raziya. Some say that she sent him to prison and that he died there in a short time of the usual illness that carries off deposed rulers in an Eastern country. But one writer says that as he cowered before her, Raziya turned away with the words, "Let the slayer be slain,"—and that the people massacred him forthwith in revenge for his murdered brother, whom they had loved.

The next heir to Delhi was only a child, so the

nobles and officers agreed to obey the firman of Altamish. Raziya was proclaimed King[1] of Delhi —the first woman to sit upon a Muslim throne, —the only woman to sit upon the throne of Delhi until the days of Queen Victoria.

And now the real tragedy begins. There are instances throughout the centuries of Muslim women exercising power "from behind the veil" as regents, from Chand Bibi of Ahmadnagar to the present Begum of Bhopal. But they ruled as women, not as men. Our Queen Elizabeth, set upon a very insecure throne, with a very imperfect title to it, among men in no way disposed to submit to petticoat government, used her sex as a weapon in the struggle, and prevailed. But Raziya, like many a woman since her time, thought that to ignore her sex was the only way to prevail. So she flung aside the woman's skirts, discarded the veil without which no decent Muslim woman would be seen in public, wore cap and tunic like a man, and gave audience every day with uncovered face.

This was too much for respectable people, such as her Turkish nobles, known as "the Forty," in whose hands was all the real power. It was nothing to them that "the King" led

[1] King or Sultan — not Sultana — "Rex Noster," like Maria Theresa.

her troops boldly and successfully against rebels, pitching her tent in the midst of her army. Courage in a woman was not needed, but decency was imperative, and what decency was left to one who allowed her Abyssinian Master of the Horse to lift her on and off her steed "by raising her up under the arms"?

So the men rose against the woman who had forgotten woman's wisdom. The Governor of Lahore, the first to revolt, was obliged to sue for pardon, but while Raziya was on the way to punish another rebel, Altuniya, Governor of Bhatinda, all the Turkish chiefs in her army mutinied. There was a conflict, in which the Abyssinian slave was killed, and the Queen was sent as a prisoner to Bhatinda, and her young brother, Prince Bahram, made king in her stead.

In prison, Raziya seems to have made the discovery that at direst need a lonely woman's best weapons are usually feminine. She worked upon her jailer, Altuniya, till either from love or from policy he married her, and having raised an army of Ghakkars, Jats, and other tribesmen, the two rode forth together to regain her throne.

Defeated near Delhi, the dauntless Queen gathered another army at Bhatinda, and again tried conclusions with her brother. Again she was defeated, her husband slain, and herself driven to fly to the jungles. As she urged her tired horse by unfrequented tracks, she found a peasant tilling his field, and begged him for food. He gave her a piece of bread, which the starving woman ate greedily, and then, worn out by sorrow, fasting, and toil, she dropped from the back of her horse to the earth and fell into a deep sleep.

She still wore a man's dress, but as the peasant eyed her, he saw the gleam of gold and pearls beneath her upper garments, and guessed her to be a woman. Then he feared her no more, and killed her as she slept. He stripped jewels and clothes from the corpse, which he buried in a corner of his field, drove the horse away, and carried some of the garments to the nearest bazaar for sale.

But the gold-embroidered stuffs that had wrapped a king's daughter were not gear for a peasant to own, and the dealer to whom he offered them haled him before the *kotwal*, who of course extracted confession with a beating. The poor body was taken from its unhallowed grave, washed, wrapped in a shroud, and reverently buried in the same place. A shrine was erected there, and pilgrims journeyed to visit the tomb of the hapless woman who had ruled Delhi for three years and a half, and known little peace until she slept in the peasant's field. At the present day, her grave is enclosed within the bounds of the new Delhi that Firoz Shah Taghlak built at Firozabad.

"She was possessed of every good quality which usually adorns the ablest princes," says Ferishta, "and those who scrutinise her actions most severely will find in her no fault but that—she was a woman."

"Sultan Raziya was a great monarch," says the historian who moralised over her brother's fate. "She was wise, just, and generous, a benefactor to her kingdom, a dispenser of justice, the protector of her subjects and the leader of her armies. She was endowed with all the qualities befitting a king, but she was not born of the right sex, and so in the estimation of men all these virtues were worthless. May God have mercy on her!"

IV.

A son and two grandsons of Altamish successively followed Raziya. It is to be hoped that the consciousness of no longer being under petticoat government was some satisfaction to the men in the kingdom, for there was no other satisfaction to be had. The Mongols took Lahore and slaughtered the inhabitants, under Raziya's immediate successor, who was murdered by his own generals; the next king fell into bad company and "thus acquired the habit of seizing and killing his nobles," who, not liking the habit, deposed him and put him into prison—"and he died." Happily for the country, during the reign of the third king, a peaceful and harmless person who supported himself and amused his leisure by making copies of the Koran "with great taste and elegance," the real ruler was one of "the Forty," Balban, a slave, who had been Chief Huntsman to Raziya.

Altamish once commissioned a merchant to buy slaves for him in Central Asia. Ninety and nine did the king approve when he returned, but when he saw the hundredth, a mean-looking little fellow, he exclaimed, "I will not take this one."

"Master of the World!" cried Balban piteously, "for whom have you bought all these?"

"For myself," laughed the king.

"Then buy me for the love of God!" pleaded Balban.

"Good!" laughed the king again, and he bought the lad, whose father had been chief of ten thousand horse in the district whence he himself had come; but taking no farther interest in him, he set him among the water-carriers.

Now astrologers had often told the king that

one of his slaves should take the kingdom from his son. For a long time he heeded them not; then it came to the ears of his wife, and she spoke of it, till he sent for the astrologers, and by their counsel ordered a review of all his slaves, that they might pick out the man who was to take the kingdom.

Class by class, they paraded before the king, and the water-carriers, who belonged to one of the lowest grades, grew very hungry as they waited their turn. So they sent Balban, "because there was none among them more despised," to buy food for them in the market. Before he could return, the water-carriers had been called, and in terror of being found out, put Balban's water-bottle and pot on the back of another youth, and made him answer to Balban's name. King and astrologers failed to find the man whom they sought, and Balban lived, to rise gradually, as Aybek and Altamish had risen before him, from slave to Sultan.

For twenty years he governed for the gentle recluse who was his nominal master, putting down rebellion, punishing conspiracy, ever alert against a Hindu revolt or a Mongol invasion, the two great perils which hung over the kingdom. When his master died, as a matter of course he stepped into his place. Inflexibly just, inexorably severe, it is little wonder to hear that "from the very beginning of his reign, the people became obedient, tractable, and submissive." He cleared the highways of the robbers who infested them, he harried the jungles where thieves took refuge, he laid waste the villages of marauders, he put brigands and rebels to the sword, he built and garrisoned forts to secure the roads. The punishments that he inflicted on the rebellious Governor of Bengal and his officers were so terrible that the beholders nearly died of fear—"such had never been heard of in Delhi, and no one could remember anything like it in Hindustan." But it was salutary severity, and when his strong hand was removed from the helm of state, men grieved bitterly for him whom they named "the father of his people."

"He was a king bounteous and powerful; an elephant in his time would avoid treading on an ant." During his forty years of power, we are told, he never jested or laughed, or allowed jest or laughter in his presence; he never conversed with persons of low extraction, and none dared recommend them to him for employment. It was once intimated to him that a *parvenu*, who had amassed vast wealth by usury, would give several lakhs of rupees in return for a single word from the throne; Balban rejected the proposal with infinite scorn. "What must his subjects think of a king who would stoop to hold converse with such a creature?"

His hopes and his pride were centred in his eldest son, Mohammad, whom in 1285 he sent forth to battle against "the accursed Samar, the bravest dog of all the dogs of Chinghiz Khan." The Mongols were drawing nearer and nearer, and it was no time to hold back even the son whom he loved more dearly than his life. Fifteen kings of Central Asia, dispossessed and driven from their realms by the tide of Mongol invasion, had taken refuge at the Court of Delhi, and their presence was a continual reminder to Balban of what might be the fate of the land he had rescued from strife and disorder.

In those days India trembled in helpless, abject fear before the advance of the hordes of Chinghiz Khan, even as Europe had quailed before the Huns. Like the Huns, the Mongols were not human beings. They were descended from dogs; God had created them out of hell-fire. "Their eyes were so narrow and piercing, that they might have bored a hole in a brazen vessel," says Amir Khusru, who, having fallen a prisoner into their hands, had more opportunity than he liked of examining them closely. "Their stink was more horrible than their colour. Their faces were set on their bodies as if they had no neck. Their cheeks resembled soft leathern bottles, full of wrinkles and knots. Their noses extended from cheek to cheek, and their mouths from cheek-bone to cheek-bone. Their nostrils resembled rotten graves, and from them the hair descended as far as the lips."

And he adds other details which are too intimate to be repeated here, though undoubtedly they give the finishing touches to the portrait.

Prince Mohammad was not fated to overcome these monsters. When the armies met near Dibalpur, after a three hours' battle, the Mongols turned to flee, followed by the victorious troops of Delhi. The Prince and some of his attendants, overcome by thirst, halted at the side of a stream, and after drinking, he prostrated himself in thanks to God who had given him to overcome. At that moment, two thousand Mongols burst from the thicket in which they had been concealed. The Prince, cheering his men, and fighting desperately to the last, was cut down, and scarcely one of his party was left alive when the Mongols were put to flight by a detachment of the Delhi army who came too late to save him.

"Not a dry eye was to be seen, from the meanest soldier to the general." To the old king, now in his eightieth year, the loss of his son was a death-blow. By day he held his Court with all the solemn formality of one who never suffered even his confidential attendants to set eyes upon him, except when he was in full dress; he transacted business with ministers and officials, "as if to show that his loss had not affected him." By night, "he poured forth cries of grief, tore his garments, and threw dust upon his head," wailing for him who was long remembered by his people as "the Martyr Prince."

He wasted away with the load of sorrow and years, and died in 1287, last of the great Slave Kings. "From the day that Balban, the father of his people, died, all security of life and property was lost, and no one had any confidence in the stability of the kingdom. His successor had not reigned a year before the chiefs and nobles quarrelled with each other; many were killed upon suspicion and doubt; and the people, seeing the trouble and hardships which had befallen the country, sighed for a renewal of the reign of Balban."

IV.

THE VENGEANCE FOR BLOOD

Jalal-ad-din Firoz Shah .	1290-1296
Ala-ad-din	1296-1316
Kutb-ad-din Mubarak Shah .	1316-1321

"La spada di quassù non taglia in fretta,
Nè tardo."

IV.

THE VENGEANCE FOR BLOOD.

I.

BALBAN, like his predecessors, had been unable to train up a son to follow him. Bughra Khan, the eldest surviving son, cared so little for Delhi that he left his father's deathbed to return to Bengal, where he could enjoy himself as he pleased. His descendants ruled that province until well into the fourteenth century.

Kai-kubad, Balban's grandson, was set upon the throne—a youth so carefully trained and guarded by his grandsire's orders, that until the day of his accession he had never been allowed to cast eyes upon a fair damsel or to taste a cup of wine, to do any unseemly act, or utter an improper word. The result was, of course, that as soon as he found himself lord of an empire, "all that he had read and heard and learned he immediately forgot." In less than three years his evil example had contaminated all classes, and he had sunk to such degradation, moral and physical, that the assassin who came to murder him in his "hall of mirrors" found him a helpless paralytic lying on a couch, and drove the wretched life out of him "with two or three kicks."

There were murders, intrigues, and civil war between the dominant race, the Turks, and the Afghan Khaljis, a clan of Pathan adventurers, before the land found peace under the Khalji Muster-Master-General, Jalal-ad-din Firoz Shah, "the mildest king that ever held a sceptre." For some time he would not enter Old Delhi, on account of the feeling against him, and when his kindness and liberality had in some degree conciliated the people, and he went in state to the "Red Palace," he dismounted at the gate, and sat in his accustomed place among the nobles in the Audience Hall, out of respect to Balban's memory.

Himself a pattern of integrity, he believed other men to be true and upright as himself, and when undeceived, he could not punish. The nobles who had made insurrection in favour of Balban's nephew, and were brought captive, "covered with dust and dirt and their garments soiled," for the new Sultan to punish, found themselves washed, perfumed, dressed in clean garments, and given wine to drink, and then dismissed with the kindly assurance that "in drawing their swords to support the heir of their old benefactor, they had taken an honest rather than a dishonest course." When thieves were haled before the Sultan for justice, he would set them free on their taking an oath to steal no more, observing to the indignant spectators that he could not slay a bound man. A Thug, taken in the city, turned king's evidence, and was the means of capturing a thousand of his fraternity. "But not one of these did the Sultan kill": he merely ordered them to be put into boats, and conveyed to Bengal, where they were to be turned loose—to exercise their talents, presumably, upon the subjects of another king. To all remonstrance from his councillors he had one reply, "I am an old man, and I have never caused a Muslim to be killed: let me go down to the grave without shedding more blood."

"Clemency is a virtue which descends from God," observes Ferishta, "but the degenerate children of India of that age did not deserve it. The king's sentiments having become public, no security was any longer found. The streets and highways were infested by thieves and banditti. Housebreaking, robbery, murder, and every other species of crime, were committed by many who adopted them as a means of subsistence. Insurrection prevailed in every province, numerous gangs of freebooters interrupted commerce, and even common intercourse. Add to which, the king's governors neglected to render any account, either of their revenues or of their administration."

There were general complaints of the Sultan's clemency, and certain disaffected nobles babbled in their cups of deposing him or putting him out of the way. "Men drink too much and talk foolishly," was all he said when he was told of their threats; "do not repeat drunken stories to me."

It happened one evening that there was a wine party at the house of one of the nobles, and as the liquor went round, the guests began to talk even wilder treason than usual. They proposed setting their host in the Sultan's place; one vowed he would slay the Sultan with a hunting knife, another drew his sword and swore to make mince-meat of him. Next morning, when reflection and severe headaches had somewhat damped their ardour, they were suddenly brought before the Sultan, who for once in his life had been stirred to violent anger by the report of their boastings over the wine. He upbraided them roundly in the presence of the Court, while they trembled, and "all men wondered where it would end." "Ah, drunken negroes, who brag together and talk of killing me!" he exclaimed, flinging his sword down among them. "Is there one of you who is man enough to take this sword and fight it out fairly with me? See, here I sit ready for him. Let him come on!"

Not one among the culprits stirred, till a witty noble, "the principal inkstand-bearer," gathered courage to speak. "Your Majesty knows that topers in their cups utter ridiculous sayings. We can never kill a Sultan who cherishes us like sons, as you do, nor shall we ever find so kind and gracious a master; neither will you kill us for our absurd drunken ravings, because you will never find other nobles and gentlemen like us."

The Sultan himself had been drinking wine—perhaps to string himself to the necessary pitch of severity. His kindly old eyes filled with tears, and he pardoned them all; only insisting that they should remain on their estates and not be seen in Delhi for a twelvemonth.

Another offender, who had written a lampoon against Jalal-ad-din in the time of Balban, came to Court with a rope round his neck, in expectation of death: the Sultan called him forward, embraced him, gave him a robe of honour and a grant of land, and enrolled him among his personal attendants. Never was Jalal-ad-din known to visit

F

offences with stripes, imprisonment, or other severity; "if he got angry with any of them, he threatened them with his second son, Arkali Khan, who was a hot-tempered man."

The strongest man about him was his nephew, Ala-ad-din, whom he had brought up from infancy and married to his daughter. The marriage proved unhappy; Ala-ad-din was on ill terms both with his wife, and her mother who had great ascendancy over the Sultan, and cast about for some means to make himself so great that however the women might intrigue against him, they could not ruin him utterly. From Karra, of which place the Sultan had made him governor, he had marched upon Bhilsa, and captured idols and plunder from the Hindus. There he heard much of the wealth and elephants of Deogir (Devagiri) in the Deccan, and made up his mind to go where no Muslim conqueror had yet penetrated. The Sultan granted permission for an expedition to some country vaguely specified as "in the north," believing "in the innocence and trust of his heart" that Ala-ad-din wished to conquer some unknown land whence he need never return to the wife and mother-in-law with whom he could not live in peace.

So Ala-ad-din led his men to Deogir, a land exceedingly rich in gold and silver, jewels and pearls, where the people had never even heard of Muslims. After he had been absent from Delhi for a twelvemonth, news reached the Sultan, who was then near Gwalior, that he was returning "with elephants and an immense booty."

The Sultan held festivities in honour of his nephew's victory, and consulted with his advisers whether he should go to meet Ala-ad-din, or return to Delhi and receive him there. The wisest of them all gave it as his opinion that elephants and wealth in abundance were the cause of much strife, and liable to turn the head of the possessor. Let the Sultan march to meet his nephew, then Ala-ad-din must needs yield up his booty to the superior force, whether he liked it or not.

But the Sultan "was in the grasp of his evil angel." "What have I done to Ala-ad-din that he should turn from me and not present his spoil?" he asked indignantly. He would take no advice, he would not even listen to those who came to warn him that Ala-ad-din and his army intended treason. The old man, who had no anger for evil-doers, grew angry with his best friends, and said that they wanted to set him against "his son."

Ala-ad-din now pretended to fear that his enemies had poisoned his uncle's mind, and to reassure him, the Sultan promised to meet him at Karra with only a small retinue. Almas Beg, Ala-ad-din's brother, acted as his agent at Court, protesting to his uncle that the victorious general was in such fear of royal displeasure that he carried poison in his handkerchief, and would swallow it at a sign. Working in concert, the brothers lured the Sultan to Karra in the rainy season, and played upon his love for "his son" until he consented to cross the river with only a few personal attendants, leaving his escort on the other bank. The river ran high, and while the boat rocked on its swollen current, the Sultan placidly read in the Koran—for it was the time of Ramazan—while those with him repeated the verses prescribed to men in imminent peril of death. Obstinate to the last, the old man would listen to no warning, and those who crossed the river with him knew that they should return no more.

When they reached the farther shore, Ala-ad-din fell at the feet of his uncle, who embraced him as if he were once more a little child, stroking his beard and kissing his face. "I have brought thee up from infancy," murmured the Sultan, patting him tenderly upon the cheek; "why art thou afraid of me?"

As the loving hand clasped his own, Ala-ad-din

gave a signal; one of his following, "a bad fellow of a bad family," struck at the Sultan with a sword, but the blow fell short, cutting the assassin's hand. Again the sword was brandished, and wounded the Sultan, who fled towards the river with the piteous cry, "Ah, thou villain, Ala-ad-din, what hast thou done?"

Another ruffian flung him down and hacked off his head, while others slaughtered his attendants. The head—grown white with eighty years' labour—was set upon a spear, and paraded up and down, while the conspirators raised the royal canopy over the head of Ala-ad-din.

Sooner or later retribution fell on all who had betrayed their master. At the end of three or four years Almas Beg was dead, and four of his confederates with him. The man who struck the first blow was eaten up with leprosy. The actual murderer went mad, and in his dying ravings cried that Sultan Jalal-ad-din stood over him with a naked sword ready to cut off his head.

Ala-ad-din went to Delhi, and "scattered so much gold about him that the faithless people easily forgot the murder of the late Sultan and rejoiced over his accession." He reigned, and for a while all things seemed to prosper to his wish. Yet over him hung the doom, while he "shed more innocent blood than ever Pharaoh was guilty of," and such a retribution destroyed his house, the chronicler tells us, shuddering, as "never had a parallel, even in any infidel land."

II.

The modern historian with the modern facility for labelling and classifying, would probably write down Sultan Ala-ad-din as a victim to "megalomania"; the Muslim historian, with unscientific common-sense, considers that high position and success turned the head of a man who was so illiterate that he could neither write nor read a word.

At first all his undertakings prospered. The late Sultan's family were blinded, imprisoned, or put to death. A Mongol invasion which swept up to the very gates of Delhi was successfully driven back by Zafar Khan, "the Rustam of the age and the hero of the time," with whose name the Mongols would rebuke their horses when they refused to drink: "Why dost thou fear? Dost see Zafar Khan?" That the great Khan lost his life in the engagement caused no distress to Ala-ad-din, who had begun to think him too powerful, and to debate whether it were better to poison him, blind him, or merely send him with a few elephants to take Bengal.

The fastnesses of the western deserts where the Rajputs had preserved their independence, the fertile plains of the Deccan where the very name of Muslim had been unknown, yielded to Ala-ad-din. His generals brought back to Delhi the spoils from the great "temple of the golden idols" in Southern India, and conquered almost to the borders of Mysore. Chitor, the sacred city of the Rajputs, was taken by storm, and sacked by Ala-ad-din—not for its wealth, say the Rajputs, for little of that was left to them, but for love of the fair Princess Padmani, whose carven palace still looks over crumbling stones and climbing weeds in her deserted city.

As success followed success he became intoxicated, and according to the idiom of the historian, "quite lost his hands and feet." "Despatches of victory came in from all sides; every year he had two or three sons born, affairs of state went on according to his wish and to his satisfaction; his treasury was overflowing, boxes and caskets of jewels and pearls were daily displayed before his eyes, he had numerous elephants in his stables, and seventy thousand horses in the city and environs, two or three regions were subject to his sway, and he had no apprehension of enemies to his kingdom, or of any rival to his throne." He talked of founding a new religion in emulation of the Prophet, of leaving Delhi in charge of a viceroy, and going forth to conquer the whole habitable world. On his coins and in his proclamations he styled himself "the second Alexander."

At one time his successes abroad seemed likely to be overthrown by rebellions at home, but the Sultan, waking from his dreams, showed a sense and a ferocity that soon reduced his subjects to order. He came to the conclusion that it was superfluity of wealth that was the chief cause of sedition, inasmuch as it gave the disaffected the means of raising disturbances. He, therefore, instituted a rigorous system of taxation; all his subjects were "pressed and amerced" on one pretext and another, until scarcely a penny of ready money was left to any but certain nobles, officials, and bankers. "The people were all so absorbed in obtaining the means of living that the name of rebellion was never mentioned." The Hindus, we are told, "had not even time to scratch their heads," and the Muslims were in little better case.

All feasts and entertainments were prohibited, since hospitality might be used as a cloak for conspiracy. A system of spies was established, and kept all men, good or bad, under such close observation that "nobles durst not speak aloud even in the largest palaces, and if they had anything to say they communicated by signs." Dicing and wine-drinking were forbidden, and detected buyers and sellers of intoxicating liquor were put into holes dug outside the Badaun gate, "which is a great thoroughfare." Here many of them died, and the sight of their sufferings deterred others from offending. Those who were unable to exist without liquor, had to go out to villages twenty or twenty-four miles away to procure it.

Then Ala-ad-din "requested the wise men to supply some rules and regulations for grinding down the Hindus," and the wise men conscientiously set to work upon them. All Hindus were condemned to pay the *jiziya*, or poll-tax, a hated imposition that continued until the days of Akbar. No Hindu was to be able to keep a horse to ride on, to carry arms, to wear fine clothes, to chew betel, or enjoy any of the luxuries of life. Such a strict watch was kept over the assessments that no revenue officer durst accept a bribe to deal gently with his victims. Payment was enforced by blows, confinement in the stocks, imprisonment and chains. The system worked so thoroughly that "no Hindu could hold up his head, and in their houses no sign of gold or silver or of any superfluity was to be seen."

An invasion of the Mongols in 1303, when they bivouacked in the suburbs of Delhi for two months, brought home to the Sultan that if he wished to do no more than maintain the conquests he had already made, he must increase and strengthen his army. In order to enable the soldiers to live upon small pay, he fixed a price for all necessaries of life. Certain districts were commanded to pay their taxes in grain, which was stored in the royal granaries and sold in lean years to the inhabitants of Delhi at the price regulated by the Sultan. There were stern laws against "forestalling and regrating," and the Sultan was kept informed of the market transactions. After a market overseer had received twenty blows with a stick, once or twice, for reporting a trifling rise in prices on account of deficiency in the rains, no one attempted further variations in the tariff. It was possible, however, to give short weight, and this the dealers did, "especially to ignorant people and children," until the Sultan's spies having brought word of it to their master, the offenders were seized by an inspector, who took from their shops whatever was wanted to make up the correct amount, and then cut from their haunches pieces of flesh equivalent to the weight of which they had cheated their customers.

After a few object-lessons of this kind, the Delhi traders became noted for their honesty; they were even known to give the purchaser something more than his due.

Many reforms can be worked by a despot who is merciless, and Ala-ad-din's cruelties were without parallel in the previous history of Delhi. "Up to this time no hand had ever been laid upon wives and children on account of men's misdeeds," but he made the families of criminals suffer death, torture, and outrage worse than death, and prisoners of war, rebels, and other offenders paid for their misdoings in such manner as cannot be described. "No consideration for religion, no regard for the ties of brotherhood or the filial relation, no care for the rights of others, ever troubled him."

There is this much to be said for him, that under his rule his subjects preserved their lives if not their property, and though stripped bare by his exactions, none else, from tax collector to highway robber, durst take a penny from them. Moreover, the Mongols were repulsed, until "all fancy for coming to Hindustan was washed clean out of their breasts," and "no one cared about them or gave them the slightest thought."

Some of his work still remains in Delhi, notably

the Alai Darwaza beside the Kutb Minar, and the extension of the court of Altamish. Fortunately he had not time to complete the great minaret which, in one of his extravagant dreams, he purposed "to raise so high that it could not be exceeded," to tower far above the Kutb Minar. Its vast base stands in the centre of the court that he built, probably as the workmen left it at his death. In constructing a new fort at Delhi, we are told, he was mindful of the condition that a new building must be sprinkled with blood, and "sacrificed some thousands of goat-bearded Mongols for the purpose."

In his latter years his successes were changed into disaster. Trusting no one, he removed all men of experience from his administration, and filled their places with eunuchs and young slaves. He lavished honours upon his commander-in-chief, Kafur, thereby alienating his amirs and khans. His sons, "brought prematurely from their nursery," gave themselves up to every form of licence; there was revolt in Gujarat, which spread to other parts of his kingdom, and the terrible Sultan, helpless with dropsy, could no longer put down the rebels, "though he bit his own flesh with fury." Whether the disease killed him, or whether he was murdered by his favourite, is an open question. In January 1316 his corpse was brought from the Red Palace and buried in the tomb by the Kutb Mosque.

The story of what followed can only be indicated faintly. Kafur seized upon the government, as regent for one of Ala-ad-din's sons, a baby of six. Murders, blindings, and spoliation continued for five weeks, at the end of which time "God be thanked that it entered into the heart of some slaves of the late king that they ought to kill this wicked fellow,"—and they did. Then another son of Ala-ad-din became king, under the title of Kutb-ad-din Mubarak Shah,—and the events of his reign of five years are best left in the comparative obscurity of the Delhi chronicles.

He was governed by a favourite calling himself Khusru Khan, a Hindu pariah. With this man for counsellor and accomplice, tortures, mutilations, scourgings, imprisonment, wholesale murders and executions, were rife throughout the land, until a wild night in March when the Sultan's headless body was cast into the courtyard of the palace, slain by the man whom he had delighted to honour.

Khursu had himself proclaimed as "Sultan Nasir-ad-din"; the horrors of his four months' reign must be left unwritten. To sum them up briefly, every man of the late Sultan's kin, all his personal attendants, all the great nobles, were slaughtered; the women of every degree were given to the outcast followers of the new Sultan. Then Taghlak, the Governor of the Punjab, came with the surviving remnant of the old nobility to Delhi, defeated the usurper—whose gold had not been able to buy the loyalty of the army—and put him to death. When Taghlak asked whether any were left of Ala-ad-din's blood whom he might set upon his old master's throne, the answer came from all men present that not a single one of the whole stock was left alive.

Jalal-ad-din was avenged.

V

SAINTS AND KINGS IN DELHI

GHIYAS-AD-DIN TAGHLAK .	1321-1325
MOHAMMAD TAGHLAK .	1325-1351
FIROZ SHAH . . .	1351-1388

"If a holy man eats half his loaf, he will give the other half to a beggar,
But if a king conquers all the world, he will still seek another world to conquer."

—*Sa'adi.*

V.

SAINTS AND KINGS IN DELHI.

I.

ONCE upon a time, in the days before Mohammad Ghori had destroyed the four great Rajput kingdoms, the chief of holy men, the venerable Khwaja Sahib of Chisht, was walking round the Kaaba when a voice came from Heaven and bade him go to Medina.

Forthwith the saint journeyed to Medina, where the Prophet appeared to him in a vision and said: "The Almighty has intrusted the country of India to thee. Go thither, and abide at Ajmir. By God's help, the faith of Islam shall be spread in the land, through thee and thy followers."

So the Khwaja Sahib, nothing doubting, journeyed to Ajmir, where the idolaters sought to slay him. But when the saint looked upon them, they were rooted to the ground with terror, and instead of crying "Ram! Ram!" to their god, they could only cry "Rahim! Rahim!"[1] to the All-Merciful. Then in fear and contrition they besought the Khwaja Sahib to remain with them, and he made his dwelling on the southern side of their city, near to where his shrine now stands; and the *yogi* who had been the spiritual guide of Rai Pithora was converted, and became his disciple.

But the heart of Rai Pithora was hardened, and he scoffed at the faith, and tempted the followers of the Khwaja to do evil, till that venerable one grew wroth, and laid a curse upon him.

Then came Sultan Mohammad, and slew Rai Pithora before Delhi, and set his slave Aybek upon the throne; and through the help of the Khwaja's prayers the whole country was brought into the hands of Aybek. The saint died in 1235; "he lived a hundred and seventy years; God knows the truth," says one of his biographers.

Since the time of the Khwaja Sahib, three other holy men of Chisht had lived in India, working miracles and instructing disciples, and the last of these was Nizam-ad-din-Aulia, known as "the Commander of Assemblies," whose shrine has been a resort for pilgrims and sightseers for nearly six hundred years.

[1] *Ram*, the Hindu invocation; *Rahim*, "the Merciful," one of the Arabic titles of God.

In his time Delhi was ruled by Ghiyas-ad-din Taghlak, who had saved the land from the nightmare of Khusru's reign, and had been elected to the throne by the voice of all the surviving nobles and officers when it was made clear that not one of the race of Ala-ad-din was left alive.

A warrior of tried reputation, who had earned his title of "Al-Malik al-Ghazi" by routing the Mongols in nine and twenty battles, Taghlak was the man whom the wretched kingdom needed in its misery. He righted wrongs, so far as he might, he punished the wrongdoers, he restored order, he settled the land revenue upon just principles. The land cultivation increased year by year under his management. The Hindus were taxed "so that they might not be blinded with wealth," yet not so as to bring them to utter destitution, and peace and prosperity returned once more to the country. It is true that his methods of restoring order were calculated to inspire terror as well as respect. On one occasion, a false report of his death having caused disaster to an expedition against the rebellious province of Deogir, when the authors of the report were discovered, he thus passed sentence upon them: "Since they have buried me alive in jest, I will bury them alive in earnest."

Now Taghlak designed a great citadel five miles east of Old Delhi, to be built of giant stones, such as no other king had ever used, with a reservoir to be hewn out of the rock, and within the fortress a tomb of red sandstone and white marble, where he should lie when his work was done. He was in haste to see it finished, because he was the king, and also because he was an old man, and might not look for many years of life. So he took all the workmen that he could find, and set them to build his fortress, and among them were the men whom Nizam-ad-din-Aulia had hired to make a tank for him.

The saint was also an old man, and loved waiting no more than the Sultan, so he bought oil, and when the workmen came away from the fortress, at nightfall, he gave them lamps and set them to labour at his tank till the dawn.

They durst not refuse, for it is ill to affront a saint, but they grew faint and weary with working double tides, and the Sultan's overseers would know the cause. Then word was brought to Taghlak that the men were too feeble to work for him by day after working for the saint by night, and he commanded that no man henceforth should presume to sell or give oil to Nizam-ad-din-Aulia.

Then the holy man betook himself to his prayers, and a miraculous light arose from the water of the tank when the sun went down, so that the workmen had no need of lamp or torch.

But the Sultan had acquired much holiness by warring against the infidel, and in his wrath he laid a curse upon the water of the tank, and it became noisome, so that no man could drink of it.

Then the saint cursed the new city of Taghlakabad, saying, "Be it the home of the Gujar, or rest it deserted."

In token whereof, to this day, the waters of the saint's tank emit a stench of rotten eggs when men and boys leap into them from the top of the surrounding buildings, in his honour, and for the amusement of visitors; and Taghlakabad, deserted by Taghlak's son because it was unhealthy and waterless, lies desolate, two small Gujar villages huddled amidst its giant ruins.

Then the Sultan went on an expedition into Bengal, where no ruler of Delhi had exercised authority since the days of Balban, and while he was busy there his eldest son, Prince Mohammad, grew impatient for the succession, and plotted against him, seeking the help of the saint, who vowed that never again should Taghlak set foot in Delhi.

When the news came that the Sultan was returning in triumph, and expressing the intention of making the saint pay for his treason, the prince and the saint's disciples were seized with fear.

"The Sultan comes!" they cried, "he is a stage nearer to Delhi each day."

"Dilli dur ast" ("It's a far cry to Delhi"), was the only reply of the saint, as he calmly told his beads.

"To-morrow will see him here. Let us fly before he comes."

"Dilli hanoz dur ast" ("It's still a far cry to Delhi"), answered the saint, without stirring a finger.

At the last stage of the journey the prince came to meet his father and younger brother, and feasted them in a wooden pavilion which he had built for them beside the river. After the feast, he asked leave to parade the elephants, and the Sultan consented.

Taghlak sat in the pavilion, with his favourite son, the boy whom he had taken with him on his campaign, and beside them was a certain shaikh, to whom Prince Mohammad said: "Master, it is time for afternoon prayer." Mohammad then left the pavilion to give orders to bring up the elephants, and the obedient shaikh descended to his prayers, without waiting to see the parade.

Scarcely were prince and shaikh outside the building when a crash was heard. The shaikh hurried back, his prayers unsaid, and found that at the touch of the foremost elephant the whole pavilion had subsided.

Mohammad feigned great distress, and ordered pickaxes and shovels to be brought at once. But he made a sign to those in command of the workmen which they understood too well to hurry. After scientifically planning his pavilion, with the help of his father's inspector of buildings, he did not intend to lose the reward of his trouble by a premature rescue. It was not till after sunset that the tools were brought, and the men began to dig in the dusk of a January evening.

The old Sultan was found under the fallen beams, shielding his boy with outstretched arms, as if he had striven to keep death away from him. The young prince was dead; there were dark rumours that the father still breathed when the workmen found him. His body was carried at night to the tomb within the fortress, and Prince Mohammad gained his heart's desire.

II.

It was a misfortune for Hindustan that Mohammad ibn Taghlak was given to trying experiments.

A few centuries later, as a man of science, with his researches under the control of legislation, he might have lived not unhappily, achieved some little good, and wrought no more harm than the generality of men: as an Eastern despot, the lord of three-and-twenty provinces—a wider realm than submitted to any King of Delhi, save Aurangzib,—he was a direful failure. His reign "was a tragedy of high intentions self-defeated."[1]

He was upright, abstemious, and devout, saying his prayers regularly, and punishing those who did not follow his example. His bravery in the field was renowned, and his private life without reproach, according to the Law of the Prophet. He was skilled in logic, astronomy, and mathematics, eloquent and overpowering in controversy with philosophers and learned men. His Persian verses were acknowledged to be good, and his Arabic and Persian letters were studied, long after his time, on account of their literary style.

[1] S. Lane Poole.

His caligraphy put the most accomplished scribes to shame. He specially delighted in the study of medicine, and went so far as to attend in person upon those stricken by any remarkable disease—a proceeding which is not likely to have alleviated their sufferings.

Add to this that he never spared himself in carrying out what he conceived to be his duty, that he established hospitals for the sick and almshouses for widows and orphans, that he was a liberal patron to learned men, and you have the outline of what might have been one of the best rulers that Delhi ever knew.

Three of his qualities spoiled all the rest—the zeal for experiment which was never satisfied, the obstinacy that caused him to go on his way without asking counsel of any man, and the hard heart which made him callous to all the suffering that he inflicted. After twenty-six years of reign, only Gujarat and Deogir remained to him of outlying possessions, and in the kingdom of Delhi revolt and disaffection beset him on all sides; there was a deficit in the treasury, and the land had returned to the poverty and misery from which his father had rescued it.

The most vivid picture of him is that given by Ibn Batuta, the Arabian traveller, who spent some time at his Court:—

"Mohammad is a man who, above all others, is fond of making presents and shedding blood. There may always be seen at his gate some poor person becoming rich, or some living one condemned to death. His distinguishing characteristic is generosity. It rarely happened that the corpse of some one who had been killed was not to be seen at the gate of his palace. This sovereign punished little faults like great ones, and spared neither the learned, the religious, nor the noble. Every day hundreds were brought chained into his Hall of Audience, their hands tied to their necks and their feet bound together. Some were killed, and others tortured or well beaten. It was his practice to have all persons in prison brought before him every day except Friday. This day was to them a respite, and they passed it in cleaning themselves and taking rest. God preserve us from evil!" piously concludes the traveller, who once fell into disgrace with Mohammad and narrowly escaped death, after being closely guarded by four slaves for ten days.

It was his distinguishing characteristic that first brought trouble upon Mohammad. Having depleted his treasury with grants to savants, poets, distinguished foreigners, and officials of every grade, he attempted to supply the deficit by laying a super-tax of five or ten per cent upon the fertile plain of the Doab, between the Ganges and the Jumna. The inhabitants were reduced to beggary, and became rebels for want of other means of support. The cultivators in adjoining districts, taking alarm, set fire to their houses and fled to the jungles, before the tax-collector should come to take all that they had. Whole districts fell out of cultivation, and famine spread through the land; in the Doab, and round about Delhi, the people died by thousands upon thousands. It next occurred to the Sultan that as Deogir was in a more central position than Delhi, he would make a new capital there; and not content with transferring his Court, he insisted that all the inhabitants of Delhi should follow him to the city which he named Daulatabad ("city of empire"). Not one might stay behind. Every family, with men-servants and maid-servants, and dependents of every sort, was uprooted; not even a dog or a cat was left in the city and its suburbs, from Taghlakabad, and the fort of Rai Pithora, where the Slave Kings had built their palaces and mosques among the ruins of Hindu temples, to Siri, where Ala-ad-din had cemented his foundations with the blood of Mongol prisoners, and Jahanpanah, the new town which had begun to rise between Old Delhi and Siri. The very trees were torn from the ground, and planted along the road to Deogir, to give shade to the travellers on their way.

The trees probably did not live long; the people bore uprooting even less well than the trees. Some fell by the wayside, others pined from home-sickness when they reached the Deccan. "The Sultan was bounteous in his liberality and favours to the emigrants, both on their journey and on their arrival, but they were tender, and they could not endure the exile and suffering. They laid down their heads in that heathen land."

An attempt to translate some of the inhabitants of other towns to Delhi fared no better; many of the strangers died, and the rest escaped back to their homes. Soon afterwards the Sultan, who had been putting down the revolt of Govenor of Multan, led his army past Delhi, and found himself, on a sudden, almost deserted, every soldier who belonged to the city hurrying back to his old home. In a spasm of good nature, Mohammad himself entered Delhi, and invited his troops to return; but after two years the old obsession revived, and he carried off all the inhabitants of Delhi a second time to Daulatabad. Even the blind and the lame were dragged away by force, and the noble city was left to the owls and the jackals.

The deficit in the treasury still continued, and the Sultan's next experiment was to issue copper tokens instead of money. The ingenious Hindu of course seized upon this opportunity of gaining a little of the wealth which was considered unwholesome for him; every Hindu house became a mint, where forged tokens were coined. The Hindus waxed fat, rode once more upon horses, and ruffled abroad in fine clothes; and the royal treasury was filled with copper tokens of no more value than pebbles. Trade was at a standstill, and the old coins rose four- and five-fold in value. The Sultan was forced to proclaim that whoever possessed copper coins should receive their equivalent in gold from the treasury. "So many of these copper coins were brought to the treasury that heaps of them rose up like mountains" in Taghlakabad—where they may still lie, beneath the surface, to reward an enterprising excavator.

Mohammad's dreams of world-wide dominion ended no better than his other dreams. He raised a vast army to conquer Khorasan, which, after being kept idle for a whole year, broke up, and each man returned to his own occupation. He actually despatched an army against China which was destroyed in the passes of the Himalayas, only ten men returning to Delhi with the news of its fate. All these experiments ended alike, in increasing the financial ruin of the country and in embittering the Sultan against the people, on whom he visited all his displeasure for the failure of his schemes.

His cruelty was beyond conception, and it increased with what it fed upon. In the earlier part of his reign he had caused a rebellious nephew to be flayed alive, and had amused himself by hunting the inhabitants of a district near Delhi as if they were wild beasts, making a *battue* and hanging some thousands of the victims' heads over the city walls. As the years went on, and his empire dropped from him, bit by bit, rebellions, famine, and pestilence wasted through the land, and the foreign adventurers, whom he preferred to the old noble families, repaid his favour by treachery, he grew more and more vindictive. Sometimes misgivings assailed him; Barni, the contemporary historian from whom the story of this reign has been taken, tells us how the Sultan, on his way to put down insurrections—his usual occupation in his later years,—asked him how kings in history had punished their subjects. Barni quoted the example of King Jamshid, who had approved capital punishment only in seven cases. The Sultan replied that the world had waxed very evil since the days of King Jamshid, and that he would continue to punish the most trifling act of contumacy with death till he died, or until his subjects mended their ways.

So he continued his severities, and afterwards regretted to Barni that he had not executed more of his amirs before they could revolt. "I could not help feeling a desire to tell the Sultan that the troubles and revolts which were breaking out on every side, and this general disaffection, all arose from the excessive severity of his Majesty," sighs the historian, "and that if punishment were suspended for a while, a better feeling might spring up." But he lacked the courage to do so, and consoled himself by reflecting that certainly it would be useless.

Deogir revolted under its Afghan viceroy, Hasan Gangu, who became King of the Deccan, where his descendants, the Bahmanid kings, ruled till the beginning of the sixteenth century. Bengal also broke off the yoke of Delhi, and was practically independent until the reign of Akbar. "No place remained secure, all order and regularity were lost, and the throne was tottering to its fall."

For a while the Sultan lost heart, and Barni notes as an extraordinary event that no one was sent to execution for some months—whereas, in the usual way, "the execution of true believers had become a passion and a practice." He then spent three rainy seasons in Gujarat, putting down rebellion, and there fell sick of fever. He struggled to shake it off, and led his army across the Indus in pursuit of a rebel leader, but his strength failed him. Barni says that he insisted upon eating some fish which did not agree with him. If this were another of his experiments, it was the last. Mohammad Taghlak died on the banks of the Indus, in March 1351.

III.

The merciless Sultan lay dead. A party of Mongols plundered the baggage-train of his army, and went off to their own country, and all the khans, amirs, princes, and officials cried in their despair, "*Dilli dur ast!* Sultan Mohammad has gone to Paradise, and the Mongols have come up against us."

It was clear that nothing could be done without a leader. Happily for the chances of peace, the late Sultan had left no sons. After long deliberation, nobles and officials elected to the throne his cousin, Firoz Shah, who had been thoroughly trained in the conduct of affairs of state by Taghlak and Mohammad, and had lately been viceroy of one-fourth of the territories of Delhi.

Firoz protested, vowing that he intended to make the pilgrimage to Mecca, but in vain. The nobles flung royal robes over the mourning garments which he refused to lay aside, the drums were beaten, and universal joy prevailed.

There was good reason for rejoicing. Firoz was no unworthy son of a noble mother who had given herself for her country.

Ghiyas-ad-din Taghlak had determined to make the fortune of his brother Rajab by marrying, and hearing that the daughters of Rana Mal Bhatti of Dipalpur were very beautiful, sent to demand one of them for Rajab. Now the Bhattis are a Rajput tribe, descended from Chandra (the moon), and when the proposal was made that the Rana should give one of his daughters to the cow-slaying Toork, he rejected it with haughty and unseemly words.

Then Taghlak demanded that all the year's tribute from the Rana's territory should be paid to him at once and in ready money.

The people durst not resist, though they stripped themselves bare, for it was in the days when Ala-ad-din sat upon the throne of Delhi, and they knew too well how he could punish contumacy. The sound of their lamentation reached the mother of Rana Mal, and she came to her son's house weeping, with torn hair, to plead for them.

Naila, the daughter of the Rana, stood in the courtyard as the old woman came to the door, and asked her why she wept.

"It is because of you that I weep," answered her grandmother. "It is because your father will not give you in marriage to the Toork that Taghlak has laid this heavy burden upon the people of the land."

"If to give me to the Toork will save my people, send me to him at once!" cried Naila. "Think only that the Mongols have carried off one of your daughters!"

The grandmother went to the Rana and told him of his daughter's words; and he yielded for the sake of the people. Naila was sent to her bridegroom, and their only child was Firoz Shah.

The new king wasted no time; he beat the Mongols in a pitched battle, and then led his army back to Delhi, which once more became the capital. Here he set himself, as far as possible, to undo or alleviate the evil wrought by his predecessor. His first act was to seek out the heirs of all those who had been executed by Mohammad, and all those who had suffered mutilation by his command, and make compensation to them. Each was asked to sign a deed declaring that he had received satisfaction, and these deeds, duly witnessed, were placed within the grave where

Mohammad slept, in his father's mausoleum, "in the hope that God in his great clemency would show mercy to my late friend and patron, and make those persons feel reconciled to him."

Taxation was lessened, judicial torture of all sorts was forbidden, and "terrors were exchanged for tenderness, kindness, and mercy." The Hindus were still forced to pay the *jiziya*, and some of their temples were destroyed, but no other special severity was shown to them. Throughout a reign of thirty-seven years, Firoz, adored by his people, found there was "no need of executions, scourging or tortures." "Not one leaf of dominion was shaken in the palace of sovereignty." His generosity was great, and his management so judicious that he could afford to be liberal without impoverishing the treasury. "Things were plentiful and cheap; and the people were so well to do and enjoyed such ease, that the poorest married their daughters at a very early age,"—aided by the Sultan, who founded an institution for the promotion of marriages.

He was a great builder, restoring and repairing the tombs, mosques, and other foundations of previous Sultans, besides constructing numerous public works of his own. He built another Delhi at Firozabad, adjoining the modern city, and laid out no less than one thousand two hundred gardens. A list of the works constructed in his reign includes forty mosques, thirty colleges, two hundred towns, thirty reservoirs, fifty dams, one hundred hospitals, one hundred public baths, and one hundred and fifty bridges.

In the third century before Christ, there had ruled an Emperor in India named Asoka, "the Beloved of the Gods," who became converted to Buddhism, and sent yellow-robed missionaries through Asia, as far as Syria and Greece, to preach the Way of Renunciation. Inscriptions on rocks and pillars tell of his mercy, his tenderness to men and animals, his aspirations for a universal toleration which anticipate the yearnings of the Emperor Akbar, seventeen hundred years after his time. At Topra and Meerut were two pillars erected by him, with inscriptions—and Firoz, to whom the Buddhist Emperor was of course "an idolater," conceived the idea of moving them to Delhi.

So all the people of the neighbourhood were commanded to help in the work, and to bring quantities of the down of the cotton-tree upon which the pillars might be laid. The removal was satisfactorily accomplished, to the joy of all good Muslims, who regarded it as a triumph of religion as well as engineering. One pillar, which was set on the ridge, was broken by an explosion early in the eighteenth century, and has suffered from being left to lie upon the ground for a hundred and fifty years; the other, "the Lat of Asoka," still stands in good preservation amid such fragments as the building operations of the Emperor Shah Jahan have left of Firozabad.

War was not to the good king's liking, though, out of respect to Mohammad Taghlak's memory, he occupied Sind, and brought its ruler to submission, at a great cost of men and treasure. His great recreation was hunting, and he once lost himself so completely in an expedition to capture elephants that no word of him reached Delhi for nine months. His only fault was that he persisted, despite the law, in drinking wine of different colours, "some yellow as saffron, some red as the rose, some white."

When in old age he set down the record of the works of his reign, he was able to thank God, "who inspired me, His humble servant," for the blessing bestowed upon him, and for all that he had been guided to do for the realm over which God had placed him. He was ninety years old when he died, "worn out with weakness," in 1388 —just a month after the Percy had yielded to the bracken bush on the borders of Northumberland.

"The whole realm of Delhi was blessed with the bounties of the Almighty" so long as he ruled, and those who survived into the evil days which followed his death, looked back with longing to the good days of Firoz Shah.

VI.

A FLIGHT OF LOCUSTS—1398-1399

"Ante faciem ejus ignis vorans, et post eum exurens flamma; quasi hortus voluptatis terra coram eo, et post eum solitudo deserti, neque est qui effugiat eum."

VI.

A FLIGHT OF LOCUSTS—1398-1399.

THE good days of Firoz Shah were the last that Delhi was to know for many a year.

His gentle rule had made for prosperity and content, but it had not made for strength, and when Hindu rajas and Muslim nobles broke loose and asserted their independence of Delhi, neither of his successors was able to curb them. The only one who showed signs of a masterful disposition died after a troubled reign of less than four years, and after his death two cousins of the race of Taghlak claimed sovereignty in Delhi, one holding his court at Firozabad and the other at Jahan-panah. Both were helpless toys in the hands of their mayors-of-the-palace, and the whole empire which they aspired to rule had shrunk to the five districts round the city of Delhi.

Then Timur the Lame, conqueror of Persia, Mesopotamia, and Afghanistan, determined to lead a holy war against the infidel, and in defiance of his amirs, who urged the obstacles put in the way by impassable rivers and impenetrable forests, the ferocity of the Rajas, and the might of their war elephants, he chose India as the scene of his campaign. In the spring of 1398 he led his army over the frozen passes of the Himalayas, crossed the Indus, and marched into the Punjab, carrying fire and sword wherever he went. Thousands of the inhabitants slew their wives and children, before meeting their own death in battle or siege, thousands more were slain in cold blood, after the capture of fort, city, or town.

By December he and his host had reached Panipat, but for once no opposing army was on the historic battle-ground. It was at the very gates of Delhi that the action was fought, on 17th December, beginning with a massacre of 100,000 Hindus who had been taken prisoner since the crossing of the Indus. These, it was suspected, might escape during the confusion of the fight and join the other side; it would therefore not be safe to leave them with the baggage, since no man could be spared to guard them, and it was against the law of Islam to set idolaters at liberty. "In fact," as Timur explains in his Memoirs, "no other course remained but that of making them all food for the sword"; and he records with pride how one of his councillors,

The Court of Timur; Bayazid in an Iron Cage.

a learned man who in all his life had never killed a sparrow, succeeded in murdering "fifteen idolatrous Hindus" in obedience to orders.

The battle was well fought on both sides, as Timur admits, and he wept with pride and thankfulness when it ended in the rout of the men of Delhi. He entered the city in triumph, cowardly Sultan Mahmud, careless of what might befall his people, fleeing away to the hills.

It was agreed that the inhabitants of Delhi should redeem their lives and property with a heavy ransom. But, as Nadir Shah was to discover, more than three hundred years later, there was little chance of keeping control over barbarian soldiers, flushed with triumph, religious enthusiasm, and greed. There were brawls and disputes, which ended in a hideous massacre, lasting for three days. By the end of the third day the whole city was sacked, every soldier had secured at least twenty captives for slaves, and the booty in rubies, diamonds, pearls, gold and silver, ornaments and vessels, and rich stuffs exceeded all account. Timur picked out some thousands of artisans and clever mechanics, as presents for his friends, and ordered that all stone-masons and builders should be reserved for himself, that they might build a mosque at Samarkand to surpass all others in the world.

"When my mind was no longer occupied with the destruction of the people of Delhi," he tells us, "I took a ride round the cities," like any modern tourist. After fifteen days' plunder and festivity, he recalled that he had come to Hindustan not to enjoy ease and splendour, but to slay the infidel, and he departed, tempestuously as he came. Meerut was razed to the ground, its men slaughtered, its women and children led into captivity. The sacred place of Hardwar, where holy Mother Ganges falls from the mouth of a stone cow, was defiled with the blood of its defenders. Through the Sivalik hills, past Nagarkot and Jammu, into Kashmir marched the hordes of Timur, wading through rivers of blood, and leaving ruin and death behind them, until they returned to Samarkand in March 1399.

Sultan Mahmud crept back to his desolate capital, and lived sometimes there, sometimes at Kanauj, till his death in 1412—the last of the house of Taghlak.

Delhi, henceforth, was no longer the queen-city in Hindustan, but fallen to the level of the chief town of a petty state. To such a low ebb had sunk the empire of Mohammad Taghlak and Ala-ad-din, that after the death of Mahmud no man cared to call himself King of Delhi. A Sayyid noble, Khizr Khan—the Sayyids are of the race of the Prophet Mohammad—ruled nominally as Timur's deputy. His son and successor was murdered by his own chief minister, who would also have murdered the next Sultan if he had not been anticipated by his Majesty. The Sayyid dynasty fell into utter contempt, and was supplanted by the Afghan house of Lodi. The two first Lodi kings, Buhlol and Sikandar, recovered some of the lapsed territory of Delhi; the third, Ibrahim, after alienating his nobles and officials by his haughtiness, disgraced, imprisoned, and assassinated them, until a rebellious section, headed by Ibrahim's uncle, Ala-ad-din, invoked the aid of a foreign power.

Hindustan was like a ripe pear, ready for the first hand with quickness to pluck it and strength to hold it. As in the days of the first Muslim conquerors, all India was divided into states, most of which were at war with each other. Bengal, which had cut loose from Delhi in the latter years of Mohammad Taghlak, was ruled in turn by a variety of dynasties, Khalji, Turk, Hindu, and Afghan. Gujarat was under Muslim kings, descended from a converted Rajput, who had held the country in fief from Firoz Shah, and they and the Rajputs of Mewar, the dominant race of Rajast'han, disputed the possession of Malwa, the Rajputs gradually gaining the upper hand until the defeat of Kanwaha broke their power, when Gujarat carried off the prize. The Deccan in the last years of the Bahmanid kings split into five states, which had little to do with Hindustan until the reign of Akbar. Beyond the Krishna lay the great Hindu empire of Vijanagar, which under various spellings, of which "Beejanugger" is the most common, became a byword for wealth and splendour with all mediæval visitors to India, although in history, art, and letters it left scarcely a trace behind it. Practically it had no concern with the story of Delhi.

Into all this confusion of warring interests, races, and creeds, came the man who was to found a dynasty that in its height of power occupied the whole peninsula, and in its effeteness and decay was a name to conjure with, in the days of Queen Victoria. It is one of history's ironies that the dynasty has always been known by the name that of all names would have been most abhorrent to its founder, who lost no opportunity of proclaiming his dislike and contempt for the Mongols. Yet because to the native of India all northern Muslims, if not Afghans, must be Mongols, "the Great Moghul" passed into history, and is a name not unfamiliar to numberless persons who would be quite incapable of saying who or what the Great Moghuls were.

VII.

THE PRINCE WHO WENT TO SEEK HIS FORTUNE—1483-1530

"The Hour's come, and the Man."

VII.

THE PRINCE WHO WENT TO SEEK HIS FORTUNE—1483-1530.

ONCE upon a time there was a prince who went out into the world to seek his fortune.

Like the princes of fairy tales, he was oppressed by cruel uncles, who robbed him of his heritage; like them, he had a few faithful friends who would not leave him; and like them, at the lowest ebb of his fortunes, he met an old woman—for all that we know, a fairy in disguise—who pointed the road that he was to take.

It was the close of the fifteenth century, when everywhere old barriers were breaking down and new worlds opening out to the adventurous. The Portuguese had rounded the Cape of Storms, while Columbus, seeking another way to India, had found instead another continent. The Turks had given the death-blow to the moribund Empire of the East, while Ferdinand and Isabella had driven the last Moorish king from Granada.

The revival of classical learning was working upon literature, upon art, upon religion. What we call modern history was beginning in the West when, in 1494, the king of the petty state of Farghana, beyond the Oxus,[1] went up to his pigeon-house to feed his pigeons.

The pigeon-house was built on to an outer wall overhanging a precipice. For some unexplained reason this wall gave way, and the king "was precipitated from the top of the steep with his pigeons and pigeon-house, and so took his flight to the other world." Humane, courageous, affable, "eloquent and sweet in his conversation," the old king was beloved of men, in spite of the passion for war which had often brought trouble upon Farghana, and in spite of the strength of his fists; "he never hit a man whom he did not knock down," says his son admiringly.

The heir to Farghana was a boy in his twelfth year, named by his father "Zahir-ad-Din," "Protector of the Faith," but known to all time as "Babar," "the Tiger," — a name given him in babyhood by his mother's father, Yunis Khan of the Mongols, who could not pronounce the letter Z. The boy had every right to have something of the tiger in him. Through both

[1] Now called Khokan.

parents he was descended from the Mongol Chengiz Khan, who had ravaged Persia, Armenia, and the land on both sides of the Oxus, from the Indian Ocean to the Caspian Sea; through his mother, from Timur the Lame, who, after overrunning Persia, Mesopotamia, and Afghanistan, had descended into India, butchering men, women, and children like sheep.

Of all his kin, Babar evidently felt the greatest respect for his maternal grandmother, a lady who upon one occasion fell into the hands of her husband's enemy, and was given forthwith as a wife to one of his officers. She made no remonstrance or lamentation, but when once the man had entered her room, superintended the stabbing of him by her maids, had the corpse flung out into the street, and sent word to his master—"I am the wife of Yunis Khan. You gave me to another man, which is against the Law of the Prophet, so I killed him. Come, kill me, if you choose."

To her enemy's credit be it said, he did not choose, and she was restored to her husband.

We hear less of Babar's mother, but the courtesy and kindness that he showed, whether as a homeless fugitive or as lord of an empire, to aunts, sisters, and other uninteresting female relations, is one of the most lovable features in a prince worthy to stand beside the "courteous knights" of ballad and romance.

Of all the figures that move across the pages of Indian history, Babar is the most attractive, as he has drawn himself with an artist's vividness and a child's simplicity in his own Memoirs, or as he appeared to his contemporaries. Never had any man more of the *joie de vivre*, the overflowing vitality that enables its possessor to take all gifts of Fortune's hand with gladness, and to put some of his own spirit into those about him. Everything, to him, was to be enjoyed as part of the great game, whether it were fighting for dear life against an enemy who had routed half his followers "about as long before as it takes milk to boil," drinking with boon companions in a garden beneath the stars, toiling through a mountain pass through many feet of snow for a week at a time, or composing verses as he galloped after a flying enemy. At a time when "Nature-study," as we call it, had not been invented, he knew the habits of every beast and bird in his dominions, and among the records of war and battle, set down the discovery of some new species. When king in Kabul he made a collection of the three-and-thirty different sorts of tulip to be found on the skirts of the mountains. When first in Hindustan, he observed "the grass was different, the trees different, the wild animals of a different sort, the birds of a different plumage," and forthwith noted all that he saw. If he had not been a king and a warrior he might have been an artist or a poet. He had the gift of seeing beauty, and the power of sketching a scene or a character in a few strokes, so that his friends whom we meet in the Memoirs are life-like figures, almost every one of whom we should recognise if they suddenly strode back to us out of the past. Capable of terrible bursts of wrath, but prompt to forgive, sharing every hardship with his followers, giving away the best that he had and keeping nothing for himself, it is impossible to read of him without seeing that he was of those princes of romance whose power to "cast the glamour" continues long after their bones have crumbled into dust and their kingdoms have vanished.

Scarcely was his father cold in his grave when his uncles, the Kings of Samarkand and Tashkand, seized upon outlying parts of his territory; Babar managed to retain the main portion, "thanks to the distinguished valour of my young soldiers," says the boy king. Later, when he was still only fifteen, the King of Samarkand died, and Babar made a dash for the throne of Timur, occupying it for "just one hundred days." His capital, Andéjan, meanwhile rebelled, and messengers sent by his mother and grandmother to urge his return to Farghana found the lad recovering from a desperate illness. "My circumstances prevented me from nursing myself during my amendment, and my anxiety and exertions brought on such a severe relapse that for four days I was speechless, and the only nourishment I received was from having my tongue occasionally moistened with cotton. Those who were with me, high and low, begs, cavaliers, and soldiers, despairing of my life, began each to shift for himself." Word was brought to Andéjan that he was actually dead; and so, when only half recovered, his speech still thick with weakness, he dragged himself back to his own country, he learned that his capital had surrendered to the enemy. "For the sake of Andéjan I had lost Samarkand, and found I had lost the one without preserving the other."

Then followed years of weary wandering with his mother and grandmother—who had been sent to him after the surrender of Andéjan—and the few who were true to him. Sometimes he was obliged to throw himself upon the very unwilling hospitality of his mother's relations; sometimes he was driven to lurk among the wild hillmen. For a little while he recovered his kingdom of

Farghana, thanks to a tardy attack of remorse on the part of the governor who had surrendered Andéjan during his illness. But he lost it again through his own act: hearing piteous complaints of the plunder and exactions of the ruffianly soldiery who had just returned to their allegiance, he issued an order that those friends of every degree who had accompanied him in his campaigns might resume possession of whatever part of their property they recognised. "Although the order seemed reasonable and just in itself, yet it had been issued with too much precipitation," he confesses. "When there was a rival at my elbow, it was a senseless thing to exasperate so many men who had arms in their hands. This inconsiderate order of mine was in reality the ultimate cause of my being a second time expelled from Andéjan." A mistake in strategy it may have been,—such a mistake as Robert the Bruce made when he delayed his army's retreat for the sake of "a puir lavendar."

"I could not, on account of one or two defeats, sit down and look idly around me," he tells us, but for the next few years there was nothing save defeat and disappointment for the lad who was only seventeen when he lost Farghana for the second time. He then made another attempt upon Samarkand, and took it by surprise, with a handful of men, only to lose it again after a long siege in which the poorer inhabitants were reduced to feeding upon dogs' and asses' flesh. Forage for the horses was not to be had, and the mulberry trees, planted in happier days for the silkworms that have made "silken Samarkand" famous, were stripped of their leaves. The soldiers and citizens lost heart, and began to desert in small parties—even Babar's friends abandoned him, and he scarcely escaped with life, and his mother. His eldest and most dearly loved sister, Khanzada Begam, was intercepted as they left the city—or, as some say, was given in marriage to the enemy, in exchange for her brother's life.

Yet still the buoyant spirit was unquenched. On the next day, as he rode away from the city of Timur, his ancestor, he tells us that he had a race with two of his officers; and he dwells with delight upon the first good meal that he tasted after his long privation—"nice fat meat, bread of fine flour, well baked, sweet melons, excellent grapes." "In my whole life I never enjoyed myself so much, nor at any period of it felt so sensibly the pleasures of peace and plenty."

Upon persuasion, the husband of Babar's aunt gave him a district among the Kuh-i-Suliman hills for his winter quarters, and there he and his followers lodged in the shepherds' huts. Babar himself lived with one of the headmen, in a house that was probably infested with vermin and reeking with pungent smoke—a sorry abode for a king; but here he was to meet his fairy.

His host's mother, then said to be of the age of one hundred and eleven, was still vigorous and talkative, and her constant theme was the conquests of Timur in India. One of her relatives had served in his invading army, "and she often told us stories on that subject," says Babar, who, wandering barefoot among the hills, like any of the peasants around him, could look down to the mists on the far horizon that showed where the hills touched the plain of Hindustan. It is a matter for disappointment to all his readers that he never tells what the stories were.

Once more he recovered Farghana, after many fights and skirmishes, which he thoroughly enjoyed, even when his wounded horse flung him on the ground in the midst of the enemy. Again, and for the last time, he was expelled, forced to fly for his life, and fell alone into the hands of "unlucky perfidious clowns," who seemed to have the worst intentions against him. Unfortunately for us, the Memoirs break off when he is in hiding in a garden in Karnan, expecting death at every moment, and concerned only to perform his last ablutions, as became a true Muslim. When he begins them again, two years later, he is on his way southwards at the head of a motley crew. "The followers who still adhered to my fortunes, great and small, exceeded two hundred, and fell short of three hundred. The greater part of them were on foot, with brogues on their feet, clubs in their hands, and long frocks over their shoulders. Such was our distress that among us all we had only two tents. My own tent was pitched for my mother." Nevertheless, only four months after thus setting out, Babar had marched upon Kabul, the star Canopus, never seen by him before, shining brightly upon his little army, and "by the blessing of Almighty God, gained possession of Kabul and Ghazni."

In Kabul he spent about ten years, more peacefully than any that he had known since early boyhood, or was ever to know again. Though nothing in his eyes would ever equal Farghana, the lost valley clipped by snowy mountains, with its melons and pears, its tulips and roses and fat pheasants which he wistfully recalled to the end of his days, he learned to love the cool gardens and running streams of the country of his adoption, and has much to say of all he found there, from the flying-foxes to the thieves in a particular district which he purposed to settle in his first moments of leisure, "if Almighty God prosper my wishes."

Shortly after he became master of Kabul, his mother, worn out by her sorrows and the hardships of their wandering life, "was received into the mercy of God." A year later, he married a noble lady of Khorasan, whom we know only by his name for her—"Maham"—"my Moon." At the age of five, for reasons of state, he had been betrothed to his first cousin; "in the first period of my being a married man, though I had no small affection for her, yet from modesty and bashfulness I went to her only once in ten, fifteen, or twenty days. My affection afterwards declined, and my shyness increased; insomuch that my mother used to fall upon me and scold me with great fury, sending me off like a criminal to visit her once in a month or forty days."

Perhaps it is not strange that this wife left him during his misfortunes—"induced," he declares, "by the machinations of her elder sister." Since then he had taken other wives, whose names and children he enters in a business-like manner; but the "Moon Lady," to the end of his days, retained the heart of the man who, courteous and kindly to all women, had little time for love-making.

There is nothing else about which we need

concern ourselves during those years of sovereignty at Kabul, except that, during a visit to some jovial cousins at Herat, he learned to drink wine. As he honestly avows, "I had a strong lurking inclination to wander in this desert," though he had never dared show it; and having once broken the strict rule of abstinence in which Chengiz Khan's descendants were brought up, he drank upon every occasion—and enjoyed it as whole-heartedly as he enjoyed everything else. Henceforth, "We had a drinking party" is a frequent entry in his Memoirs; or "I was miserably drunk," "I was completely drunk," and, best of all, "looking down from my tent on the valley below, the watch-fires were marvellously beautiful; that must be the reason, I think, why I drank too much wine at dinner that evening." Indeed, on his march from Kabul to India, he seems rarely to have been sober for a single day.

The chatter of the old woman in the shepherd's hut was at last to bear fruit; after a third unsuccessful attempt on Samarkand, Babar realised that if he were to sit upon the throne of Timur, it was not the throne of Central Asia, but the throne of the land beyond the hills, that had seemed to beckon him ever since he reached Kabul. After one or two raids, in the style of former invaders, a way opened before him; Ala-ad-din, a prince of the Lodi race of Afghans who had ruled Delhi for the last seventy years, came to Kabul, imploring help against his graceless nephew, Sultan Ibrahim, who had revolted even his own kin. "India was seething with faction and discontent" beneath the Afghan yoke, and the Afghan Amirs, who held the chief offices of trust and the principal fiefs, were divided amongst themselves. A dash upon the Punjab in 1524 gave the inhabitants a foretaste of what they might expect when, in November of the following year, Babar descended upon the plains, his best-beloved son, Maham's child, Humayun, leading a contingent of allies from Badakshan.

It was in the spring of 1526 that he met the forces of Sultan Ibrahim upon the plain of Panipat, near Delhi, where the fate of India has been decided over and over again—where the belated wayfarer may still hear the shouts of phantom warriors and the neighing of their steeds. The King of Delhi had an army of 100,000 men and 1000 elephants; Babar had no more than 12,000 men. But he entrenched his camp, linking 700 gun-carriages and baggage-waggons, with hurdles between each pair, and bided his time, quickly realising that his adversary was "a young man of no experience, who marched without order, retired or halted without plan, and engaged in battle without foresight." After a night attack which was repulsed, battle was joined "by the time of early morning prayers." By midday the enemy were completely routed, and by afternoon prayers, the head of Sultan Ibrahim, found dead under a heap of slain, was brought to the conqueror, who took possession of Delhi and Agra forthwith.

The booty was incredibly great, and Babar distributed it royally. To Prince Humayun he gave £20,000 and a palace with all its contents. The family of the slain Raja of Gwalior, in gratitude to Humayun for his protection, had given him an enormous diamond—none other than the Koh-i-Nur—which, after years of straying from one hand to another, bringing misfortune wherever it went, now rests in the Tower of London. Humayun delivered this to his father, who bade him keep it for himself. To his chief officers Babar gave from £1700 to £2800 apiece; every man who had fought had a share of prize-money, and even the clerks, traders, and camp-followers received gratuities. Friends at home were not forgotten. Every soul in Kabul, man or woman, slave or free, received elevenpence "as an incentive to emulation." Babar's daughter, Gul-badan Begam, tells how all the ladies of the royal harem at Kabul were summoned into the garden of the Audience-hall, to receive the Emperor's presents. To each princess was given a dancing-girl from Delhi, and a gold plate full of gems, and four trays of coins, and nine sorts of Indian stuffs—kincobs, and muslins, and so forth—all chosen for her by Babar himself. Jewels and stuffs were distributed to all the harem nurses, and to his foster-brethren, and "to the ladies, and all who pray for me,"—so numerous a list that it was three days before all was divided, and the solemn prayer and thanksgiving made by the assembled ladies in conclusion, as Babar had required. "They were uplifted with pride," the princess tells us, and there was no small cause for it, when the master of Delhi found time himself to choose out gifts for each of those whom he had left behind him.

The hot season of that year was unusually oppressive at Agra, and many men dropped down and died where they stood; Babar's officers were homesick for their hills, and demanded to return. Babar himself was of opinion that "Hindustan is a country that has no pleasures to recommend it . . . no good horses, no good fish, no grapes or musk-melons, no good fruits, no ice or cold water, no good food or bread, no baths or colleges, no candles, no torches, not even a candlestick." But he had no intention of giving up what he once had grasped. He summoned his chief officers to a council, and spoke shortly and sternly, concluding, "Let not any one who calls himself my friend henceforward make such a proposal. If there is any among you who cannot bring himself to stay, let him depart." The malcontents were silenced, all but one Khan, who returned to Kabul with the Emperor's presents, after having, to Babar's great indignation, scribbled the following couplet upon the walls of several houses in Delhi:—

> "If I pass the Sind safe and sound,
> May shame take me if I ever again wish for Hind!"

It was well for Babar that he had brought his officers to his mind; while in Agra he was designing baths to allay the three chief curses of Hindustan—heat, winds, and dust—and planting gardens with roses and narcissus, there came the news that a new enemy was at hand. Rana Sanga of Mewar,[1] "the sun of the Hindus," the greatest and noblest chief in India, who had defeated the Lodi rulers of Delhi in eighteen pitched battles, was laying siege to Biana, followed by 80,000 horse, seven Rajas of the highest rank, nine Raos, and one hundred and four lesser chieftains, with five hundred war elephants.

[1] Now the state of Udaipur.

Babar.

Babar went to meet him, and encamped on the plain of Kanwaha, near Biana. As at Panipat, he chained his gun-carriages and baggage-waggons together to cover his front. "Among his ordnance was the cannon known as the 'Victorious One,' which Ustad Ali, the chief artillery officer, was hereafter to distinguish himself by firing at the unprecedented rate of sixteen times a-day." His men were in a panic; a preliminary skirmish had shown them that the Rajput was a different foe from the mercenary rabble of Delhi, and the royal astrologer, "a rascally fellow," "loudly proclaimed to every person he met in the camp that at this time Mars was in the west, and that whoever should engage coming from the opposite quarter would be defeated."

It was the decisive hour, and Babar was not found wanting. As he went round his outposts on a Monday morning, he was struck with the reflection that he had always intended, at one time or another, "to make an effectual repentance." So, sending for all the gold and silver goblets used in his drinking parties, he there and then ordered them to be broken, and the fragments distributed among dervishes and the poor, vowing never to drink wine again, and, if victorious over "the pagan," to remit the stamp-tax upon his Muslim subjects. That night, and the following, amirs and courtiers, soldiers and others, to the number of three hundred, made vows of reformation, and poured upon the ground the wine that they had brought with them.

"Having thus knocked with all our might at the door of penitence," Babar called all his officers about him, and made a last appeal to the old fanatical spirit of Islam:—

"Noblemen and soldiers: every man that comes into the world is subject to dissolution. When we are passed away and gone, God only survives, unchangeable. Whoever comes to the feast of life must, before it is over, drink from the cup of death. He who arrives at the inn of mortality must, one day, inevitably take his departure from that house of sorrow, the world. How much better is it to die with honour than to live with infamy!

> "'With fame, even if I die, I am contented:
> Let fame be mine, since my body is death's.'[1]

"The most High God has been propitious to us, and has now placed us in such a crisis that if we fall in the field, we die the death of martyrs; if we survive, we rise victorious, the avengers of the cause of God. Let us then, with one accord,

[1] A quotation from Firdausi.

swear on God's holy word that none of us will even think of turning his face from this warfare, nor desert from the battle and slaughter that ensues, till his soul is separated from his body."

The words vibrated to the heart of every man there; from amir and beg to common soldier, great and small seized the Koran and vowed to conquer or to die.

On March 16, 1527, the armies faced each other in battle array. On the one side were the Muslim, burning with religious zeal and desperation, under their Emperor, still young, despite his forty-four years, above the middle height and strongly made, his piercing dark eyes under the heavy arched eyebrows glancing to right and left, as he rode up and down to see that every man was in his place. On the other were the "sons of princes," tried warriors whose banners had waved over many a stricken field, and ardent youths who thirsted to win themselves a perpetual name. Their leader, "the Lion of Battle," once strong and muscular, with fair complexion and unusually large eyes, was no more than the wreck of a man; an eye and an arm had been lost in fight, one leg was crippled by a cannon-ball, and on his body were the scars of eighty wounds. But the old lion was not to be held back from the prey, and he rode that morning beneath his standard, the golden sun's disk, with its motto, "Whosoever keeps his faith steadfast, God keeps him."

At first it seemed that once more the Lord of Mewar was to prevail over the Lord of Delhi. Never before had the Emperor's men faced a Rajput charge, and as one after another the long lines of saffron-robed horsemen dashed down upon the right of their foe, their helmets garlanded with the bridal coronet, their eyes reddened with opium, their lances and swords dripping blood, the Muslim fell thick and fast. But they held their ground stubbornly, and for hours the battle wavered, the Rajputs, for all their reckless valour, unable to force the entrenchment, the Emperor's troops unable to gain one step. Then Babar sent word to his flanking columns "to wheel and charge, while at the same time he ordered his guns forward, and sent out the household troops at the gallop on each side of his centre of matchlock men, who also advanced firing." At that instant, a traitorous ally who led the Rajput vanguard, turned and went over to the enemy.

"The whole raging sea of the victorious army rose in mighty storm," says the official despatch of Babar's secretary: "the valour of all the crocodiles of that ocean was manifested. The blackness of the dust, spreading over the sky like dark clouds, raced backward and forward over all the plain, while the flashing and the gleaming of the sword within exceeded the glance of lightning." The Rajput hosts wavered and broke, while Ustad Ali's "huge bullets" ploughed through their ranks. "They were scattered abroad like teased wool, and broken like bubbles on wine." The crippled Rana was hurried away, to die of grief within the year, and some of his host followed with him, but the greater number remained on the field, where the dead lay so thickly that there was not space to plant a foot.

On a little hill overlooking the camp, Babar piled a tower of the heads of his enemies, in true Mongol fashion, as his fathers did before him. The astronomer had the assurance to come up and congratulate him upon his victory. "I poured forth a torrent of abuse upon him," says Babar, "and when I had relieved my heart by it, although he was heathenishly inclined, perverse, extremely self-conceited, and an insufferable evil-speaker, yet, as he had been my old servant, I gave him a present," and a caution never to show himself again.

Henceforth India lay at Babar's mercy. There was another victory over the Rajputs when Chanderi, the chief fortress of Malwa, was taken by storm; Sultan Ibrahim's brother and the

Afghan troops fled before him, and the independent kingdom of Bengal which had showed signs of sympathy with the Lodi claimant, was forced to make a treaty of peace. Babar was now able to send for Maham and the ladies of his family, who had been left in Kabul. He had intended to meet her on the way, but she travelled post-haste, and at evening prayer-time, one Sunday, "some one came and said to him, 'I have just passed her Highness on the road, four miles out.' My royal father"—it is Gulbadan who tells the story—"did not wait for a horse to be saddled, but set out on foot," and met her. She would have dismounted from her litter, but he forbade it, and walked in her train till he reached his own house. The Memoirs only tell us, "It was Sunday at midnight when I met Maham again."

His eldest sister, Khanzada Begam, had returned to him after an unhappy married life, and his father's sisters came also to Agra, to see the wonders of the infidel country that he had conquered. The state architect was told that whatever work the aunts required to be done for their palace was to be given precedence over everything else. Babar visited the old ladies every Friday. "One day it was extremely hot, and Maham Begam said, 'The wind is very hot indeed; how would it be if you did not go this one Friday? The princesses would not be vexed.' His Majesty said, 'Maham! it is astonishing that you should say such things! They have no father or brothers; if I do not cheer them, how will it be done?'"

Maham was doubtless nervous at the thought of Babar's exposing himself to the burning winds of Agra. He had been renowned for his strength; he could run along the battlements of a fort carrying a man under each arm, and leaping over the embrasures in his way; it was his custom to swim over every river to which he came; and he once rode from Kalpi to Agra, 160 miles, in two days. But his constitution was breaking down under the strain of incessant toil in the Indian climate, huge doses of opium, and perhaps also from the effects of sudden and total abstinence from wine after a long succession of drinking-bouts. He was constantly suffering from fever. The last entry in the Memoirs, September 7, 1529, records his forgiveness of a rebellious subject.

In the following year, Humayun fell ill at his fief of Sambal, near Delhi. Maham started at once for Delhi, "like one athirst who is far from the waters." She brought the invalid by water to Agra, where his father's doctors confessed that they were powerless to cure him. Then a holy man suggested to Babar that the sacrifice of some most precious thing might be accepted by God in return for the prince's life. The mullahs —perhaps with an eye to their own advantage —proposed that the great diamond should be offered, but Babar rejected the counsel; what were diamonds to him in comparison with his favourite son? He would offer his own life as a sacrifice. Three times did he walk round his son—(as men do even now, in India, "to take away the evil")—crying aloud, "O God! if a life may be exchanged for a life, I who am Babar, I give my life and my being for Humayun." He retired to pray, and was heard several times to exclaim, "I have prevailed! I have borne it away! I have saved him!" That very day, Babar fell ill, and Humayun rose from his bed and came out to give audience in his father's place.

Babar grew daily weaker as Humayun recovered strength. He fretted for his young son Hindal, whom he had not seen for a long time, asking "how tall he was?" His last care was to arrange marriages for two of his daughters. He then called his nobles round him for the last time, saying, "For years it has been in my heart to make over my throne to Humayun, and to retire to the Gold-scattering Garden.[1] By the Divine grace I have obtained all things, but the fulfilment of this wish in health of body. Now when illness has laid me low, I charge you all to acknowledge Humayun in my stead. Fail not in loyalty to him. Be of one heart and one mind with him. Moreover, Humayun, I commit to God's keeping you and your brothers, and all my kinsfolk and your people; and all of them I confide to you."

"Three days later" (December 26, 1530) "he passed from this transitory world to the eternal home. Black fell the day for children and kinsfolk and all. They bewailed and lamented; voices were uplifted in weeping; there was utter dejection. Each passed that ill-fated day in a hidden corner."

[1] A garden near Agra.

VIII.

THE ADVENTURES OF HUMAYUN—1530-1556

"Humayun, always more distinguished by courage than by conduct."—H. G. KEENE.

VIII.

THE ADVENTURES OF HUMAYUN—1530-1556.

So Babar slept beside a cool running stream amid fragrant flowers, in that northern land for which he had vainly longed, and Humayun his son, "the Fortunate," reigned in his stead. To hold, and to weld together, what Babar's hand had grasped, would have been a hard task for any man; only an eighth part of all India—equivalent to what are now the Punjab and United Provinces—had been brought into any kind of order. To the east lay Bengal, not even nominally under Moghul rule, and to the south Malwa and Gujarat, united under a powerful king, Bahadur Shah, who was backing a rival claimant to the throne of Delhi — one of Humayun's own cousins. Rajputana was ever ready for revolt, and a brother of the late Sultan of Delhi was stirring up a rebellion in Bihar. To meet all these dangers, Humayun had little help from his own kin or followers; the heat of the plains had sapped the fibre, moral and physical, of the men who marched down with Babar through the gates of the North, and the old spirit of religious fervour had died away. Worst foes of all were the three brothers, Kamran, Hindal, and Akbar, whom the dying Babar had recommended to Humayun's care: each not only failed the Emperor, but betrayed and revolted against him, over and over again, to be forgiven almost to the limit of "seventy times seven." Any other monarch of the time, in East or West, would have made short work of them and their treasons; but Humayun, violent, hasty, subject to sudden fits of rage, was merciful, even to weakness.

In spite of all the good advice and the tenderness which Babar had lavished upon his Moon Lady's son, Humayun had fallen victim to the fatal habit which had wrecked his father's health, and was to be the ruin of many of his descendants: at the age of three-and-twenty, when he ascended the throne, he was already a slave to opium. Poet and warrior, like his father, brave with something of a fantastic chivalry that makes him spiritual brother to the knights-errant who had vanished from Europe before his day, alternating bouts of fiery energy with long periods of inaction, when he shut himself in his palace and would see no one, combining a marked reverence for holy things and holy names with a marked taste for exceedingly bad company, good and evil were inextricably blended in his character. To women on the whole, and especially to Khanzada Begam, he showed the courtesy and kindliness that we should expect from Babar's son. Once we hear of his going off by himself in a rage because the ladies of his household had kept him waiting when he wished to take them out on a picnic to gather wild rhubarb. Another time, there was what we gather must have been an unpleasant scene when they ventured upon a joint remonstrance because he had left them unvisited for many days; they were compelled to sign a declaration that they would be equally pleased whether his Majesty came to see them or not. He had his father's love of a joke, and once, in the midst of a magnificent festival, we hear of great confusion caused by a schoolboy trick played by Humayun, who, sitting with Khanzada Begam under pearl-strung draperies, turned the water-pipes upon some of the guests engaged in scrambling for gold coins at the bottom of a dry tank. Some men loved him, and some respected him, though not as they had loved and respected his father; but with many picturesque and estimable qualities, he was not the man to guide the ship of state through the very stormy waters now closing upon her.

It would be tedious to follow in detail all the changes in his fortunes. Kamran began by declaring himself sovereign of Kabul and the Punjab, thereby cutting off Humayun from the chief recruiting-ground for his armies. Good luck, rather than skill, gave him the victory over Bahadur Shah of Gujarat, whom he chased from place to place, driving him even out of the strong fort of Champanir, which was finally scaled by means of seventy-nine iron spikes driven into its walls, Humayun climbing up the forty-first amongst the Moghul soldiers. Gujarat and Malwa and inestimable spoil fell into the conqueror's hands, and demoralised both Emperor and army. Humayun wasted a year in revellings in Malwa, careless that Bahadur had stolen back to Gujarat and was winning the hearts of the people, that Prince Askari had set up an independent sovereignty at Ahmadabad, and that a new and terrible foe had risen against him in Bengal.

This was an Afghan,[1] Sher Khan, who had once taken service with Babar, but soon left him, contemptuously vowing, "If fortune favour me, I can drive these Moghuls out of Hindustan!" Fortune favoured him now, as with artful show of retreating he lured the Emperor, step by step,

[1] "Tiger Lord"—so called from his slaying a tiger that had leapt upon the King of Bihar.

Humayun.

into Bengal, to find the country laid waste on all sides, and the capital strewn with corpses. Here for six months Humayun feasted amid desolation and death, while Sher Khan cut off all the approaches to Bengal, well knowing that not one of the Emperor's brothers would stir a finger to help him.

After marching along the bank of the Ganges beyond Patna, the forces of Humayun entrenched themselves in a fortified camp opposite to the forces of Sher Khan, and there the two armies remained confronting each other for two months, neither feeling strong enough to risk a battle. Then, finding that his cattle and horses were all dying, and that his faithless brothers sent no reinforcements from Agra, Humayun entered into negotiations with Sher Khan. A treaty was arranged, and the Emperor's forces were breaking up their camp, in careless security, when before the dawn of a May morning Sher Khan fell upon them and cut them to pieces. Some were killed in their sleep, some were cut down as they fled, some were drowned. The Emperor himself, hurried away by a few watchful followers, spurred his horse into the river, where it sank exhausted in mid-stream; a water-carrier, seeing the lord of Delhi like to be swept away by the current, took him across to the opposite bank on an inflated skin, in the manner in which Eastern rivers have been crossed since the beginning of time.[1] All his possessions had to be left for the enemy, including his wife, for whom he appears to have cared very little. "I have nothing to give thee now," said Humayun to Nizam the water-carrier, as he turned his horse's head westwards, "but come to me in Agra, and, if I live, thou shalt sit on my throne for a whole day."

At Agra he met the brothers whose selfish treachery had helped to work his undoing. "What is past, is past," he told them; "we must now all join manfully to repel the common enemy." If such generous forgiveness shamed them for the moment into a better mind, it was soon forgotten when, amid the bustle and stir of preparations for another campaign, the water-carrier appeared to claim his reward.

Humayun kept his word royally: the peasant was king for a day, and the skin sack that had saved the Emperor's life was cut into little pieces and stamped by the royal mint. The man seems to have been too ignorant to use his brief power either for others' harm or to an undue extent for his own advancement, but sulky Prince Kamram resented this new folly of his brother's, and remembered it against him.

[1] See the Assyrian sculptures.

After a year of preparation the armies took the field again, and again found themselves camped opposite to each other—this time for a month, on the opposite banks of the Ganges, near Kanauj. There were constant desertions from Humayun's army, and the leaders had lost all heart; on the day in May 1540, when battle was joined, twenty-seven of the amirs, overcome with fear, hid the yak-tail standards which it was their right to display. "Before the enemy had let fly an arrow," wails the Moghul historian, "we were virtually defeated, not a gun was fired, not a man was wounded, friend or foe." In the headlong flight the bridge over the Ganges was broken down; Humayun, pulled up a steep bank out of the press of drowning and smothering fugitives by a rope made of two turbans fastened together, fled once more to Agra, shattered in nerve and wandering in mind. Babbling of strange portents, of supernatural allies that had fought on the side of the Afghans, he only stayed in Agra long enough to gather together a little of his treasure before making for the deserts of Sind with a few faithful friends. The Moghul Empire in India had vanished, and Sher Khan ruled in Delhi and Agra as Sher Shah, and "from the day that he was established on the throne, no man dared to breathe in opposition to him."

Kamram, thinking as usual only of himself, had taken possession of Kabul, made peace with Sher Shah, and declined to help his brother, or even to receive him.

The story of the banished Emperor's wanderings in the fifteen years during which he disappeared from Indian history would fill a volume. One of the first places to which he drifted was Pat or Patr (twenty miles west of the Indus), where Dildar Begam, Hindal's mother, received him kindly and made a feast for him. At the feast he saw among Dildar's ladies a girl named Hamida, daughter to Hindal's shaikh, of the race of the Prophet, and fell in love with her there and then. She was sixteen; he was thirty-three, an opium-drinker, and already extensively married.

Humayun went to pay a visit of ceremony to his step-mother, and not finding Hamida there, sent for her to come. The girl refused. "If it is to pay my respects, I was exalted by paying my respects the other day. Why should I come again?" This scene was repeated day after day; once Humayun sent Hindal—who was furiously jealous, having intended to take Hamida for himself—to bring back the wilful child, sometimes other messengers, who each complained, "Whatever I may say, she will not come." To all their remonstrances Hamida returned, "To see kings once is lawful; a second time it is forbidden. I shall not come."

It speaks well for Humayun's forbearance—or for the real amount of power exerted by women in a land where they are commonly supposed to be of no account—that for forty days the girl "resisted and discussed and disagreed." Then Dildar Begam, having pacified Hindal, tried the effect of a little motherly reasoning upon Hamida. "After all, you will marry some one," she urged. "Who is there better than a king?" "Oh yes, I shall marry some one," retorted Hamida, "but he shall be a man whose collar my hand can touch, and not one whose skirt it does not reach." Dildar "again gave her much advice," and at last the shaikh's daughter yielded to fate.

A dreary fate it must have been for the next few months, wandering up and down the country with a banished king who, for all his titles and dignities, had not a roof over his head. At length Humayun determined to throw himself upon the protection of Maldeo, Raja of Marwar, the second kingdom among the Rajputs. It was a desperate device, for the Rajputs had no cause to love "the Turk"; and moreover, Humayun at the beginning of his reign had allowed Bahadur Shah to sack Chitor, the crown of Rajputana, without attempting to save it, though summoned to its help by the Queen-Mother.

To reach Maldeo's city of Jodhpur, Humayun and his followers must pass through a desert where neither food nor water was to be had; the fugitives lived for the most part upon the ber-berries that they gathered by the way. There is little nourishment in the sharp-tasting fruit, no bigger than a bullace, but the juice is refreshing, and it saved the fugitives from dying of thirst. Jodhpur was not far off, and they were looking forward to the luxury of good food and water for themselves and their weary steeds, and a bed for Hamida, whose sorrowful hour was at hand, when they were met by a goldsmith whom Humayun had sent on in advance, to sound Maldeo's purposes. The hearts of all sank as he drew near, and they saw that with one hand he grasped the little finger of the other—the signal arranged beforehand by the Emperor to show that the Raja was plotting treachery.

Maldeo had heard that Humayun was only bringing a small band of followers with him, and had determined in that case to give him up to his enemies. "Their only chance of escape was to plunge into the Indian desert known as 'the region of death'—a waterless sea where the wind piles up the sand in waves from twenty to a hundred feet high. Here and there a few wells or a spring may yield a little fresh water, but the wells are from seventy to five hundred feet in depth. The lives of all depended upon their steeds, and those who fell by the way must leave their bones to whiten the sands where the mirage added mockery to their sufferings."

At midnight, Humayun and his handful of followers began their flight to Amarkot, a fort near the Indus, where they hoped to find refuge. On the way the Emperor's horse fell dead; "he desired Tardi Beg, who was well-mounted, to let him have his, but so ungenerous was this man, and so low was royalty fallen, that he refused." Maldeo's troops followed hard at their heels, and Humayun might have been captured but for a more loyal officer, who dismounted his own mother from her horse to give it to his lord, placing her on a camel and running by her side.

"The Moghuls were in the utmost distress for water; some ran mad, others fell down dead; nothing was heard but dreadful screams and lamentations." There were false alarms of the enemy's approach, and actual skirmishes with them; the rear lost their way in a night march. There were three horrible days without water, and when a well was reached, the people, mad with thirst, flung themselves on the first bucket before it reached the brink of the well, "by which means the rope broke, and the bucket was lost, and several fell headlong after it. Some lolling out their tongues, rolled themselves in agony on the hot sand; while others, precipitating themselves into the well, met with an immediate, and consequently an easier, death."

Only seven, with their Emperor, reached the brick fortress of Amarkot, where the Raja not only received them with every kindness, but offered to help them to gain a footing in Sind. Humayun, in one of his fits of untiring energy, started off at once, with such forces as the Raja could lend him, and on the way was overtaken by a messenger to say that three days after his departure, on October 15, 1542, Hamida Begam had brought forth a son, Akbar, "the Great." The royal father of a son was accustomed, on receiving the glad tidings, to distribute jewels and costly dresses among his courtiers. Hamuyun had less to give than the poorest beggar who held out a hand for alms at the gates of a mosque; but forms and ceremonies must be observed, and a musk bag, that he carried with him, was solemnly cut into little pieces and distributed among those who shared his rejoicing.

When Hamida and the child were able to travel they followed Humayun in his march upon Kandahar, which Prince Askari held as Kamran's viceroy, and refused to yield to its rightful lord. They had braved the desert sands, and were now to face the terrors of the hills. The cold was so intense that the broth turned to ice as it was poured from the camp-kettles; warm clothing was not to be had, and Humayun, in a moment that recalls his father, divided his own fur cloak between two of his followers.

They had halted for the night at a place about 130 miles south of Kandahar, when an Usbeg youth urged his worn-out pony into the camp, crying "Mount, mount, your Majesty! I will explain on the way. There is no time to talk!" Humayun mounted Hamida on his own horse, and they fled through the night towards the Persian frontier, followed by thirty men alone. Scarcely were they gone when into the camp rode the troops of Askari, the prince himself at their head. "Where is the Emperor?" he demanded of the attendants who had remained behind with the baby Akbar. "He went hunting long ago, your Highness." Askari might rage, but the prey had slipped through his fingers, and he must needs content himself with seizing upon all that Humayun had left behind. Akbar and his devoted nurse Maham were taken to Kandahar, where Askari's wife took charge of the forlorn baby.

As Humayun and his little band rode to Persia, sick at heart and despairing, it chanced one day that they rested during the heat of noon, and Humayun slept. Then—so men told at the Court of Delhi in later years—a mighty eagle swooped from the sky, and hovered above the head of the banished Emperor, keeping the sun from him with its pinions until he woke. Then his attendants cried out with joy, saying, "Surely thou shall yet be Lord of Hindustan once more."

Now Mahommedans are divided into two great sects, the Shias and the Sunnis, who, broadly speaking, have for each other the cordial regard that the Greek Church entertained for the Church of Rome at the time of their severance. The Turks are Sunnis, the Persians are Shias, and as emblem of their faith wore the peculiar cap from which they styled themselves "Kazlbash"—"Red-head." On reaching Persian territory Humayun sent one of his most trusted officers, Bairam Khan, as ambassador to Shah Tahmasp. After conventional civilities, the Shah told Bairam plainly that if he came to a Shia court, he must wear a Shia cap.

"I am the servant of the Emperor," returned Bairam, "and I may not change my dress without my master's leave."

The Shah was not one to brook refusal. "Do

as you please," he told the ambassador, "but learn what comes to those who disobey me." And he ordered certain offending officers to be brought into the presence, and there and then put to death. Bairam gazed unmoved upon their dying agonies, and still thrust aside the cap, scornful as any of his contemporary Lutherans who might have been invited to wear a scapulary. He escaped with his life, to the wonder of all men.

Humayun, of less uncompromising nature, and with more at stake, was forced to apostatise. Vainly did he offer his great diamond as a bribe; he must wear the loathed cap. If, according to orthodox Sunnis, he lost his soul by compliance, at least he gained some substantial advantages by it, when Shah Tahmasp sent 14,000 horse to help him conquer Afghanistan.

The gates of Kandahar were opened when Humayun knocked upon them with his army behind him; but the greatest treasure of all was not within its walls. Kamran had sent orders that Akbar was to be transferred to Kabul. Travelling through rain and snow, over roads infested by robbers, the boy was brought at peril of his life to Kabul, where he fell into the keeping of his great-aunt, Khanzada Begam, who wept as she kissed his hands and feet because they reminded her of Babar's. Old and weary as she was, she went to and fro between Humayun and his brothers, labouring for peace, till illness overtook her on one of her journeyings, and she died —a worthy sister of the brother beside whom she was buried at Kabul.

Kamran fled from Kabul as Humayun advanced; and Akbar, safe and sound, was given back to his parents.

Fate had not yet finished her sport with Humayun; on an expedition to Badakshan he fell ill—apparently the same sort of illness that had lost Babar Farghana and Samarkand. For days he lay in a trance, nourished only by the juice of a pomegranate which one of the Begams squeezed into his mouth; when he came to himself, it was to find that Kamran had taken advantage of his absence to seize upon Kabul and Akbar once more.

Through the heavy snow the Emperor hurried back to Kabul, and summoned the fort to surrender. In reply, Kamran dangled from the battlements, at the ends of ropes, the children of two begs who were with Humayun; he had already slain three whose only crime was that they were the children of one of his brother's officers, and thrown their bodies over the walls; he would do the like with these, unless their fathers would forsake Humayun and come over to him—or at least open a way through the lines, so that he might escape.

Then one of the fathers, Keracha Khan, Humayun's prime minister, made answer, as he watched his sons hanging in mid-air: "The children must die some day, and how can they die better than now, to serve their lord? As for my own life, it belongs to the Emperor,—but if Prince Kamran will return to his allegiance, it shall be devoted to him from henceforth."

Kamran did not fulfil his threat, though some say that he brought his nephew Akbar out on the battlements, as a mark for the besiegers' fire, to be saved by his nurse, Maham, who covered the child's body with her own, while the shot fell around them. Both were unhurt: Kamran could hold the fort no longer, and escaped by connivance of his brother Hindal, while Humayun once more regained possession of his capital and his son.

Still his troubles were not yet over while Kamran remained to stir up strife. Time after time was the prince forgiven, time after time, in sheer wantonness, did he break away and join himself to any rebels who might be in arms against his brother. Once Humayun had to fly, wounded, from Kamran's men in such desperate haste that he flung off his quilted silk cuirass as he rode, and was forced, when at length he reached a place of safety, to borrow an old woman's silk drawers to cover himself.

The tide was turning, however, and Humayun's worst enemies were to be removed. Askari, kept a close prisoner for some years after the taking of Kandahar, was sent to Mecca. Hindal was killed on almost the only occasion recorded when he was true to his salt, pursuing after Kamran during a night attack, and was as passionately mourned by his brother as if this exception had been the rule of his life. Finally, Kamran, discredited and deserted, was given up to Humayun by the mountain tribe among whom he had taken refuge. Amirs, begs, courtiers and officers, all pleaded for his death; scarce one among them but had lost kin and gear in one or other of his continual rebellions. Humayun could not bring himself to shed the blood of his father's son; at the same time, in common justice to his subjects, he could not set the prince at large. He compromised by blinding him, and sending him to Mecca. Cruel as it seems, it was no more cruel than Kamran had done to others, and far less than he deserved,—in fact, according to the ordinary custom of Oriental monarchs of that time, Humayun might have saved himself and every one else much trouble by having the operation performed on all his brothers as soon as he had succeeded his father.

Meanwhile, Sher Shah, having proved himself a just ruler and an excellent man of business, as stern in putting down robbery upon the high-roads as in checking peculation in the palaces, had been mortally wounded while besieging a fortress in 1545. The red sandstone mosque that he built at Indrapat near Delhi still links his name with the city where he was too busy to dwell. "In a very short period," says a chronicler, "he gained the dominion of the country and provided for the safety of the highways, the administration of the government, and the happiness of the soldiery and people. God is a discerner of righteousness."

His son was an incompetent and futile person, whose reign of nine years left all things in confusion. Then came the usual anarchy, reports of which reaching Humayun at Kabul, made him turn his thoughts southwards. Was it to be with him as it had been with his father, and was Kabul once more to be the stepping-stone to Delhi?

Men noticed his gloom and abstraction, and one day, on a hunting party, he opened his mind to his nobles. Some of the inhabitants of Delhi and Agra, weary of the strife between the three

Afghan princes who severally pretended to the throne, had invited him to come back; but he had no means of raising a sufficient army.

Some were for venturing it, others were for prudence, and argued that it would be folly to lose Kabul again in a mad attempt upon Hindustan. Then one of those who were ready to take all risks, spoke again: let them try fate as the wisdom of their fathers had tried it many a time, by sending on three of their number in advance to ask the names of the first persons whom they met. If the names were of evil omen, they would know that Heaven was not on their side.

Humayun agreed, and the three horsemen galloped away, and returned again.

"I met a traveller named Daulat (Empire)," said the first.

"And I a man who called himself Murad (Good Fortune)," said the second.

"And my man was a villager whose name was Saadat (the object of desire)," cried the third.

Therefore Humayun doubted no longer, but descended into the Punjab with 15,000 horse. Lahore fell into his hands, the Afghans were defeated, and Delhi and Agra owned him for their lord once more.

Six months after his return to Delhi, fate shot its last bolt. Close to the mosque of Sher-Shah is a three-storied building, known as the Sher Mandal, and used at that time as a library. Hither the Emperor came on a January day in 1556, and after walking to and fro upon the terrace, sat down to enjoy the fresh air. Hearing the muezzin's call to prayer from the mosque, with his usual scrupulous reverence he rose, repeated the Muslim confession of faith, and sat down upon the narrow staircase leading to the ground floor until the crier had finished. In rising again he caught his foot in his robe, and the staff on which he leaned slipped upon the polished stone. The ornamental parapet was no more than a foot high, and the Emperor fell headlong over it to the ground. On the fourth day after this he was a corpse.

"If there was a possibility of falling, Humayun was not the man to miss it," says a modern writer. "He tumbled through life, and he tumbled out of it."

To this day his mausoleum is one of the sights of Delhi. In spite of the green trees that surround it,—a rare delight in a land where all is flat and dust-coloured,—in spite of the solemn grandeur of its red sandstone walls and marble tomb, there is a shadow on the place; "old unhappy far-off things" seem to whisper there among the sunshine and the flowers. For here, with Humayun his ancestor, lies Dara Shukoh, son of Shah Jahan, murdered a hundred years later by order of his own brother Aurangzib, while he called upon the name of the Son of Mary; and here, a hundred years after Dara's death, the last sons of the house of Timur took refuge from the English who had come to avenge murdered women and children.

IX.

AKBAR PADISHAH—1556-1569

"His Majesty, King of Kings, Heaven of the Court, Shadow of God."

IX.

AKBAR PADISHAH—1556-1569.

ONCE upon a time there was a king who dreamed a dream.

Sitting on the throne of Delhi, he looked out over Hindustan, and saw how marauders had despoiled it and parcelled it out among themselves, how chief warred with chief, and none was strong enough to bid them cease. He heard the complaints of the poor in time of war, slain, driven forth homeless, carried away captive, because the great men had quarrelled with one another, or in time of peace ground down into the dust, stripped bare, because the tax-gatherer extorted many times more than was due to put into his own pocket. He saw men persecuted and oppressed, shut out from all honourable employment because they held to the gods of their fathers, and he saw how the poor among them might not even worship in their holy places because they could not pay the tax upon pilgrimages imposed by their conquerors. He saw what the women endured—made to know the pangs of childbirth when they themselves were but children; bound, living, to a husband's corpse on a funeral pyre, while the Brahmans lit the flames beneath them. Alien in race, his heart yearned over the land, as the hearts of many aliens have yearned since his day; and he dreamed a dream. He saw Hindustan at peace under the rule of a strong hand, men of every tongue and race and creed rising to honour and place in camp and court, or dwelling in security on the land and in the city, with no one to make them afraid. He saw the women, grown to full strength, the mothers of strong sons, who should all unite under the banners of the Empire to repel a common foe. He saw the multitude free to worship as they pleased, unhindered and unmulcted, so they kept the laws; and he saw the wise bowing before the One God who is not contained in temples made by hands, the Father of all men, the Spirit who clothes Himself with this material universe as with a garment.

It was a dream. Akbar himself knew that it would not last. Before he was laid in his tomb at Sikandra, his books, raiment, and weapons placed around him ready for his waking, with mullahs to patter the Koran at his side, and the Crucifix and the Virgin Mother to look down upon his rest, the dream had faded away. Even in our own day, after three hundred and fifty years of progress, it has not been realised in full. Yet it is something to have seen it,—infinitely more to have made it come true, though only in part and for a little while. "Akbar's dream" has become a byword among many of those who have the vaguest ideas as to when he lived or what he dreamed; comparatively few know how much he did to turn the dream into reality.

It was no time for dreams when Humayun tumbled headlong down the stone staircase. The Afghans were in possession of Bengal and the Ganges valley, and an army from Bengal was advancing upon Agra and Delhi. The Moghul leaders were divided in their counsels, and the new emperor was a boy of thirteen.

So desperate seemed the prospect that the general cry was for a retreat upon Kabul; but there was one who had the wit to see that the Moghuls must stand or perish, and this was the "King's father," as men called the newly appointed regent, Bairam Khan—the same who had defied Shah Tahmasp in the matter of the Shia head-dress. He had come down from the north with Babar, he had fought and fled with Humayun, and his judgment prevailed.

Fervently must the Emperor's counsellors have

wished that they had never listened to him when news came that Agra had surrendered without a blow, and then that Delhi had fallen. Tardi Beg, —the churl who refused his horse to Humayun on the night march through the desert,—left in charge there, had been routed under the city walls, and came flying with the remnant of his men to Akbar's camp. To crown all, word came from the north that the Prince of Badakshan had seized upon Kabul, which had been placed under the nominal regency of Akbar's baby brother, Mirza Hakim.

Bairam, in no way dismayed, while the hearts of those about him were trembling like reeds in the water, prepared to meet the crisis. First of all he ordered the execution of Tardi Beg, who had forsaken his post when he should have held it or died at it; Tardi Beg and he had been rivals for a long time, and even if death and ruin were to overtake him to-morrow, there was a grim satisfaction in the thought that he had won the last move against his old enemy. Tardi Beg's subordinates were put under arrest to discourage the faint-hearted from following their example, and Bairam reminded his army that in case of defeat it was useless to run away, as their homes were a thousand miles distant.

Needless to say it was at Panipat that the

armies met for the decisive battle. On the one side was the boy Emperor, with the survivors of the men who had followed his grandfather from the north—grizzled veterans, fair of face and sturdy of limb, their ruddy colouring blanched with many years' scorching in the plains, but the old spirit coming back into their hearts as they turned to bay where, thirty years ago, they had smote the infidel, and piled a tower of victory of the heads of the slain.

Facing them was a vast army of Afghans and Rajputs, with fifteen hundred elephants and thousands of horsemen, under the command of Himu, the Hindu who had risen from a chandler's shop to the command of an army. About twenty years before he had offered to put down a rebellious petty chief of Biana if he were given a small force. Adil Shah of Delhi had consented, either for the jest's sake or because he considered the matter of no importance. The Biana chief, when he heard that a shopkeeper was coming against him, sent his head groom to meet the foe, and went off on a hunting expedition. The head groom was soon disposed of. The furious chief himself, hurrying to retrieve the blunder, was surprised in a night attack, and his army cut to pieces. Himu presented himself with folded hands beneath the throne at Delhi, and when the delighted monarch would have dressed him in a robe of honour, waved it aside. "It was his Majesty's soldiers who won the victory; let his Majesty's favours fall first upon them, not on this unworthy slave who is only a poor tradesman."

Since that day he had gained two-and-twenty actions for his master, though always ailing, and so feeble in body that he could never ride to battle, and must be borne in a litter. From his elephant "Hawa," "the Wind," he now directed his army, a vast host, but held together only by the strength of his personality.

The Moghul left yielded to the charge of the elephants, and Himu penetrated to the centre, where the Moghul archers kept up such a hail of lances, arrows, and javelins, that the beasts could not face it, and turned, regardless of their drivers' blows, throwing their own ranks into confusion. An arrow pierced through Himu's eye; he sank upon the floor of his howdah in agonies of pain, and the troops of Bengal, thinking his wound mortal, broke and fled in all directions. With a supreme effort Himu tore out the arrow, though the eye came with it, and encouraged those about him with voice and gesture. But he was alone, in the very heart of the Moghul army, and his mahout, terrified for his life, betrayed him to the foe. A body of horse surrounded the elephant and urged it to the camp five miles in the rear, where Akbar had been kept during that November day.

Bairam Khan exulted savagely as the elephant grunted and swayed into the boy's presence with its dying burden. Here was a chance for the Emperor; let him draw his sword and make an end of this infidel, and so earn the title of Ghazi, —a title as honourable and as sacred to Muslim chivalry as was ever knighthood to a Christian warrior when won on a stricken field after battling against the Paynim.

Akbar turned fiercely upon his guardian. "How can I strike a man who is as good as dead?"

For answer, Bairam's sword gleamed in the air, and at one blow Himu's head and body rolled apart, while the boy burst into tears of shame and indignation. Never was that blow to be forgiven: in slaying a defenceless man, Bairam had slain his own influence over his pupil.

For the next few years the lad chafed in silence beneath the yoke. Arrogant and masterful, Bairam was not one to conciliate by a show of deference, even if Akbar had been one of those who are content to take the shadow for the substance. No man loved the Regent, and he had a dangerous enemy in Maham Anaga,[1] who had more influence with the boy she had nursed than any other human being.

At the age of sixteen Akbar went on a hunting party, and was joined near Sikandra by Maham, who declared that his mother was lying sick unto death in Delhi. Whether the Emperor knew the truth, or whether he was deceived, like every one else, he hurried to the city, and once there issued a proclamation that he had taken affairs into his own hands, and that no orders were to be obeyed unless issued under his own seal. He sent word to Bairam, "Let our well-wisher withdraw from all worldly concerns, and taking the pilgrimage to Mecca on which he has for so long been intent, spend the rest of his days in prayer far removed from the toils of public life."

Needs must; but the old warrior's heart was suffocating with rage. He to be cast aside at the whim of a boy, and to be sent to tell his beads, as if he were good for nothing else! He went obediently to Gujarat, it is true, avowing an intention of taking boat to Mecca, but at the last moment he could not bear the thought of leaving place and power. He gathered troops around him and broke into open rebellion—only

[1] *Anaga:* the title given to a foster-mother.

to meet total defeat, escaping barely with life to wander among the Siwalik hills.

Thence he sent his slave to Akbar, owning his wretched plight and asking for pardon. Back came the answer: if Bairam Khan sues for pardon, let him come and receive it from the Emperor.

Was this the prelude to a more than usually ceremonious execution? the Khan must have asked himself, when a guard of honour came out to meet him at some distance from the camp and brought him into the royal presence. There was all the Court, gathered to see the disgrace of the man whom all had hated, eyeing him in contemptuous triumph,—men who a year ago would have crawled at his feet. There in their midst was the boy whom he had taught and trained, for whom he had won victories, and against whom he had rebelled. The old man burst into passionate tears as he hung his turban about his neck in token of deepest humiliation, and prostrated himself before the throne.

An arm was cast about him, a hand was raising him; he was standing once more in his old place at the Emperor's side, at the head of all the nobles, while a robe of honour was hung on his shoulders. Bewildered he listened while the Emperor's voice pronounced his sentence—if he still hankered after a military life, the governorship of Kalpi; if he preferred the Court, an honourable place and a pension; if he purposed to go to Mecca, an escort suitable to his rank to accompany him.

The old soldier could have faced death, but this kindness was more than he could bear. Broken down with shame, he faltered that he could no longer venture to remain in the presence; let him forget the world, and seek forgiveness for his sins.

So to Mecca he went, after taking leave of his pupil, who settled on him a pension of 50,000 rupees. Whether the "suitable escort" despatched with him would have kept him out of mischief is uncertain; perhaps it was as well for his virtuous resolutions that before he could leave Gujarat he was assassinated by an Afghan whose father he had slain in battle with his own hand.

Not yet, however, was Akbar free from tutelage; now that Bairam was removed from her path, Maham Anaga was prime minister in all but the name, using her influence to push the fortunes of her family, and in particular of her ill-conditioned son, Adham Khan, said to have been the child of Humayun. Akbar could deny nothing to the woman who had shielded his body with her own, and to the youth who might be doubly his brother, and Adham was honoured with place and dignity which he knew not how to support.

By this time the Afghans had been driven back into Bengal, and the Ganges valley conquered as far as Jaunpur and Benares. The Emperor's men held Ajmir and the strong fortress of Gwalior. The next step was to be the reduction of Malwa, then under the easy sway of an Afghan governor, Baz Bahadur, so steeped in indolence and love of pleasure that he allowed the Moghul troops to approach within twenty miles of his capital "before he would quit the pillows of ease." At the first onset he was defeated and sent into captivity, "with streaming eyes and a broken heart." His treasures, his family, and his harem fell into the hands of Adham, who was in command of the imperial forces. He sent a few elephants to Agra, and kept everything else for himself.

Now Baz Bahadur had a Hindu mistress, one of the fairest women ever seen in India, as renowned for her skill in making verses as for her beauty. "Seven long happy years did they live together, while she sang to him of love." Rupmati, weeping for the lover she had lost, was told to dry her tears, for the Khan designed to show her favour.

Rupmati indignantly spurned the suggestion: she had belonged to Baz Bahadur; she would be the toy of no other man on earth. Adham sent back word that he could take what he wanted by force if it were not given to him.

Rupmati listened in silence, and appointed an hour at which she would receive her new master; she put on her richest dress and jewels, covered herself with perfumes, and lay down upon a couch to wait for him. Attendants knelt beside her, and whispered in her ear that the Khan was at the door; she must rise to receive him. There was no answer or movement, and when they ventured to pull back the veil that her own hand had drawn over her face, they found that she would never wake again.

The scandal could not be hidden; it reached the Emperor's ears, and in haste he rode from Agra to look into these matters for himself. Word of his coming reached mother and son, and while Adham laid treasure and spoil at the Emperor's feet, vowing that he had only retained it in order to have the honour of presenting it in person, Maham superintended the murder of two other women of Baz Bahadur's harem, that they should tell no tales. The Emperor saw through the flimsy excuse, and in bitterness of heart went back to Agra, though for the sake of

Akbar Learning to Read.

the ties that were between them, he would not punish Adham save by refusing henceforth to trust him with any command.

Dwelling at court, Adham brooded in sullen inaction, jealous of all around him, most jealous of the prime minister, Shams-ad-din, to whose influence with the Emperor he attributed his disgrace. One night when the Emperor had retired to the harem, Shams-ad-din was sitting in the hall of audience, reading the Koran aloud. Adham swaggered in, followed by a band of Uzbegs; the prime minister continued his reading without noticing the Khan, who suddenly drew his dagger and stabbed him, then gave a signal to the Uzbegs, who completed the work. Then he sprang upon the terrace leading to the harem, and knocked violently upon the door. Hearing the noise, Akbar came out in his night clothes, sword in hand, and saw the body of his minister lying in the courtyard, whither he had dragged himself in the last agony, and the murderer standing on the threshold. "What is this?" he cried. "Hear me!" answered Adham, seizing his hands. A blow from Akbar's clenched fist brought him to the ground. Then the Emperor gave command to the bystanders to fling the murderer over the terrace wall. Some say that Akbar himself took the wretched man in his arms and kissed him once ere he sent him toppling over two-and-twenty feet into the court below.

This much is certain, that he himself went to break the news to Maham Anaga. "Maham, we have slain Adham," he told her. "His Majesty has done well," she made answer, bowing her head; but she could neither forgive nor forget. Within forty days she was dead of a broken heart, and Akbar buried her with her son at Delhi. Maham's tomb has disappeared, but her son's tomb, on the walls of the Lal Kot citadel, is yet to be seen in all distant views of the Kutb.

Two or three years later Akbar was going in procession through Delhi; as he passed by the mosque, built by Maham in the days of her prosperity, an archer on the roof, pretending to aim at a bird overhead, lodged an arrow span-deep in the Emperor's shoulder. The assassin was seized, and the nobles implored that before his execution a little pressure should be put upon him to reveal the names of his accomplices. But Akbar refused; confession under torture might incriminate the innocent; and if there had been fellow-conspirators he had no desire to learn who they were. So the man was cut to pieces there and then, before the surgeons had taken out the arrow from the Emperor's wound.

Akbar was not yet twenty when the death of Maham set him free to govern according to his will. Looking at him in the opening years of his reign, there is much to recall Babar. He had the same inexhaustible physical strength, seeming not to know the meaning of fatigue. He could ride from Agra to Ajmir (240 miles) in a day and a night; he was an unwearied polo player (using fire balls when the sudden darkness of an Indian night fell upon the game), and a mighty hunter, who could cut down a royal tigress with a single stroke when she crossed his path. With only a part of Babar's unquenchable *joie de vivre*, there were moments when he forgot kingdom, dignity, and responsibilities, and flung himself into whatever fate had provided in whole-hearted exultation. We read of him coming, in pursuit of a rebel, to a ferry where there were no boats, urging his elephant into the river "which was then deep," despite the remonstrances of his officers, and, careless of the fact that only a hundred of his bodyguard had been able to follow, sounding his kettle-drums before the enemy's camp. We read, too, of a glorious day during the campaign in Gujarat, when the Emperor crossed a river with only one hundred and fifty-six men and fell upon a thousand, drawing up his handful of followers in a narrow lane formed by hedges of the prickly pear where only three horsemen could ride abreast, himself in advance of them all, with two Rajput princes to guard his head while he plied sword and bow.

He had Babar's infinite capacity for being interested in everything and every one, and his experiments were the horror of orthodox Muslims at his Court. He experimented in all directions, from religion to metallurgy. It was bad enough that an Emperor should soil his fingers by making new kinds of gun-barrels—warranted not to burst—or machines for cleaning guns, or other devices which should have been left to a craftsman. It was worse when he smoked tobacco—seduced by "a handsome pipe three cubits long," which a courtier presented to him, although, after a first trial, his Majesty did not care to smoke again. When, with a view to ascertaining the primitive religion, the Emperor took some luckless babies from their mothers and shut them by themselves in a house at Fatehpur-Sikri, with attendants who were forbidden or unable to speak a word to them, the orthodox bore it philosophically: much harm was not likely to come of the experiment—especially as the poor children grew up dumb; but when his Majesty caused the Hindu sacred books and the Gospels to be translated for his own reading, and held conferences with Brahmins, Guebres, and Jesuits, all respectable persons were outraged.

He had little or nothing of Babar's delight in sensuous pleasures; he ate once a-day, and only took meat twice a-week; his drink was Ganges water; he slept three hours out of the twenty-four, and was never idle. The only luxury that he allowed himself was perfumes, of which he was fond beyond measure. Like Babar, he was subject to sudden fits of rage, in one of which he flung from the battlements a servant whom he found asleep when he should have watched; like Babar, he would build a pyramid of the heads of his enemies after a battle; like Babar, he could forgive over and over again, as only the strong can forgive.

A story is told of him that during the campaign in Gujarat, just before an action, he found a young Rajput prince weighed down by a suit of armour far too heavy for his boyish limbs. Akbar took it from him, and gave him a lighter suit to wear. Just then, happening to see another of the Rajputs unarmed, he bade him put on the heavy mail which the prince had stripped off. Most unluckily, this last Raja happened to be the deadly foe of the other's house, and the boy, furious that his armour should be profaned in this way, tore off the Emperor's gift, vowing he would go "baresark" into the fight. Akbar thereupon stripped himself of his armour. "I cannot allow my chiefs to be more exposed than myself; if they ride to battle unarmed, so do I."

"He is affable and majestical," says a contemporary; merciful and severe; skilful in mechanical arts, . . . curiously industrious, affable to the vulgar, seeming to grace them and their presents with more respective ceremony than the grandees; loved and feared of his own, terrible to his enemies."

He was beardless, of middle height, with a stout, sturdy body, abnormally long arms, and black eyes and hair. A wart on the left side of his nose was considered to be an additional beauty and a sign of extraordinary good fortune. His voice was loud, clear, and ringing. "His manner and habits were quite different from those of other people, and his countenance was full of godlike dignity," adds the son who did much to break Akbar's heart in the last sad years of his life.

Like his father, Akbar at the beginning of his reign had to contend with a rebellious brother, and rebellious cousins, who, one by one, were brought to order. Then, by degrees, he added the outlying provinces to his empire; Chitor, the stronghold of the Rajputs, was stormed in 1567, and since that hour, when its garrison perished sword in hand, lighted by the flames of the pyres on which the women were burning, it has been a forsaken city, where the doleful creatures of the night cry in the palaces. Bengal and Gujarat, Kashmir, Sind, and, in an evil hour, part of the Deccan, owned the ruler of Delhi as their master.

With scarcely a year in his life in which he was not at war, reducing a rebellion, putting down a usurper, or annexing new territory, it is marvellous that he accomplished so much as he did in the way of internal reforms. In the year of Adham's death the Rajput lord of Amber, ancestor of the present Maharaja of Jeypore, gave his daughter in marriage to the Emperor. It was unspeakable pollution for the descendant of the moon to mingle his blood with that of the unclean "Toork," but it was sound policy for Amber, and for the Hindus in the Emperor's dominions. Henceforth Hindus were chosen for the highest offices, civil and military; a Rajput chief, Man Sing of Jodhpur, was the first "Commander of Seven Thousand," and fought against the "Sun of the Hindus," the Rana of Udaipur, at the Emperor's command.

For many years, in scrupulous observance of the Prophet's commands, the Muslim conquerors had levied a poll-tax upon all unbelievers; Akbar remitted this, after his marriage with the princess, and also took off the tax upon Hindu pilgrims, saying to those who remonstrated at this last proceeding, that "although the tax fell on a vain superstition, yet as all modes of worship were designed for a great Being, it was wrong to throw an obstacle in the way of the devout, and to cut them off from their mode of intercourse with their Maker."

The Hindus were not equally pleased when he forbade child marriage and animal sacrifice. The burning of widows was horrible to him; the daughter-in-law of the Raja of Jodhpur, doomed to the flames, found means to send him a bracelet, whereby, in accordance with old Rajput custom, he became her "bracelet-brother," bound to do whatever service she required of him. Akbar rode himself to save her, and forbade burning for the future, save with the widow's consent. While the Hindus murmured at these interferences with their traditions, the Muslim were equally indignant at the ordinance which forbade that captives taken in war should be used as slaves.

Akbar's greatest achievement was the reconstruction of the revenue. "The land-tax was always the main source of revenue in India, and it had become almost the sole universal burden since Akbar had abolished not only the poll-tax and pilgrims' dues, but over fifty minor duties."[1]

[1] S. Lane Poole.

It is impossible to give an adequate account of the system worked out by Todar Mal, the great Hindu financier; his threefold object was (1) to obtain correct measurement of the land; (2) to ascertain the amount of produce of each half-acre and the proportion it should pay to government; and (3) to settle the equivalent in money. Though the actual amount yielded in revenue was lessened, and the taxes and fees paid to the revenue officers were abolished, more money actually reached the treasury, as defalcations were checked. The present land-revenue system of British India is founded upon the principles that Akbar and Todar Mal laid down more than three hundred years ago.

Great was the disgust of the Muslim when they saw the rise of Todar Mal; greater still, when everywhere in court and camp Hindus were equally eligible with Muslims for office. Their remonstrances had as little effect upon the Emperor as his wise sayings about toleration had upon them. There is a story told during the campaign in Rajputana, of a Muslim who asked a brother officer how he was to order his men to fire without injuring the Hindu allies who were covering their front. "Bah!" said the other, with a faith as robust as that of Bishop Folquet at the siege of Albi, "let fly in the name of God! He knows His own."

X.

THE PASSING OF A DREAM—1569-1605

"O God, in every temple I see those who see Thee,
And in every tongue that is spoken, Thou art praised.
Polytheism and Islam grope after Thee.
Each religion says, 'Thou art One, without equal.'
Be it mosque, men murmur holy prayer; or church, the bells ring for love of Thee.
Awhile I frequent the Christian cloister, anon the mosque.
But Thee only I seek from fane to fane.
Thine elect know naught of heresy or orthodoxy, whereof neither stands behind the screen of Thy truth.
Heresy to the heretic—dogma to the orthodox—
But the dust of the rose petal belongs to the heart of the perfume-seller."

—*Abu-l-Fazl.*

X.

THE PASSING OF A DREAM—1569-1605.

TWENTY-TWO miles away from Agra, on a ridge overlooking the plain, lies Fatehpur-Sikri, a city of dreams, built of red sandstone that takes marvellous colours at sunset and sunrise. Built by Akbar, it was abandoned even in his lifetime, and five years after its founder's death an English traveller found it "ruinate, lying like a waste district, and very dangerous to pass through at night." To the traveller of our own day it scarcely seems "ruinate"; in many places the angles of the carven stone are as sharp as if the chisel had left them last year. You may walk beneath the balcony where Akbar stood each day to give justice to the people, and through the courtyard where he played at chess in the cool of the evening, his pawns sixteen beautiful slave-girls, richly dressed and covered with jewels, who became the prize of the victor. Here are the palaces of his wives—"the house of the Turkish Sultana,"—the house of Bibi Mariam, where over the door may still be traced the golden wings of the angel of the Annunication, drawn by a Portuguese artist,—the house of a Hindu princess, with its little temple where she worshipped her own gods. Here, too, are the dwellings of his three dearest friends, Raja Birbal, the Hindu minstrel, witty and wise, whose keen-edged sayings were remembered long after he and Akbar had gone to their appointed places; Faizi, the Poet Laureate; and Abu-l-Fazl, his brother, scholar and mystic. These men came on Thursday evenings to the lofty hall of the Diwan-i-Khas, when the Emperor took his seat on the platform above the carved central column from which run four stone causeways, each leading to a niche at the corner of the building. In these niches sat representatives of different religions,—mullah and Brahman, Jesuit missionary, Jew, or philosopher, and each argued his case,—sometimes with much violence on the part of the mullahs, who thought the sword the best argument to use against heretics.

The empty courtyards now echo only to the click of Western shoes and the gabble of the guide; they were crowded to suffocation at the vernal equinox or on the Emperor's birthday, when the ground was spread with two acres of

Akbar.

Abu-l-Fazl.

Raja Birbal.

Three Friends.

silk and gold carpets, when many hundred elephants defiled before him, the leading one of each company wearing gold plates set with rubies on breast and head, followed by rhinoceroses, lions, tigers, panthers, cheetahs, hounds, and hawks. There were squadrons of cavalry, blazing in cloth of gold; there were the nobles "sparkling with diamonds like the firmament," wearing herons' plumes in their turbans; and in the centre of all was the solitary figure upon the throne, arrayed in plain white muslin.

When the moonlight is steeping halls and courtyards, sitting in the old Record Office, near the entrance gate, or climbing the narrow staircase by which Akbar's ministers went up to the "House of Dreams," where the Emperor slept, you may hear the dreams and the ghosts rustle their wings, and whisper all night long. Or you may come forth at dawn and sit in the courtyard where he used to sit, meditating on Life and Death till the sun rose, and he bowed before the symbol of Him who gives light to the world. As has well been said, "Fatehpur-Sikri is now a body without a soul"; but the shadow of Akbar's soul yet seems to hover within the charmed city that he built and then deserted.

Babar had had the simple faith of a child and a soldier, Humayun, though devout, had been anything but orthodox; in Akbar, a penetrating sense of the reality and constant presence of God was joined to a complete indifference as to religious forms,—or rather, looking through the form to what lay behind it, he was ready to accept all forms for the sake of what they were intended to convey. The Jesuit fathers from Goa found him ready not only to listen to them, but to incline to their side in their disputes with the champions of other faiths. One of his sons was given religious instruction by Padre Rodolfo Acquaviva,—said to have been the Jesuit who, by way of clinching a dispute with one of the chief mullahs at the Emperor's Court, offered to enter a fire, Bible in hand, if his adversary would do the like, armed with the Koran. On certain days "the Emperor came forth to the audience-chamber with his brow marked in Hindu fashion, and jewelled strings tied by Brahmans on his wrist to represent the sacred thread." His bowings before the sun, and his command to the Court to rise, every evening, when the lamps were lighted, have made some writers pronounce him a fire-worshipper; those who remember the "grace for light" that used to be said in cottage homes in certain glens of Ireland when the candle was lighted, may deem that the reverence was for the Giver of Light.

As the years went on he disregarded or set aside observances practised by the most lax of Muslims. The profession of faith, "There is no God but God, and Muhammad is his Prophet," no longer appeared on the coins; the scandalised orthodox beheld instead the characters "Allahu Akbar," which might read either "God is most Great" or "Akbar is God." When men saluted each other, they were bidden to say "Allahu Akbar" instead of the "Peace be with you" which their fathers had used. In the great mosque of Fatehpur-Sikri, on a Friday in 1580, the worshippers gathered to hear the Emperor conduct the service. Islam, unlike most other religions, has no separate priestly caste, but mullahs and doctors of the Law wagged their beards in pious horror as he ascended the pulpit and began to read "the bidding prayer," to which Faizi had added the lines:—

> "The Lord to me the Kingdom gave,
> He made me wise, and strong, and brave,
> He girded me in right and ruth,
> Filling my mind with love of truth;
> No praise of man can sum His state.
> *Allahu Akbar!* God is Great!"

Their joy must have been uncontrollable when, after the first three lines, Akbar's voice faltered and broke. Whether it were emotion or stage fright, he could go no farther, and was obliged to resign the pulpit to its rightful occupant, the Court preacher.

As if this were not shock enough to all good Muslims, Akbar's next proceeding was to employ the father of Abu-l-Fazl and Faizi—a Shia and a free-thinker who had been expelled from Agra for heresy—to draw up a proclamation: "We have decreed and do decree that the rank of a Just Ruler is higher in the eyes of God than the rank of a Chief of the Law,"—which from that ominous beginning deduced that in all religious disputes his Majesty's decision was binding upon his people. "Further, we declare that, should his Majesty, in his wisdom, issue an order (not being in opposition to the Koran) for the benefit of the people, it shall be binding and imperative on every one; opposition to it being punished with damnation in the world to come, excommunication and ruin in the present life."

Henry VIII., declaring himself Head of the Church, had spoken in much the same tone fifty years previously; but the heathen Emperor, for whose conversion, were he living at the present time, good people would subscribe to send out missionaries, was more merciful in practice than the Christian king. When he tried to bring Raja Man Sing to his way of thinking, and got for answer: "I am a Hindu; your Majesty does not ask me to become a Muslim, and I know of no third faith," the Rajput was not racked, hanged, or burned, but suffered to go his own way in peace. Though in Akbar's lifetime there were conversions to the Monotheism which he strove to teach, it died with him; it was too vague, too pure for the mass, who must needs have something concrete whereon to stay their souls.

With his firm belief that he was the chosen of God, His viceroy in spiritual as well as temporal affairs, there was an overpowering sense of the danger lest he should be unfaithful to his trust. He would never administer justice to his people sitting upon the throne; he stood beneath it as a sign to them that he was only the instrument of God, Who had given the power into his hand. As every one knows, there is a season in the year when the male elephant becomes wild and unmanageable, frequently killing his keeper unless properly secured. One of Akbar's practices was to mount an elephant when the frenzy came upon it, and let it fight another elephant, goading or checking it, heedless of the terrible risk to himself. When a friend ventured to remonstrate, he answered that he did it, praying that, if he had failed in his duty, God would suffer him to be torn in pieces rather than continue in sin.

In the latter part of his reign he had sore need of what comfort he might draw from religion; his luck had turned, and the closing years of his life were marked by disaster, the loss of friends, and the misconduct of those who should have been his stay.

Dearest of all the little band whom he called "the elect," was Raja Birbal, whose influence was thought by the orthodox to be the reason of Akbar's listening to Brahmans and yogis. The two were almost inseparable, and Akbar opened his heart to the minstrel as he would to no other man. In 1586 an expedition was to be sent against the Yusufzais, a wild Afghan tribe inhabiting the valleys of the Hindu Kush. Abu-l-Fazl and Birbal drew lots who should command one of the divisions; Birbal won, and rode away from Akbar's camp on the east side of the Indus, doubtless with a merry quip at Abu-l-Fazl, who remained behind in great mortification.

The expedition was foredoomed to disaster: the other commander of the imperial forces was Zein Khan, one of the Emperor's foster-brothers (son of that Shams-ad-din whom Adham had murdered in the Emperor's audience-hall), and he and Birbal detested each other. There were continual quarrels; Birbal insisted upon attacking the Afghans, contrary to Zein Khan's judgment, and was drawn into a mountain pass where his forces were overwhelmed by showers of stones and flights of arrows. His division was cut to pieces, and Zein Khan's, which had remained in the plain, fared little better. The Khan escaped on foot to Attock, where Akbar refused to see him.

Birbal's body was never found, and the story rose that he still lived, a prisoner, among the Yusufzais. Long after the disaster, an impostor appeared, calling himself Birbal, and Akbar sent command for him to come to Agra. It would have been impossible for him to play the part successfully before Birbal's dearest friend, and he was lucky in dying on the way to Court, honoured beyond his deserts, in that the Emperor put on mourning for him.

It is said that the Emperor and the minstrel had made a compact together that if there were a life after death, whichever of the two died first should come back to the survivor. Perhaps it was after vainly sitting, night after night, in the "House of Dreams," where he and Birbal had often "tired the sun with talking and sent him down the sky," vainly listening and looking for the curtain, "always rustling but never rising," to be drawn aside, that Akbar determined to leave his City of Victory.

The official reason was that there was no water

supply—a drawback that might have been ascertained before the city was built. A modern writer has imagined the cause to be Akbar's heartbreak over the son whose birth had been the cause of its foundation.

For, up to the fourteenth year of his reign, none of the sons born to the Emperor had lived, until, returning from one of his campaigns, he halted at the foot of the hill of Sikri, and there found a very holy man, the Shaikh Salim Chishti, living in a cave. The shaikh had a little son, only six months old, who noticed that after the Emperor's visit his father seemed heavy and dejected. "Why do you grieve, O my father?" asked the child, who—we are rather unnecessarily told—had never spoken before. "O my son," answered the shaikh, "it is written that the Emperor will never have an heir unless some other man will sacrifice to him the life of his son, and surely none is capable of such an act."

"Nay, father," cried the child, "if you forbid me not, I will die in order that his Majesty may be consoled." And forthwith he lay down and died. In proof of the truth of this story, his grave may be seen in an enclosure near the quadrangle, where stand the mosque built by Salim Chishti and the domed tomb where the saint lies beneath a sarcophagus inlaid with mother-of-pearl, and surrounded by pendent ostrich eggs.

Akbar left his wife, the Amber princess, at Sikri for some months; after the birth of a son, named Salim, after the holy man, he began to build the city on the hill.

Other sons were afterwards born to the Emperor, only to bring grief and shame upon him. Not one had any thought of carrying out his father's work, or helping him in any way; all three were incorrigible drunkards, the curse of their house having fallen on them. Akbar himself, worn and harassed beyond endurance, had yielded to it so far as to take opium.

Whether it were grief over lost friend or living sons that moved him, the Emperor abandoned Fatehpur-Sikri after Birbal's death, and for the next fourteen years of his life made his capital at Lahore.

The two brothers, Faizi and Abu-l-Fazl, were spared to him for some time longer. Faizi, the first Muslim to study Hindu literature and science, had been set by the Emperor to translate portions of the Mahabharata, Ramayana, and other Hindu works. Most of us have to be content to take it on trust that he was also "one of the most exquisite poets India has ever produced." Abu-l-Fazl compiled the "Ain-i-Akbari," the

"Acts of Akbar," which is partly a history of the Emperor, partly a most minute account of the revenue, household, treasury, military regulations, and other matters, with a gazetteer of India, and a collection of his Majesty's sayings and teachings. No other work gives such a picture of contemporary India, its learning, traditions, and customs, and under the pompous style of a "Court Journal" the most vivid glimpses of Akbar the man are disclosed, amid details of etiquette, cookery recipes, or treatises upon religion.

It was some nine years after the disastrous expedition against the Yusufzais, that word was brought to Akbar at midnight that Faizi was desperately ill. Hurrying to his friend's room, he bent over him, raised his head, and called him by the familiar name that had long been used between them. "Shaikh-ji! I have brought Ali, the doctor." The dying man, nearly insensible, could make no answer. "Why do you not speak?" implored the Emperor; then, recognising that Faizi was slipping away beyond his reach, he flung his turban upon the ground and gave himself up to passionate grief. Abu-l-Fazl, unable to see his brother die, had gone to his own room, and there the Emperor went and remained for a long time, trying to comfort him, before going back to the palace.

Akbar was called from his private griefs to make a decision that was to bear ill-consequences for those who came after him. Beyond the Vindhya mountains which form the southern boundary of Hindustan, lies the table-land supported on all sides by hill ranges which is known as the Deccan. Conquered and despoiled by Ala-ad-din of Delhi early in the fourteenth century, it shook off the yoke in later years, and from the reign of Muhammad Taghlak no king of Delhi had been acknowledged south of the Vindhya mountains. The Bahmanid sultans ruled it for a hundred and eighty years,—a fierce and cruel race, one of whom used to hold great feasts whenever he had succeeded in massacring over 20,000 Hindus at a time. When their dynasty came to an end, just at the time when Babar was making his way to Delhi, their dominions were split into the five states of Bijapur, Ahmadnagar, Golkonda, Berar, and Bidar, all ruled by Muslim princes.

A glance at the map will show that the Deccan is divided from Hindustan by natural barriers, and very little acquaintance with history will prove the truth of the saying that "Nature never intended the same ruler to govern both sides of the Vindhya mountains; people, character, and geographical conditions are dissimilar. Nevertheless, to conquer the Deccan has been the ambition of every great king of Delhi, and the attempt has always brought disaster."[1]

Unluckily for all parties, Akbar had a good pretext for interference in the condition of the Deccan. In 1595 there were no less than four separate claimants to the throne of Ahmadnagar; one of them called upon the Moghuls to aid him, and, nothing loath, Akbar sent out an army under his second son, Murad.

When the Prince and his host arrived beneath the walls of Ahmadnagar, they found the conditions not what they had expected. One of the four rival claimants, a mere child, had been put under the guardianship of the widow of Sultan Ibrahim, his uncle. Chand Bibi—"the resplendent lady"—was one of the noblest women who have ever appeared in Indian history. No longer young, and childless, her day might have seemed over, when she was called to fight for her husband's heir, and bravely grappled what had seemed a hopeless task. The pretender who had appealed to Delhi was expelled from Ahmadnagar; and Chand Bibi made a solemn appeal to her kinsman, the King of Bijapur, who was backing another claimant, to cease this internecine strife, and to join against the foe who

[1] S. Lane Poole.

would eat them up, one by one, unless he were expelled at the outset.

The appeal from a woman to a man's better self succeeded for the time being; the King of Bijapur combined with two of the rival armies and marched against the Moghuls, while the leader of the third, Nehang, an Abyssinian, cut his way through the lines of the besiegers, and came to reinforce the garrison in Ahmadnagar.

Chand Bibi was the soul of the defence, exposing herself freely on the walls or down below in the darkness, where besieger and besieged mined and countermined. One mine was fired before the garrison were ready to meet the danger; a yawning breach opened in the walls, and the besieged fled in terror from their posts, leaving the way open to the storming party. Then down among her panic-stricken men came a slight figure, sword in hand, recognised at once by the richly decorated suit of armour and the silver veil that floated over her helmet. She rallied them, she led them back to the wall; all day till evening they stood in the breach, keeping off the assailants, and when night brought a truce she toiled with the men, who brought wood, stones, earth, even dead carcases, and built up the wall again until it was too strong to be forced without another mine.

In after generations, when Ahmadnagar was no longer a kingdom, men told how the Queen defended her city, making balls of copper when all the shot was expended, then silver, then gold, and at last firing away her jewels when nothing else was left.

The Moghuls were obliged to make terms, for the King of Bijapur and his allies were approaching, and they feared to be taken in the rear. So peace was arranged; the Emperor's forces drew off, and Chand Bibi was left to rule for her nephew.

Freed from the common danger, men returned to plot and intrigue, and the Queen's wisdom and valour availed her nothing. Ghand's own prime minister turned traitor, and sought the help of Prince Murad, and before the year was out the Deccan was once more invaded. The imperial forces gained a victory, and made no attempt to follow it up. Then Akbar himself came to take command, sending on a force under his third son, Daniyal, to Ahmadnagar, where Chand held out, dauntless, but at the end of her resources. The city was a mass of disaffection and rebellion, and Nehang had broken out into revolt, and had been besieging her until the Moghul forces arrived. Nothing remained but to make conditions of surrender. While she was striving to gain the utmost that she could for her ward and her people, some of the rebels stirred up the soldiery to mutiny: "the Queen had betrayed them to the Moghuls." They broke into the women's side of the palace, calling for Chand Bibi; the old woman faced them, a queen to the end, and fell beneath their swords.

There is some comfort in remembering that, a few days later, the imperial troops stormed Ahmadnagar and slaughtered every man of the garrison. The poor little king was sent to Gwalior, where innumerable state prisioners have ended their days in the fortress on the hill.[1]

In the Deccan campaign, Abu-l-Fazl at length obtained his heart's desire, and went on military service for the first time, proving himself as brave and capable as he was loyal. A quarrel had arisen between Akbar and his vassal, the King of Khandesh, whose brother-in-law Abu-l-Fazl happened to be. To the king it seemed perfectly natural to send costly gifts to his brother-in-law in order to gain Akbar's favour; Abu-l-Fazl sent them all back. "The Emperor's bounty has extinguished in my mind all feelings of avarice." He succeeded in capturing the fort of Asirgarh, on an isolated hill of the Satpura

[1] See Meadows Taylor's 'A Noble Queen' for the whole story of Chand Bibi.

range, one of the most famous strongholds in India, Khandesh was annexed, and when Akbar returned to Agra he left his friend to command in the Deccan.

It was no pleasant errand that took the Emperor back to Agra before his conquests in the south were completed. Prince Salim, his heir-apparent, had been left to conduct the war with Udaipur in his father's stead, with Man Sing to help him. A revolt in Bengal sent the Raja hurrying to put it down, and Salim thereupon seized upon Allahabad and proclaimed himself king.

Akbar had already lost one son, Prince Murad having drunk himself into his grave during the war in the Deccan, and he could not treat the graceless prince as he deserved. A touching letter, warning Salim of the consequences if he persisted in rebellion, and assuring him of the undiminished love and free pardon that waited for him if he repented, brought a half-submission. Salim retired to Allahabad, and Akbar, catching at any sign of grace, made him a grant of Bengal and Orissa, in hope that independence might bring a sense of responsibility.

In August 1602, Abu-l-Fazl, relieved from his command in the Deccan, was making his way across the plains to his Emperor at Agra. He rode with only a small escort, for the land was at peace, and who would dare to touch one of the royal household? He had nearly reached Gwalior when he was surrounded by a body of freebooters under Narsing Deo, the Hindu Raja of the petty state of Orcha. He and his men sold their lives dearly, but they were overwhelmed by numbers.

When Akbar heard that the last of his three friends had perished, he refused to eat or sleep for two days and nights. Then he came forth, terrible in his anger, and sent a force to Orcha; the raja and all his family were to be seized, the country was to be ravaged, the whole state should mourn Abu-l-Fazl's death. For a short space the relentless, indiscriminating cruelty of his barbarian forefathers woke within him.

He did not know—it is to be hoped he never knew—that Narsing Deo had been only the tool of Salim, who, madly jealous of Abu-l-Fazl, had seized this opportunity of removing him. There was bitterness enough in the thought that at one time the prince had succeeded in poisoning his mind against his friend, so that when Abu-l-Fazl had first gone to the Deccan, it had been intended as an honourable banishment.

In Allahabad Prince Salim gave himself over to every kind of debauchery, drinking at least ten pints of wine a-day, and subject to such terrible fits of rage that his attendants durst not come near him. Akbar was told that his son had ordered an offender to be flayed alive, and could not suppress his indignation. "How can the son treat a human being like this, when the father cannot endure to see a dead sheep skinned without pain?" he asked in the bitterness of his soul.

There was a l st hope that a meeting between father and son might reclaim the prince from his evil ways. Akbar set out to Allahabad to wake his boy's better self if he might,—at least, to snatch him from his companions in sin. He had only gone a little way from Agra when a messenger overtook him to say that the Queen-Mother was at the point of death. It gives something of a shock to find Hamida Begam, after all the breathless flights, the privations, the long-drawn wanderings, and the heart-sickening anxieties of her early youth, living on almost to the end of her son's reign. The Emperor hurried back to Agra, in time to be with her at the last. Mother and son were united by a very close affection, and to the end of her life, we are told, the first dishes of food that Akbar tasted after the yearly fast, were sent to him from his mother's house. He already knew the loneliness of mind which is the penalty of all who are in advance of their fellow-men; he was now to know loneliness of heart. Save his mother, no woman had ever counted for much in his life: there were five thousand in his harem, each dwelling in her own apartment. As Abu-l-Fazl observed, "the large number of them—a vexatious question even for great statesmen—furnished his Majesty with an opportunity to display his wisdom," but not one of these was ever to him what the Moon Lady had been to Babar, or even Hamida to Humayun.

In a transient spasm of better feeling Salim now came to Agra, and being placed under a doctor's care, regained his health, thanks to the iron constitution of Babar's descendants. His temper, however, was no better than could be expected of a suddenly reformed drunkard; he was on the worst possible terms with his eldest son, Khusru, whose mother (Raja Man Sing's sister) had poisoned herself in desperation at the dispute between her husband and his heir. Khusru was doing his utmost to excite his grandfather's anger against his father, and, if possible, to gain the throne for himself, backed up by Man Sing, who certainly had no reason for loving Salim. The whole Court was seething with jealousies and plots, and the Emperor's heart was broken. Vainly did he warn those about him that they must lay aside their disputes and work together for the common good, if they would not see the empire go to pieces; he was not the man that he had been, he could no longer control bursts of temper, the result of overstrung nerves and overwrought strength, and all men knew that his time would soon be over. His dream had faded, not into the light of common day, but into the clouds of the gathering storm.

In 1604 died his youngest son, Daniyal; he had been put under supervision, like his brother, to keep him from drink, and, unable to bear enforced sobriety, he had intoxicating liquor smuggled into his palace in the barrel of a fowling-piece, until it killed him. It was the last blow, and Akbar could bear no more. He took to his bed in the September of the following year, after having been ill for some time. Salim at first refused to come to his father, having intelligence that Man Sing intended to proclaim Prince Khusru as Akbar's successor, and fearing to be seized by the Rajput if he set foot in the palace. But when the Emperor had repeatedly declared his will that Salim should reign in his stead, even Man Sing dared not attempt anything, and reluctantly promised to be true man to his brother-in-law.

It was the 4th of October 1605,—in England certain foolish and misguided men were unwillingly deferring the execution of their design to blow up Westminster Hall, because Parliament had been prorogued unexpectedly. In the great red fort at Agra which he had built, Akbar lay on his deathbed, and the son for whom he had asked continually, stood at his side. Round him were the omrahs and the ministers whom the Emperor had bidden Salim call into the room. "I cannot bear that any misunderstanding should subsist between you and those who have for so many years shared in my toils and been the companions of my glory." Looking on them for the last time, he asked their forgiveness if he had injured or offended them in any way. Repentant too late, Salim flung himself down in a passion of tears; the Emperor could not speak, but pointed to his sword and signed to the Prince to gird it on. In a momentary revival of strength he threw his arms round his son's neck, and bade him care for the women of the family who would be left desolate. The last commendation came brokenly: "My servants and dependants—when I am gone do not forget the afflicted in the hour of need. Ponder, word for word, on all I have said: again, forget me not." In the night the weary soul found freedom.

At the northern end of the ridge on which Fatehpur-Sikri is built, stands one of the finest portals in the world, the Baland Darwaza, on which may yet be read the inscription that Akbar placed there in 1602. The latter part, which follows the record of his titles and his conquest of the Deccan, perhaps embodies some of the wisdom that he learned during those last years of loneliness and disappointment. "Said Jesus (on Whom be peace!), 'The world is a bridge, pass over it, but build no house there. He who hopes for an hour hopes for an eternity. The world is but an hour; spend it in devotion, the rest is unseen.'"

XI.

THE WEST IN THE EAST—1608-1618

"Neither will this overgrown Elephant descend to Article or bind himself reciprocally to any Prince upon terms of equality, but only by way of favour admit our stay so long as it either likes him or those that govern him."

—Sir THOMAS ROE (August 21, 1617).

XI.

THE WEST IN THE EAST—1608-1618.

It was on an August day of 1608 that Captain William Hawkins, trading for the East India Company, brought his ship the *Hector* into the Swally Roads, the harbour for Surat, and prepared to deliver the letters and presents with which King James I. of England had intrusted him "to the princes and governors of Cambay." He soon found that he had set his foot in a hornet's nest. The Portuguese, who had once commanded the European trade with the East, from the Cape of Good Hope to China, now had to endure the competition of the Dutch, and were not disposed to admit another rival company. Hawkins was told by the Portuguese officials in Surat that his king was "King of Fishermen and of an Island of no import," and that the seas belonged to his Catholic Majesty, the King of Spain and Portugal, without whose licence no one must presume to come hither.

Now William Hawkins was the nephew of that Sir John Hawkins who started the trade in African slaves, took part in repelling the Armada, and died on Drake's last voyage to the West Indies, and by his own showing he had inherited much of the family temper. "The King of England's licence is as good as the King of Spain's," was his reply; "and so tell your great Captaine that in abusing the King of Englande, he is a base villaine, and a traytor to his King, and that I will maintaine it with my sword if he dare come on shore."

Some of the Emperor's officials interfered to prevent the duel; but the Portuguese, for the time, had the upper hand. The *Hector*, sent by Hawkins to trade at Bantam, was captured by their ships as soon as she left Surat, and men and goods taken to Goa, the chief Portuguese settlement. Hawkins, who, with many an Englishman of all times up to our own, cherished the faith that a Jesuit was *capable de tout*, accuses the padres of Surat of suborning men to stab and poison him while he waited for an opportunity of presenting his credentials to the Emperor. At last he succeeded in getting an escort, with which he reached Agra in April 1609.

Immediately on his arrival, the Emperor sent for him with such urgency that Hawkins had no time to unpack suitable offerings for his Majesty—for it was a strict rule of Court etiquette that no one might enter the presence without bringing a gift. He was well received, and the Emperor commanded "an old Jesuit" to translate King James's letter. Anxious to lose no opportunity of hindering a rival in trade, the padre began "discommending the stile, saying it was basely penned." "My answer was unto the King," says the undaunted Hawkins, "'And if it shall please your Majesty, these people are our enemies; how can this letter be ill-written when my King demandeth a favour of your Majesty?'" This appeal to common-sense was at once admitted, and the Emperor took the Captain into the private audience-chamber, where they talked together for a long time. The Court language was Persian, but Hawkins, in the course of his voyáges, had picked up Turkish, which, properly speaking, was the native tongue of Babar's descendants, and they could converse without an interpreter.

"Both night and day his delight was very much to talk with me," says Hawkins, who was soon to find this favour rather burdensome. The Emperor took a violent liking to the Englishman whose honest bluntness made him as amusing a companion as his capacity for drinking. When the envoy asked leave, in the name of the East

India Company, to establish an English factory at Surat, the Emperor swore "by his father's soul" to allow this upon the most favourable terms, on one condition — Hawkins must take service with him.

After thinking the matter over, the captain decided not to refuse, considering, as he told the Company, that in a few years they would be able to send someone to replace him, and meantime "I should feather my nest, and do you service." So Captain Hawkins became "Inglis Khan," one of the nobles of the Court, to the furious jealousy of "the Portugalls," who became "like mad dogs," and the righteous indignation of devout Muslims.

He had to pay for his favour; for twelve hours out of every twenty-four, day or night, he must serve his new master. Then he and all his company suddenly became ill—a catastrophe not unlikely to happen to Europeans in Agra at any time, particularly in the summer months. The Emperor, however, had his suspicions, "and presently called the Jesuites, and told them if I died by any extraordinary casualtie, that they should all rue for it." As a further precaution, Hawkins was made to marry an Armenian girl, who could cook his food and so prevent poison from getting into it. Mrs Hawkins must have proved a singularly good cook, for though the bridegroom was at first unwilling to be tied to her, on discovering in after years that their marriage had not been legal, he was married to her again with all due formalities.

Hawkins was not the first Englishman to visit the Court of the potentate whom the English, with their usual inaccuracy in regard to foreign titles, styled "the Great Moghul." In the reign of Akbar, three Englishmen had appeared at Fateh-pur-Sikri, bearing a letter from Queen Elizabeth: one vanished from history, one entered the Emperor's service, and one, Ralph Fitch, a London merchant, returned home to found "the Company of Merchants of London trading to the East Indies," incorporated by Royal Charter in 1600, whose representative was Captain Hawkins. A hundred years later it was amalgamated with its most powerful rival, "the General Society trading to the East Indies," and the joint firm became the "John Company" that ruled paramount in India till 1858.

Salim, who had taken the name of "Jahangir" ("World Grasper") on his accession, by this time had sat on his father's throne for nearly four years, and had not proved himself as wholly unworthy a son of that father as had seemed likely to those who noted the debauchery and folly of his youth. He had gratified the mullahs by his professions of orthodoxy, and by restoring the Muslim declaration of faith to the coins, and had lessened the uneasiness of those who were interested in public morality by forbidding his subjects to drink wine or smoke tobacco, and by restricting the use of opium.

Unfortunately it became apparent all too soon that his subjects were to have no encouragement in the paths of virtue from their Emperor's example. Jahangir might tell his beads at break of day,—"eight chains of beads, four hundred each," rubies, diamonds, pearls, and precious stones,—but the pictures of Our Lord and the Virgin were engraved at the head of the "goodly set stone" on which he prostrated himself, with a lambskin for a praying mat. His subjects were commanded to be sober, but Jahangir, between wine and opium, was not able to feed himself by supper-time, and must have the food put into his mouth bit by bit. Akbar's large-minded tolerance had in him become a determination to do exactly as the moment's fancy seized him, in religious matters or in anything else.

Once—it is Manucci, the Venetian physician, who tells the tale—the Emperor invited himself to dine with certain Jesuit fathers at Agra, and drank wine and ate pork to his great contentment. On his return to the palace he called together the doctors of the Law, and asked them what religion allowed men to enjoy wine and pork,—to which the learned men made stern reply that such shameful indulgence was allowed only to Christians. His Majesty at once declared that if such were the case he would be a Christian, and live and dress as the Christians did, and forthwith commanded that tailors should be brought to the palace to cut out garments for himself and the Court, "and that search should be made for hats."

Whereupon the doctors suddenly discovered that the Law, while binding upon meaner men, said nothing about an emperor's diet, and Jahangir talked no more of becoming a Christian, although he allowed the baptism of two of his nephews—who afterwards recanted when they were not able to obtain Portuguese wives. One of his delights was to hold drinking bouts during Ramazan, that great yearly feast when a Muslim will not suffer even cold water to pass his lips from sunrise to sunset. If it chanced that among his guests were any who prayed to be excused, Jahangir gave them their choice between feasting as he bade them, or being thrown to the two lions that were kept chained beneath the windows of his palace—"Eat or be eaten."

Not content with carousing in the palace, he

would go out "to obscure punch-houses" in the city, and hob-nob with men of the lowest class —from which it may be gathered that his edict against drinking had been as successful as most attempts at making men sober by legislation.

The ferocity of the Tatar, latent through many generations of Timur's descendants, blazed out in him. Impalement was his favourite punishment for rebels. He delighted "to see men executed and torn in pieces with elephants." He had elephant fights five times a-week for his amusement, and whenever, as was inevitable, one of the keepers was badly hurt, he was thrown into the river. "Despatch him! for as long as he liveth he will do nothing else but curse me, and therefore it is better that he die presently." At one time he set men to "buffet with lions," and many lost their lives in this way, he continuing "three months in this vein when he was in his humours," until the keepers of his menagerie succeeded in training fifteen little lion cubs to box with them, "frisking between men's legs."

Yet there were glimmerings of better things about this ruffianly drunkard. Daily he held a public levee, as his father had done, and any one with a grievance might call for justice by pulling at "a rope hanged full of bells, plated with gold," which was fastened to two pillars near the Emperor's seat. If his subjects dared there was frequent cause for laying hand on the rope; "the country is so full of outlaws and thieves," grumbled Hawkins, "that almost a man cannot stir out of doors throughout all his dominions without great forces."

In one way at least he was careful to maintain his father's custom; never a newly-made widow in Agra but was summoned before him and asked whether she purposed of her own free will to burn with her husband's corpse. He would use every argument and inducement to keep them from the sacrifice, but not one was ever turned aside from her purpose. In our own days, when English law has long withheld a woman, even in the native states of India, from thus winning salvation for herself and her husband, many a widow, doomed to wear only a single garment, to lay aside all her jewels, to eat but once in the day, her presence an ill omen wherever she goes, has longed for the fire. "They were much better off when they were burned," said a Rajput a few months ago, describing former times. "She rode on a horse, and men walked on each side carrying trays of jewels and gold, and she scattered them among the crowd; and then she mounted the pyre and took her husband's head on her knees, and they gave her plenty of opium,—and she had had that one good day."

So Jahangir found the Hindu women of Agra insistent in demanding their "one good day"; and though for himself he cared nothing for public opinion, he durst not keep them back from getting to Heaven as they chose.

He professed great reverence for his father's memory, ordaining that Sunday should be kept as a holy day because it had been observed by Akbar, and walking on foot from Agra to superintend the building of the tomb at Sikandra. "If I could I would travel this distance upon my head or my eyelashes." He vowed that his father's tomb should be like none other, and he fulfilled his vow: that many-storied building of red sandstone and white marble, standing in the garden where the scarlet pomegranates and white jasmine swing with the breezes, is unique in Indian architecture. Remorse for the conduct that had hastened his father's end seems never to have touched him. Narsing Deo, Abu-l-Fazl's murderer, who had escaped from Akbar's justice "with blistered feet," was received by him at Court and promoted to high station. In his Memoirs he frankly avows that he instigated Narsing Deo, and that "God having rendered

Jahangir.

his aid to the success of the enterprise," the slain man's head was sent to him. "Although my father was exasperated at this catastrophe," he concludes, "yet in the end I was able to visit him without any anxiety or apprehension."

His Memoirs often recall Babar in their keen interest in flowers, animals, and other natural objects. An unknown bird, sent to him from Goa, was so marvellous that the Court painter was summoned to take its portrait: Jahangir's long description shows it to have been a turkey-cock. Like his father, he loved to experiment: having heard that saffron in sufficient quantities would bring on death amid convulsions of laughter, he fed a condemned criminal upon saffron one day, with no result; next day he doubled the dose, but still "it did not cause him even to smile, much less to laugh,"—to the great disappointment of the Emperor.

To an Englishman of the day, and a sailor to boot, Jahangir's fondness for strong drink seemed venial, if not praiseworthy, as setting one whom the honest captain in his heart must have termed "a black heathen" more on a level with ordinary Christian folk. But the Emperor's frequent changes of mind were beyond endurance; the permission to build the factory was alternately given and revoked, according to the influence that happened to be in the ascendant, for over two years, until Hawkins, beyond all patience, took leave of the Court, and started for England with his Armenian wife. He died on the voyage home, and never lived to tell his tale to the Company by word of mouth, but his written narrative of his mission happily remains to us.

Some few years later an Englishman of a very different type came to Jahangir's Court. The affairs of the Company had declined sensibly since the days of Hawkins's nightly carouses with the Emperor. "Master Edwards," their representative at Surat, honest and conscientious, was of a gentle disposition, and could not hold his own against the tyranny of the government officers and the insolence of the Portuguese and Dutch. He had "suffered blows of the Porters, base Peons, and been thrust out by them with much scorn by head and shoulders without seeking satisfaction." Surat was nominally under the rule of Prince Khurram (better known as Shah Jahan), who favoured the Portuguese, and the Portuguese had drawn up a treaty—not yet confirmed—by which all English traders were to be expelled from the Emperor's dominions. Altogether, matters looked ill for our interests, when four English ships cast anchor in Swally Roads in September 1615, bringing Sir

Thomas Roe with letters and presents from James I. to the Emperor.

At his arrival he was met by a demand from the governor—the prince's deputy—that he and all his companions, as well as their luggage, should be searched. He had already claimed an Ambassador's privileges, but "at this name of an Ambassador they laughed one upon another; it being become ridiculous, so many having assumed that title, and not performed the offices." It was the custom of the Emperor's officials "to search everything that came ashore, even to the pockets of men's clothes on their backs," and they intended to abide by it.

A stately figure was Sir Thomas Roe as he landed amid a salute from the English ships, with a face inclining to fleshy, curling locks rubbed very thin on the forehead, firm mouth, and the keen gaze that still looks round-eyed from his portrait. The chief officers of Surat, "sitting under an open Tent upon good carpets in grave order," did not rise, as he came, whereupon he sent word that he would come no farther if they sat still. Perforce, they rose; he entered the tent, and taking his place "in the middle of them," explained his embassy. Then the right of search was hotly debated; Roe would pledge his honour that none of his followers "had the worth of a *Pice* of trade or Marchandice," but he would never dishonour his master by submitting to such slavery.

The officers, who in the previous year had "very familiarly" searched poor Mr Edwards and his company "to the bottom of their pockets, and nearer too, modestly to speak it," when Roe had turned as if to go back to the ship, suggested a compromise. He, and five whom he chose, should go free; and the rest of the party they would embrace, for form's sake, in order to be able to certify that they had laid their hands on them.

On the way to the town a treacherous attempt to search some of the Englishmen in defiance of this agreement was defeated by the Ambassador, who called for a case of pistols, and hung them at his saddle. The officers then tried fair words, but to no effect, and he came to the house assigned to him in great dignity, "the sackbuts of the town going before, and many following me."

Thereafter ensued a prolonged duel between Roe and the governor, in which the Englishman's inflexible honesty at last got the better of the Oriental's cunning. He would not abate one tittle of the ceremony due on either side; he would not give bribes or valuable presents, "thinking it begat an ill custom": he would not be frightened or diverted from his purpose. When, after more than a month spent in this way, there came an order from the Emperor, bidding all governors of provinces or towns to attend the Ambassador with sufficient guard, and not to meddle with anything that was his, the governor "was very blank, desiring my friendship, and offered me anything I would demand. I answered it was now too late. . . . He demanded if I were friends. I said until I heard new complaints, which I expected hourly." And so the Ambassador departed, clean of hand and fearless of spirit as he came, and after a long and tedious journey reached Ajmir, where Jahangir had been staying for the last two years, carrying on a campaign against the Rana of Udaipur.

On the way he had been taken with such a violent attack of fever—which, unlike Captain Hawkins, he did not attribute to the Jesuits—that he nearly died, and though the Emperor sent messages commanding his attendance, he was not able to appear at the Durbar for more than a fortnight.

It was unfortunate for him that King James and the Company had exercised the parsimony with regard to presents which has often, in later days, caused our representatives in the East to blush for shame. A pair of "virginalls," in charge of an English player, an English coach with an English coachman, and some scarlet cloth, were not fitting to either giver or recipient, and Roe was obliged to substitute a sword and scarf of his own for the cloth. At first Jahangir seemed amused. "At night, having stayed the coachman and musician, he came down into a Court, got into the Coach, into every corner, and caused it to be drawn about by them. Then he sent to me, tho' ten o'clock at night, for a servant to tie on his scarf and sword, the English fashion, in which he took so great pride that he marched up and down, drawing it and flourishing it. So that in conclusion he accepted your presents well; but after the English were come away, he asked the Jesuit[1] whether the King of England were a great king that sent presents of so small value, and that he looked for some jewels."

To this blunder, Roe added another of his own, by neglecting to propitiate the Emperor's chief wife, Nur-Jahan Begam. He was determined, as he told the Company, "as well out of necessity as judgment to break this custom of daily bribing." Unluckily, Nur-Jahan's influence was paramount with the Emperor, and her brother, Asaf Khan, the most powerful man at Court, had

[1] Padre Corsi, the Portuguese representative at Jahangir's Court.

an inexhaustible appetite for bribes. Roe was thwarted at every turn in his endeavours to place the position of English merchants on a firm basis, by obtaining a concession for them to trade in all ports belonging to the Emperor. Such a concession, duly sealed, could not be over-ridden by any local authorities, and Roe toiled hard to wring it from the Emperor, often seeing it within his grasp, never succeeding in obtaining it.

Jahangir himself was friendly, and treated the Ambassador with marked favour. Having had it repeatedly dinned into his ears by the Portuguese that the English were nothing but low-born huckstering traders—"a nation of shop-keepers," in fact,—for which class the Moghuls had the greatest contempt, and having formed his own ideas of the English from jovial Captain Hawkins and meek Master Edwards, it took him some time to discover that the representative of English traders could be a soldier and a gentleman. Roe, who had been Esquire of the Body to Queen Elizabeth, and the close friend of Henry, Prince of Wales, and whom the Prince's sister, the "Queen of Hearts," called her "Honest Tom" in familiar correspondence, insisted upon being treated with the courtesy that was his due, and would not enter the presence by the way set apart "for mean men."

A great obstacle to good understanding was the want of a language in common. Roe knew neither Persian nor Turkish nor "Portugall," and all communications had to be made through the medium of an interpreter, who was not always reliable. One of the most amusing passages in Roe's diary tells of an evening when he came to speak his mind plainly to the Emperor, "being in all other ways delayed and refused," and Asaf Khan having at first shut out the interpreter, "an Italian jeweller, a Protestant, that useth much liberty with his tongue," when forced by the Emperor's command to let him enter, strove "to awe him by winking and jogging." As the interview proceeded, and Roe's plain-speaking grew more objectionable, the Khan made an attempt to stop the interpreter by force, "but I held him, suffering him only to wink and make unprofitable signs." "We were very warm," confesses Roe, who gained an admission from the Emperor that his "demands were just, resolution noble,"—and nothing more, except leave to stand where he pleased at Court ceremonies.

The Court did not greatly impress him. "I never imagined a Prince so famed would live so meanly." He admits that the Audience-Chamber "was rich, but of so divers pieces and so unsuitable that it was rather patched than glorious, as if it seemed to strive to show all, like a lady that with her plate set on a cupboard her embroidered slippers,"—one of the shrewdest criticisms ever made of Indian magnificence. "Religions, infinite; laws, none. In this confusion, what can be expected?" he writes, in despair. The Nautch-girls who performed for his diversion he dismisses with a scriptural epithet which cannot be transcribed by a modern writer. The Emperor's drinking-parties were a continual disgust to him, though it was a mark of favour to be bidden to them. On several occasions he had to grope his way out of the room in the dark, because the Emperor had fallen asleep, after "drinking of our Alicant," and "the Candles were popped out." At another time, on the Emperor's birthday, the Ambassador was obliged to drink his health in a cup of mingled wine "more strong than ever I tasted, so that it made me sneeze"; however, he was told to keep the cup, which being of gold set with jewels, with a jewelled cover and stand, may have been some consolation for his sufferings.

This was the most handsome present that Roe ever obtained from the Emperor, whose chariness in giving was a matter for deep regret to the Rev. Edward Terry, who acted for some time as chaplain to the Embassy. According to custom, an ambassador was the guest of the monarch to whom he was accredited; in spite of this, Roe was obliged to defray his own charges, and was always in straits for money. During the first months of his stay at Court, Jahangir sent him, at different times, some game, a man who had been condemned for theft, and a woman who was turned out of the royal harem for misconduct. In some degree this was his own fault; he would not scramble with the grandees for hollow almonds of gold and silver when the Emperor flung them about on his birthdays. When Jahangir sometimes asked him "Why he did not desire some good and great gifts at his hands, he being a great King and able to give it," Roe would reply that he came not to beg anything for himself; all that he desired was "a free, safe, and peaceable trade for the English," and when assured that this would be granted, and again pressed to ask something for himself, his rejoinder was, "If the Emperor knew not better to give than he to ask, he must have nothing from him." Finally, when he was seeking justice for some injury to the English traders, and a Court official would have soothed him with promises of a robe of honour and a grant for his travelling expenses, he returned answer, "That he had no need of a Babylonish garment, nor needed money."

Jahangir's own greed would have been laughable if it had not caused intolerable inconvenience. There were continual delays in sending up the presents brought in 1616 by the English fleet, and it was not until the beginning of 1617 that they were despatched from Surat, under the charge of Mr Terry, who had lately been appointed chaplain to the Ambassador. The Emperor had left Ajmir on a hunting expedition, and was now encamped near Ujjain, the chief city of Malwa.

Great was Roe's indignation to hear that on their way Mr Terry and his party had encountered Prince Shah Jahan, who demanded to be shown the presents for his father, "to fulfil his base and greedy desire," and being met with a firm refusal, had laid hands on bag and baggage, and carried everything off with him. The Emperor had left camp on an elephant "to speak with a saint living on a hill, who is reported to be 300 years old." Roe had "thought this miracle not worthy my examination," and remained behind; he now rode out to intercept his Majesty on return. "He turned his monster to me and prevented me: 'My son hath taken your goods and my presents; be not sad, he shall not touch nor open a seal nor lock; at night I will send him a command to free them.'"

Roe could say no more at the time; but when he went to attend the Emperor in the evening, he reverted to this and other grievances, while his Majesty did his best to appease the storm by fair words, and divert the discussion to safe general subjects, such as "the laws of Moses, Jesus, and Mahomet; and in drink was so kind as to declare that he meddled not with the faith of Christians, Moors, or Jews who lived under his safety, and none should oppress them." "And this often repeated; but in extreme drunkenness he fell to weeping and to divers passions, and so kept us till midnight."

It is to be feared that even the Rev. Edward Terry's presence was inadequate restraint to the Ambassador's emotion at the next news of his "presents and goods"—namely, that they had been surrendered by Shah Jahan, and that the Emperor, on their arrival, had forced them open, and helped himself to anything that he fancied, including Sir Thomas's own wearing apparel.

The furious Ambassador made his way at once to the Presence: "trouble was in my face," he grimly observes, and Jahangir began to pour out excuses. It mattered nothing that some of the presents had been intended for the Empress and the Prince, since he, his wife, and his son "were all one." He had taken only a few trifles that pleased him—two mastiffs, two embroidered cushions, and a barber's case; surely he need not return them? And there were "two glass chests, very mean and ordinary"; as one had been intended for him and one for the Empress, surely if he were "contented with one," that was very reasonable. And then there were some hats; his Majesty confessed, with masculine readiness to own where blame was due, that "his women liked them." "One of them was mine to wear," observed Sir Thomas. The Emperor was equal to the occasion. "Then," he said, "you will not take them from me, for I like them, and yours I will return if you need it, and will not bestow that upon me"—"which I could not refuse," sighs the Ambassador. After similar discussions over pictures, a saddle, some carved figures, and "some other small toys," the Emperor concluded the interview by asking if Roe had "any Grape Wine?" "I could not deny it. He desired a taste next night, and if he liked it he would be bold" (to take it all); "if not, he desired me to make merry with it."

There is small wonder that Sir Thomas was reluctant to yield to the Emperor's request that he should remain another year at the Emperor's Court. The prospects for English trade just then were more hopeful, the Empress for her own ends having gone over to their side, followed, of course, by Asaf Khan. In the end, however, he could not gain the fulfilment of any of their fair promises. "You can never expect to trade here upon conditions that shall be permanent," he sadly warns the Company in February 1618. "All the government depends upon the present will, where appetite only governs the lords of the kingdom." The most dangerous rivals were now the Dutch, who, with characteristic insolence, used every means of robbing and injuring the nation that had befriended them in their worst extremity. "They traduce (King James's) name and royal authority, rob in English colours to scandal his subjects, and use us worse than any brave enemy would, or any other but unthankful drunkards that we have relieved from Cheese and Cabbage, or rather from a chain with bread and water. You must speedily look to this maggot; else we talk of the Portugal, but these will eat a worm in your sides."

In the following year Roe took his departure, succeeding at the last in obtaining not the unrestricted liberty for English merchants to trade in all ports, which had been his aim, but concessions which "he thought as much in general as he could expect or desire,"—and this he had gained by the force of his own personality. He had shown an Oriental Court what was the best type of an English gentleman, and while they cursed him fervently, they had the wit to respect him for being entirely unlike themselves. "For his sake all his nation there seemed to fare the better," avows Mr Terry.

So he vanished from Indian history, this Ambassador, whose boast it was, "I never gave a knife for mine own ends, nor used the least baseness of begging; my riches are accordingly." Many Englishmen since his day have passed the Exile's Gate to represent their country's interests in one capacity or another, and it is matter for thankfulness that the greater number of them could echo his words in full truth.

His later life was spent in diplomatic service at Constantinople, in Sweden, and in Germany. In 1643, when member for Oxford, he retired to Bath for the benefit of his health. "At length," says Anthony à Wood, "this worthy person, Sir Thomas Roe, did after all his voyages and ramblings take a little breath; but soon after, seeing how untowardly things went between the King and his Parliament, did willingly surrender it to Him that first gave it, on the 6th day of November 1644."

His best epitaph would have been the verdict delivered upon him by the Emperor Leopold, a few years before: "I have met with many gallant persons of many nations, but I scarce ever met with an Ambassador till now."

XII.

THE LOVE OF AN EMPEROR—1606-1628

"To have one rose, we suffer from a thousand thorns."—*Jami.*

XII.

THE LOVE OF AN EMPEROR—1606-1628.

LITTLE as good Sir Thomas Roe would have suspected it, Jahangir had become a reformed character since the days when Captain Hawkins had first taken part in his carouses, and it was a woman who had worked the reformation.

In the days of Akbar, Mirza Ghaias-ad-din, a noble Persian of Teheran, having fallen upon evil days, was journeying to India to seek his fortune with his wife and three children. They had reached Kandahar, when the wife gave birth to another child; they were penniless and friendless in a strange land; the baby was only a girl, and therefore of no value. So they laid her down by the roadside, and left her there.

Now it happened that a rich merchant who was travelling by the same caravan as the Mirza, as they passed along the road next morning, saw the forsaken baby, and picked her up, resolving to adopt her. When he asked whether any one in the caravan could act as nurse, the child's mother came forward, and in a little while the whole truth was confessed. The merchant employed Ghaias and his eldest son for a while, and then recommended them to Akbar, who gave them official posts.

Thus it happened that Muhr-i-Nisa, "Seal of Womankind," as the baby was called, was about the Court in her childhood, and came to the monthly fairs instituted by Akbar, where the ladies of the royal harem sold their own work—at the high prices which usually reward royal industry—or chaffered with the merchants' wives who brought goods from every part of the kingdom. Once she had strayed from the gabble and the bustle around her to a quiet corner of the garden, where Prince Salim, then no more than a boy, passing by, saw her, and bade her take care of his two tame doves while he went off somewhere else.

On his return only one dove was there, and in answer to his peremptory demand the child confessed that she had "let it go."

"Stupid! how did you do it?" stormed the angry boy.

"So, my lord," answered Muhr-i-Nisa, throwing

her arms apart, and letting the second dove fly to rejoin its mate.

From that hour Salim fell in love with the Seal of Womankind, who showed such an "oncoming disposition" that the elders on both sides took alarm; the prince was lectured by his father; the loveliest woman in India was married forthwith to Sher Afkan, a young Persian in the Emperor's service, and went with her husband to his governorship of Bardwan, in Bengal.

It is commonly believed that Jahangir, some little time after his accession to the throne, had Sher Afkan assassinated. If so, he did no worse than King David, and with far more excuse; but the truth appears to be that, hearing complaints of Sher Afkan's rule, the Emperor sent a new governor to take over charge of Bardwan, while the Persian came to Court to answer the charges against him; that Sher Afkan refused to obey, ran one of the new governor's suite through the body, and was thereupon cut down by the others. His family were sent to Court, and his widow was given into the austere charge of the Empress-Dowager, Akbar's first cousin,[1] who had been married to him in his childhood. Here she

[1] She was the daughter of Prince Hindal.

remained for four years, supporting herself by painting and needlework. If any at Court remembered her, it was probably only to pity one whose day was over.

One day as she sat at work among her slaves, the Emperor entered. As she rose and saluted him with downcast eyes, and arms folded on her breast, he looked from the figure in the plain white robe to the richly dressed slave-girls, and a question broke forth, abruptly as at their first meeting in the garden, long years since—

"Why this difference between the Sun of Womankind and her slaves?"

"Those born to servitude must dress as it shall please those whom they serve," she answered. "These are my servants, and I lighten the burden of bondage by every indulgence in my power, but I, who am your slave, O Emperor of the world, must dress according to your pleasure, and not my own."

The old love that had leapt to birth at a word from her lips woke again; in a little while Jahangir had married Muhr-i-Nisa, and changed her name, first to "Nur-Mahal," "Light of the Palace," and then to "Nur-Jahan," "Light of the World."

Her first step was to remove, "either by

marriage or in other handsome ways," all women of the harem who might be troublesome—no small number, probably, since Hawkins estimates the expenses of "the King's women" at thirty thousand rupees "by the day." In a little while she was supreme: she sat aloft on the royal balcony, where the officers came to receive her orders; her name was placed on the imperial seals, and on the coinage, with that of the Emperor,—"a conjunction unparalleled in the history of Mahommedan money." She cut down the expenses of the Court while increasing its magnificence; she invented a becoming Court dress; and, greatest feat of all, she reduced the Emperor's potations.

A scandalous story, current in the time of Jahangir's successor, told how Nur-Jahan, having made her husband promise to drink no more than a certain number of cups of wine at supper, brought in musicians to divert him, and he, imperfectly satisfied, demanded more drink, and, on its being denied, began to cuff his Empress—and how she retaliated by slapping and scratching, until both went to bed in the worst possible of humours.

Next day Jahangir was penitent, and ready to own that all had been intended for his good. Nur-Jahan, however, was irreconcilable, and shut herself up in her rooms, declaring that she would have nothing more to do with the Emperor until he had bowed to her feet to ask her forgiveness.

It would have been impossible for the Padishah to bow himself before a mere woman, even though the woman were Nur-Jahan, and for some days the situation was at a deadlock: the Empress sulked and the Emperor moped. Then an old woman came forward with words of wisdom: if the Emperor stood in his balcony while Nur-Jahan walked in the garden below, he might bow to her, so that hls shadow should kiss her feet, and yet abate nothing of his dignity.

Nur-Jahan was growing tired of seclusion—perhaps a little afraid of the consequences to herself should she continue it any longer. So she accepted the compromise, and made preparations for a great festival to celebrate their conciliation.

Next morning going down into the garden, she was angered to find an oily substance floating in the tanks which had been filled with rose-water at her command. At first she thought that someone had disobeyed her, and bathed there; then, after trying with a finger-tip, she realised that she had made a great discovery. The rose-water, heated by the sun, had given off the precious essence known as "ata," whereof a few

Nur Jahan Dressing Herself.

drops in dull glass bottles may sometimes be found in old dressing-cases, relic of the days when it was a gift between princes, worth its weight in gold.

This cannot have been the only time when the cords by which she held the Emperor in leash had nearly snapped asunder. A man of over forty, soaked in drink, accustomed to absolute power, was not an easy subject for reformation. Her task was aided, in part, by the fact that Jahangir's health had begun to break, and that the physicians, with her to back them, spoke plainly of the consequences to follow if the Emperor persisted in drinking several quarts of "double distilled liquor" in the day. Even when most alarmed about his health, however, the royal patient was anything but tractable. When a violent illness had reduced him to living upon gruel, his complaints were incessant. "From the time I arrived at years of discretion, I had never, so far as I recollect, drunk such broth," he grumbles in his Memoirs, "and I hope I may never be obliged to drink it again."

As he drank less he took larger quantities of opium, thereby, no doubt, weakening his will, and bringing him to the state of good-humoured indifference in which he used to say to his ministers that Nur-Jahan Begam had been selected and was wise enough to conduct matters of state, and that he only needed a bottle of wine and a piece of meat to keep himself merry. For all this, there must have been terrible moments when she trembled inwardly lest the lion that she had tamed would rend her in one of his outbursts of fury. But through all danger she held him fast, to die as he had lived, her lover. One little touch in his Memoirs shows the terms on which they were. In his fiftieth year the Emperor was seized with a transient fit of religious emotion, and vowed never again to take the life of any animal with his own hand. Shortly afterwards, he was told that a fierce tiger was infesting the neighbourhood, and set out at once to put an end to its ravages. At the critical moment, when the beast was about to spring, he remembered his vow, and bade the Empress shoot in his stead. He triumphantly records that "Nur-Jahan killed at the first shot."

Of public events in Jahangir's reign there are scarcely any to note. The Rana of Udaipur had at last been brought to make submission, thereby giving peace to Rajputana, for the time. There were the usual revolts in Bengal, the usual campaigns in the Deccan. Within the bounds of Hindustan was as much peace as could be expected in a land where the ruler had four sons, and there was no law of succession.

Prince Khusru, the eldest, who had intrigued with Man Sing while Akbar lay on his deathbed, had broken into open revolt, some four months after Jahangir's succession, and seized upon Lahore. Totally defeated in an engagement with the Emperor's troops, he fled for his life, was captured, and brought in chains before his father. His chief advisers, and many of the rank and file in his army, were also prisoners. Jahangir had no mind to have his ease disturbed by incessant rebellions, and he determined to teach his subjects what they might expect if they helped his sons against himself. On a given day the gates of Lahore were opened, and a royal procession passed out—Prince Khusru on an elephant preceded by a mace-bearer, and surrounded by attendants. With its slow swaying movement the elephant passed down a long lane stretching from the gate. There, impaled on stakes, writhing in an agony that might last for three days and three nights, were seven hundred of the prisoners, and as they moaned or cried aloud through blackening lips, the mace-bearer bade the wretched prince receive the salutations of his servants.

Khusru, overcome with terror, would neither eat

nor drink for three nights and days, "which he consumed," observes his father, "in tears and groans, hunger and thirst, and all those tokens of deep repentance peculiar only to those on earth who have sustained the character of prophets and saints, but who have, nevertheless, found that a slight daily repast was still necessary to the support of life."

In spite of this terrible lesson the people were still ready to risk everything if they might set Khusru on the throne: the Emperor himself is said to have loved his eldest son, though he was forced to keep him prisoner. When Shah Jahan, the second son, went to the Deccan, in the latter part of Jahangir's reign, Khusru was sent with him, because Shah Jahan, unpopular himself, durst not leave one whom all men loved behind him at Court. Khusru never returned: it may be true that, as was officially declared, the Deccan fever killed him.

Upon the whole, Nur-Jahan's influence over Emperor and empire had been for good: it was not in woman's nature, however, that her own kin should fail to profit by her good fortune, and father and brothers were soon advanced to high office. Ghaias-ad-din, scholar, poet, and shrewd man of business, was renowned for his benevolence to the poor—which he could well afford, seeing that his audacity in taking bribes excited the wonder and the wistful admiration of every annalist who mentions his name. He died before the end of the reign, and is buried beyond the Jumna at Agra, in the white marble tomb with lace-like screens and mosaics of coloured flowers which still remains one of the glories of the city, although the Taj-Mahal and the Pearl Mosque have arisen since the day when Nur-Jahan mourned her father.

A more important person was Asaf Khan, his son, who became to all intents and purposes the ruler of the empire.

In the latter years of Jahangir's reign he became subject to violent attacks of asthma, and his sons began the usual intrigues for the succession. Shah Jahan, so far as abilities went, was marked out for the future Emperor; he had proved himself a general and an administrator. But his impassible, unsmiling countenance and the cold reserve of his manners were a tacit reproach to his father, who had vainly endeavoured to make him drink wine, and rendered him generally unpopular. By way of strengthening his position, he had married Asaf Khan's daughter,—an alliance which apparently became something more than the ordinary *mariage de convenance* for reasons of state, since it was over her grave in years to come that he erected the Taj-Mahal as a monument of his undying love and remembrance.

So far as the Emperor had any feeling, he was thought to prefer his third son, Parviz, "who could drink level with himself"; but Nur-Jahan could twist him round her finger, and his inclinations counted for very little. It is said that, knowing her husband's life could not be long, and that she would have no chance of influencing the cool, level-headed Shah Jahan, she married her daughter to Shahriyar, Jahangir's youngest son, handsome as a god, and an absolute fool, henceforth exerting all her wits to make him his father's heir.

Shah Jahan, recognising the position, followed the time-honoured precedent, and rebelled. After various excursions and alarums he was obliged to submit, and send two of his sons as hostages to Court, having been defeated and chased from place to place by his brother Parviz and Mahabat Khan, the Emperor's Pathan general.

Mahabat Khan was one of the few at Court whom the Empress had failed to bend or cajole to her will; and there was ill-feeling between himself and Asaf Khan. Whether he guessed what she was plotting and prepared to oppose it, or whether she intended to goad him into rebellion, knowing that he must be moved from her path at all costs, this much is certain—that he was summoned to Court to answer charges of oppression and embezzlement.

It was usual for persons of high rank to ask leave of the Emperor before marrying any of their children: perhaps Mahabat feared that he should not return from the presence, and meant to ensure his daughter's safety. At any rate, before setting out he betrothed his daughter to a young noble without asking leave of any man. It was foolish, for it gave Jahangir a pretext for making a quarrel; and it proved to be most unfortunate for the bridegroom, who suddenly found himself bidden to Court, and there stripped naked in the Emperor's presence, cruelly beaten with thorns, and all his property taken from him, including his wife's dowry.

Jahangir, on his way to put down an insurrection at Kabul, had reached the bridge of boats across the river Behat.[1] He sent the main body of his army across, meaning to follow with Nur-Jahan and their attendants when the press and crowding was over. Mahabat, arriving with five thousand Rajputs, was told that the Emperor would not see him.

It was the hour before daybreak on a March

[1] Better known as the Hydaspes.

morning. Nur-Jahan was in her tent among her women; Jahangir lay on his couch sleeping off the effects of the last night's carouse, when the tread of feet and the clank of arms resounded in his ears, and he started up to find the tent full of Rajput warriors, and recognised the general's face. "Ah, Mahabat Khan! Traitor! what is this?"

As he prostrated himself to the earth, Mahabat bewailed the unprincipled conduct of his enemies which obliged him thus to force his way into the presence of the Emperor of the world.

The scene that followed was like a fencing-bout between two well-matched adversaries. First of all, Mahabat implored the Emperor to show himself in public "to remove alarm, and check the misrepresentations of the ill-disposed." Jahangir cheerfully agreed, and would go at once into the other tent to dress himself. This meant communication with Nur-Jahan, so it was respectfully represented to him that he had better change his garments where he was. Jahangir again agreed, and after dressing, mounted his favourite horse, when again the Khan interposed; an elephant was the better conveyance, for safety and for conspicuousness. Resistance was useless; two thousand Rajputs held the bridge, and Rajputs surrounded the royal tents. Jahangir's mahout was cut down at Mahabat's command, as he tried to make his way through the throng to his master; but the cup-bearer, managing to scramble up on the elephant, with bottle in one hand and glass in the other, Jahangir found consolation, even though he was at once taken off to Mahabat's quarters.

Meanwhile, in the midst of panic and dismay, Nur-Jahan had not lost presence of mind. As soon as she realised what had befallen the Emperor, she disguised herself, entered a common palanquin, and crossed the bridge unhindered by the Rajputs. Once upon the other side of the river, she sent for the Emperor's generals. "This has all happened through your neglect and stupid arrangements!" she cried, and scourged them with her tongue until they vowed to save their master from captivity.

While they debated the means, a messenger arrived, bearing Jahangir's signet, and his commands that they would not attack. Whether this were done at Mahabat's compelling, or whether the Emperor were really afraid of what might happen to himself in the *mêlée*, Nur-Jahan treated it with indifference. She would attack when she pleased, but that should not be until she knew in what part of the camp the Emperor was imprisoned.

In the night one of the Khans tried to rescue the Emperor by swimming the river, but barely escaped with life, many of the small body of horse that followed him being shot down by the Rajputs or drowned. Next morning it was Nur-Jahan herself who led down the troops to battle on a tall elephant, her bow in her hand, and her baby grandchild, Prince Shahriyar's daughter, with its nurse, seated in the howdah beside her.

The Rajputs had burned the bridge, and the imperial troops had to splash through a dangerous ford to reach their enemies. Some were swept down-stream, some slain as they gained the beach; all were drenched and had their powder wetted. The engagement ended in a rout, many of the imperial troops being trampled underfoot or drowned. The driver of Nur-Jahan's elephant was killed, the elephant, wounded by a sword-cut, plunged into the river, and sank in deep water. An arrow went through the howdah and entered the nurse's shoulder.[1] When at last the elephant had struggled to shore, the women who gathered round it found the Empress seated within her blood-stained howdah binding up the wound, after having taken out the arrow, calm as in her rose-gardens at Agra, though all around her was lamentation and outcry.

[1] Another version of the story makes the baby the victim.

The strong arm, the power of man, had failed; it remained for the woman to try her weapons. Nur-Jahan left the army and set off to Mahabat's camp, where she entreated to be allowed to share her husband's captivity.

Her star was at its lowest point by this time; Asaf Khan, her brother, had fallen into the hands of the rebels, and she was told by Mahabat that the Emperor, weary of her intrigues, had signed an order for her execution.

Still Nur-Jahan was unmoved: she was ready to die if it was her lord's pleasure; all she asked as a last favour was to be allowed to kiss the hand that had showered benefits upon her. After that audience, which Mahabat durst not refuse, no more was heard of the death-warrant. She remained with her husband, and though the Khan might fear and suspect, he was never able to detect her hand on the threads that were weaving themselves about him night and day.

Jahangir seconded her nobly: he pretended to rejoice at being rid of Asaf's domineering; he took Mahabat aside and warned him, sadly, that he must not be deceived by the Empress, who, unhappily, cherished a grudge against him and would do him an ill turn if she had the chance. Mahabat fell into the snare: believing that his influence with the Emperor was established, he gave himself no trouble to propitiate others, and his insolence disgusted every one.

The whole party—Mahabat Khan, his army, and his prisoners—were advancing towards Kabul, and for fear of the Afghans the Emperor's body-guard must be increased. There was a violent quarrel between the Rajputs and the Emperor's troops, leading to an affray in which life was lost on both sides. Meanwhile Nur-Jahan's agents were recruiting men everywhere in the neighbourhood, where sympathy with the Emperor ran high, and sending some by twos and threes to enlist in the camp, while the rest waited for orders at certain stations.

Then she made Jahangir propose a review; Mahabat Khan demurred on the ground of risk. The Emperor was willing to listen to reason, but he had set his heart upon the amusement; besides, it was really necessary that he should see with his own eyes what troops were at his disposal for going against these rascally Afghans. It would surely be quite safe if Mahabat did not accompany him to the review, but remained in the camp ready to appear at the least symptom of disorder. In fact, it would be the wiser course, since—who knows?—he might be assassinated by some scoundrelly fellow at Nur-Jahan's instigation.

So Mahabat remained in his tent, and Jahangir

went forth alone. No sooner had the Emperor reached the centre of the line than Nur-Jahan's levies closed round him, cutting off the Rajputs, and he and she were borne away in triumph.

Mahabat Khan saw that the game was lost; luckily for him, the Empress durst not go to extremities while her brother remained in his hands, and terms of peace were arranged. Asaf Khan was released, and Mahabat covenanted to go down to the Deccan and keep in check Shah Jahan, who, owing to the recent death of Prince Parviz, had become formidable once more. This scheme was not altogether successful, as in a little while Mahabat, having again thrown off his allegiance, joined the prince instead of fighting him.

Jahangir, after restoring order at Kabul and Lahore, had gone up to Kashmir, where Akbar's successors generally spent the summer months. Here he was seized with one of his violent attacks of asthma, and as autumn was at hand the Empress hurried him down to the plains, meaning to winter in Lahore. On the way down, though ill and feeble, he ordered an antelope drive, and while he stood with his gun waiting for the herd to pass, a beater fell over the precipice and was dashed to pieces, almost at his feet.

From that moment the ghastly face of the dead man was always before the Emperor's eyes; he rejected wine, and muttered that he had seen a vision,—that Azrael, the angel of death, had taken the shape of the beater. He died in his tent when he had only gone about one-third of the way to Lahore, in October 1627.

Shahriyar, always a fool, happened to be out of the way at that time. Shah Jahan was also absent, which tended to equalise the circumstances. Nur-Jahan declared for her son-in-law. Whether she would have ruled the son as successfully as the father, can never be known, for in making her calculations she had not reckoned with a father's ambition. Asaf Khan might be grateful to the sister who made him the first man in the state, but after all she had had her day, and it was only fair to give his daughter her turn. So he sent an urgent summons to the Deccan to invite Shah Jahan to take possession, and then marched upon Lahore, where Shahriyar, who had seized upon the treasury, came out to meet him. The prince was defeated, and when he took refuge in the fort his own followers betrayed him to Asaf Khan. He was put to death by Shah Jahan's command. After all, perhaps this was the truest kindness for a pretender to the throne, as it undoubtedly was for the country.

Jahangir Embracing Shah Jahan.

When he was little more than a baby Shahriyar had taken blows from his father without a whimper, because "princes must not cry"; it is to be hoped that the same spirit sustained him when he had to face the executioner.

Nur-Jahan, at first held under some sort of restraint by her brother, put on the white robe of widowhood, and never appeared in public again. In the days of her prosperity "she was an asylum for all sufferers," devoting herself especially to endowing portionless girls in marriage: she now gave herself up entirely to prayer and good works, renouncing all worldly pleasure. Shah Jahan, to his credit be it said, allowed her a pension of £250,000 a-year until her death in 1646.

Asaf Khan was suitably rewarded for his loyalty. We have a glimpse of him, in the last year of his life, from the 'Itinerary' of Padre Manrique, an Augustinian missionary who visited India in 1640, and was present at a banquet given by the minister in his palace at Lahore to the Emperor Shah Jahan. The pictures on the palace-walls included scenes from the life of St John the Baptist. The Emperor came accompanied by "a great train of beautiful and gallant ladies," who were unveiled, and after four hours' feasting the company were entertained by "twelve dancing women, who performed in a manner unsuited to Christian society."

In Akbar's fort at Agra you may see "Jahangir's palace," with the great dragons carved upon the stone cross-beams of the roof.[1] He lies far away, in the Shahdara Garden at Lahore. The Sikhs used his tomb as a quarry for the material of their "Golden Temple" at Amritsar, and "the illustrious resting-place of his Majesty, the Asylum of Mercy," is shorn of its proportions. Here Nur-Jahan prayed for nineteen years of widowhood; and close beside it she built the tomb where she sleeps to this day.

[1] Experts consider this palace to be one of much earlier date than the time of Jahangir.

XIII.

SHAH JAHAN THE MAGNIFICENT—1628-1658

"The monarch who erected the Mosque at Ajmir, the Pearl Mosque at Agra, and the Taj-Mahal, left the world richer than he found it."

—G. W. FORREST.

XIII.

SHAH JAHAN THE MAGNIFICENT—1628-1658.

If there is any city in the East where the splendours of the Arabian Nights are still credible, where emeralds as big as turkeys' eggs, palaces with golden roofs, female slaves with voices of nightingales, afrits and enchanted princesses would seem only to be in their proper place, it is within the red sandstone walls, a mile and a half in circuit, of the fort that Akbar built at Agra.

For when Shah Jahan the Magnificent came to his own, it was here that he raised palaces and halls such as no ruler in Hindustan has built before or since his time. Above all rise the marble domes and glittering spires of the Pearl Mosque—a revelation to those who only know "white marble" as the dank, lifeless substance seen in Western lands, and have never realised the exquisite tints, from that of old lace or old ivory to an almost golden glow to which the Eastern sun ripens it. There is the Audience Hall, where the Emperor sat daily to give justice, robed in cloth of gold, a diamond aigrette in his turban, ropes of enormous pearls round his neck; the private Audience Hall, with groups of natural flowers that almost seem to grow upon the marble slabs; the Grape Garden, the soil of which was brought from Kashmir; the White Pavilion, where Shah Jahan sat with his Queens, looking out upon a red sandstone court, and fished in the tank below. In the walls of the ladies' rooms are recesses, too small for any but an Eastern woman's hand, where they kept their jewels at night. To the little "Gem Mosque," three tiny aisles, crowned by three domes, they came to pray, by a screened passage. In the vaults below there was given proof that neither the splendours of the Court nor the consolations of religion could satisfy every woman: some of the caged birds tried to slip out between the bars, and being discovered, were led down to the cell where was a pit, and over the pit a silken rope dangling from a beam.

Once upon a time, they say, the flowers in the Jasmine Tower (the Queens' pavilion) were inlaid with emerald, rubies, and sapphires, but those were picked out long ago, and sold to supply Shah

Shah Jahan.

Jahan's feeble successors with bread, though torquoise, cornelian, and jasper are still left in the place where Italian workmen laid them. Otherwise these fairy buildings, that seem like the work of enchantment, have suffered comparatively little with years: the worst damage was done in 1875, when, to celebrate the Prince of Wales' visit, the red sandstone pillars of the Audience Hall were whitewashed and striped with gilt.

Looking across the river, you may see among a knot of green trees, between the cobalt of the sky and the yellow of the sand, like a gigantic bubble, the dome of the Taj-Mahal. So Shah Jahan, in the midst of his splendours, must have looked over and over again, for the monument he had raised to his wife Aliya Begam, Arjumand Banu, or Mumtaz-i-Mahal (the last signifying "Elect of the Palace"), as the annalists confusingly name her. Nearly eighteen years did it take in building, and when it was finished—so tradition says—Shah Jahan put out the eyes of the principal architect, that he might never build its like. Down to the Jasmine Pavilion Shah Jahan was borne, after seven years of captivity in the Gem Mosque, that his dying gaze might rest once more on the tomb of the wife he had loved and lost, and never sought to replace.

From the time when he ascended the throne

in 1628, Shah Jahan had laid aside the cold, repellent manner which had made him disliked in his youth; his kindliness won the hearts of all who were brought in contact with him, and his passion for show and state delighted the multitude. Hindu, Muslim, and Christian united to praise his equity, his justice, his generosity, and his toleration. His rule was compared to that of a father over his children. Curiously enough for one who was three parts Hindu,[1] he was a more orthodox Sunni than his father or his grandfather—it is said owing to the influence of his wife, who, like most good wives and mothers, was orthodox. But the Hindus rose to civil and military honours under him, as in the days of Akbar, and Jesuit missionaries were welcome at Agra, though their church, built by the favour of Jahangir, was partially destroyed. Perhaps the Emperor could not endure the clang of its bell, which we are told could be heard all over the city.

Reading the descriptions of his state given by Tavernier, Mandelslo, and other visitors from Europe, the thought rises that someone must have paid for all this magnificence, and the taxpayers might have told another tale of the Emperor's benevolence and generosity. But it is certain

[1] His mother was a Rajput; both his grandmothers had been Rajputs also.

that the prosperity of the empire increased greatly in his time, aided by the comparative peace and quietness both internally and externally. At his accession Shah Jahan had disposed of pretenders to the throne; there was always fighting in the Deccan, to be sure, but that was far away.

So the Emperor was free to enjoy himself, to spend the summers in the cool valleys of Kashmir and the winters in Agra, or, as he grew older and found the climate of Agra trying, in the new city "Shahjahanabad," which he built at Delhi, within a circuit of walls seven miles round. Bernier, the French traveller, who saw it in its glory, has left us a description of it in the days when the private rooms of the palace alone covered more than twice the space of any European palace, when the Audience Hall was roofed with silver, and the throne, standing on four feet of solid gold set around with pearls, blazed with rubies, emeralds, and diamonds, a peacock flashing a tail of sapphires and other stones above it, and the Koh-i-Nur sending a dull gleam from the front of its pearl-fringed canopy.

The glory had departed long before the time of the Indian Mutiny; when Bishop Heber visited the palace, early in the nineteenth century, "all was dirty, desolate and forlorn." Shining roof and glittering throne had been carried off by spoilers, and birds built their nests in the throne recess. At least in these days it is kept clean, and what is left of gold and inlay work gives a faint shadow of the glory of the time when Shah Jahan set up the inscription on the panels on the north and south sides of the Audience Hall—"If a Paradise be on the face of the earth, it is this, it is this, it is this."

An existence spent in building palaces and moving from one to another of them was not likely to strengthen moral fibre, and as Shah Jahan advanced in years he became more and more given over to ease and comfort, less and less inclined to trouble himself about the heterogeneous parts of the empire that he was supposed to govern, provided that all went smoothly in his immediate neighbourhood. Even his better qualities contributed to his downfall: for many years he had been practically the husband of one wife, the lady of the Taj, and when she died in giving birth to her fourteenth child, although he had consolations of a different sort, it was to her children, and not to other wives, that he turned for companionship.

Innumerable fairy tales begin, "There was once upon a time a king who had three sons"; the tragedy of Shah Jahan's life might begin, "There was once upon a time a king, and he had four sons." He had daughters as well, whom he loved so much that, like Charlemagne, he would never give them in marriage,—with precisely the same consequences. The elder, Jahanara Begam, has two claims to remembrance, independently of her own doings. It was in her honour that her father built the great mosque at Delhi, which every tourist knows; and it was for her sake that her father once sent a message to the English factory at Surat, commanding that their doctor should come to Court immediately. The princess had a favourite dancing girl, whose skirt had caught fire one day when she was with her mistress: in trying to save the girl, Jahanara had been terribly burned, and the Emperor was in misery at the thought of injury to her extraordinary beauty. There was an English doctor at the factory, Gabriel Boughton, who came in haste, and succeeded in curing the patient, in spite of the obstacles thrown in the way of European practitioners by harem etiquette. When the Emperor bade him name his reward, he would take neither gold nor jewels, neither a place at Court nor a grant of land; all he asked was that the East India Company should have leave to trade in Bengal from that time forth. He obtained what he wanted, and went his way,—one of the many Englishmen who at all times have been content to spend themselves without reward for the sake of England.

Jahanara, to whom her father gave the title of "Padshah Begam," was allowed to accompany him everywhere, and to live in her own palace, instead of being shut up in the harem with the rest of the women. A younger daughter, Roshanara, less clever, less beautiful, though more given to mirth and light-heartedness than her stately sister, had less influence and was less privileged. "She was generous," we are told, "and drank wine when she could get it"; otherwise there is not much good to be said of this princess, who was as intriguing as she was hard-hearted.

Of the four sons, Dara Shukoh, the eldest, his father's favourite and Jahanara's idol, contrived to alienate more by his arrogance and overbearing temper than he conciliated by his frankness and generosity. He would not take advice, even from those who were devoted to his interests; where he despised or disliked, he would not dissemble. Shuja, though clever, was a drunkard, and if Murad had ever possessed any wits he had addled them by gluttony and self-indulgence.

Aurangzib, the third son, is one of the most extraordinary riddles in history. In his religious zeal, his narrow-minded conscientiousness, his attention to petty detail, he recalls Philip II. of Spain; but even when accepting the worst that partisan writers have laid to Philip's charge as

Shah Jahan and his Sons Visiting a Holy Man.

a private individual, such as the strangling of his son and the poisoning of his half-brother, there is nothing to approach what can be proved against Aurangzib. None of his own family loved him except the Princess Roshanara, who was his spy and his confidant,—though only to a certain extent, for he suspected all men, and never trusted any one entirely. His father and grandfather disliked him, even as a boy, and had nicknamed him the "White Snake," in allusion to his fair complexion. A legend was current in the palace that before one of her numerous confinements, the lady of the Taj had an irresistible longing for apples, which were not to be found. Shah Jahan, going himself in search of them, met a holy faquir, who gave him an apple, with two solemn warnings—to expect death when his hands should not smell of apples during an illness, and to beware of the White Snake, who would be the destruction of his race.

When only twenty-four, Aurangzib had declared his intention of renouncing the world—much to the relief of his brothers, who had nothing in common with the cold reserved youth. He put on a faquir's dress, retired to the Western Ghats, and practised asceticism in various forms. It may have been a genuine though short-lived longing after holiness, or it may have been a ruse to throw dust in the eyes of his brothers, and make them believe him devoid of ambition: his later life shows either motive to have been equally probable. Whatever was his real purpose, he came back to the world after an interval of retirement.

Then Shah Jahan committed a fatal error: disliking to be troubled as he advanced in years, he divided the empire into four parts, giving one to each of his sons to rule as his viceroy. Shuja had Bengal, and Murad revelled in Gujarat. Dara, nominally lord of Multan and Kabul, remained at Delhi with the father who could not bear to lose his company, and had his chair of gold set close to the throne, though out of respect to the Emperor he would never sit upon it.

Aurangzib, originally sent to Multan, soon wearied of a post where he had no chance of distinguishing himself, and turned longing eyes to the south, where the five kingdoms were falling to decay. He wrote to Dara, with whom he had quarrelled, pleading that his health was suffering from the climate of Multan; would not his brother use his influence with their father to have him sent to command in the Deccan? Dara bore no malice; Shah Jahan yielded to his entreatics, with the unheeded warning, "You act on behalf of a venomous snake, and you will have to suffer from its poison."

Aurangzib had already commanded in three campaigns in the North-West, one beyond the Hindu Kush, and two undertaken in the hope of regaining Kandahar, which had been seized by the Persians. Each time he was unsuccessful, but he gained experience, and the army had learned confidence in him. As soon as he had arrived in the Deccan, he began a vigorous harrying of the Kings of Golkonda and Bijapur, who, as Shia heretics, were even more deserving of chastisement than the infidel over whom they ruled.

He was everywhere successful: the Muslim kingdoms of the Deccan, like the Moghul empire, were rotten at the heart, and their rulers could no longer hold what they had held. Without declaration of war, on pretence of marrying his son, Aurangzib marched towards Hyderabad, the capital of Golkonda, and took it by surprise, while the King was actually preparing to entertain him as a guest. Among the spoils was the "great diamond" once surrendered by Humayun to Shah Tahmasp, which had found its way southward, and, as usual, brought ruin wherever it went. Aurangzib sent it to his father as a sign of victory.

It was now the turn of the King of Bijapur, who was endeavouring to obtain peace which Aurangzib refused to grant, when news came from the north that turned the Prince's energies into another direction: the Emperor was desperately ill, symptoms had appeared that usually portend death within twenty-four hours.

"This produced much derangement in the government of the country and the peace of the people," says a Muslim historian pathetically. Dara took the affairs of the state into his own hands, and closed the roads of Bengal, Ahmadabad, and the Deccan against messengers,—too late, however, to prevent the news reaching his brothers. Shuja and Murad, "each of them vying with the other," had coins struck, and prayers read in the mosques in his own name. Shuja set out to march against Agra; Murad, with great presence of mind, sent an expedition against Surat, to demand contributions from the merchants of that town; he demanded fifteen lacs of rupees, but after much parley condescended to accept six.

Aurangzib bided his time, and made no movement.

Shuja was sleeping off his wine in his camp near Benares, when a division of the imperial army, sent by Dara, came down upon him, and routed his forces completely. He fled, while all his camp, treasure, and artillery fell into the hands of Dara.

Then Aurangzib suddenly declared himself the devoted ally of his dear brother Prince Murad. "I have not the slightest wish to take any part in the government of this deceitful, unstable world," he wrote; "my only desire is that I may make the pilgrimage to the temple of God." But it behoved dutiful sons to rescue their father from "the presumption and conceit of that apostate," for whose forgiveness they would beseech the Emperor when once order was restored.

The united forces of Aurangzib and Murad marched together, until they met the Emperor's army under the Maharaja Jaswant Singh, the Rajput, on the banks of the Narbada. Murad charged across the ford, regardless of the hail of arrows and javelins, and "every minute the dark ranks of the infidel Rajputs were dispersed by the prowess of the followers of Islam." The Muslims in the imperial army broke and fled; the Rajputs, all but six hundred, died on the field. When the Maharaja Jaswant went back to his castle in Marwar with the survivors, his wife would not open the gates to him. She was no wife to a coward; if he knew not how to conquer, he should have known how to die.

In wrath and amazement Prince Dara gathered the imperial forces together, and set forth from Agra—contrary, it is said, to the wish of the Emperor, who by this time had recovered, and talked of going himself to expostulate with his younger sons. He would not even wait for the return of his victorious division from Benares, but sent an advance-guard to secure the fords of the Chambal, and followed with the main body of the army. He had marched one stage from Agra when he found that his brothers were close at hand, having crossed the river before him.

It was the beginning of June 1658. For a whole day the armies confronted each other at Samugarh, Dara's presenting a front nearly four miles in width, while neither attacked. "The day was so hot that many strong men died from the heat of their armour and want of water." Next day the battle began "with discharges of rockets and guns, and thousands of arrows flew from both sides."

Dara had the advantage in numbers and equipment, but the pick of his army had not yet returned from Benares, and many of the leaders were half-hearted in his cause.

Over and over again he led his centre against Aurangzib, who had chained his guns one to another in the fashion that his forefathers learned in Central Asia. The battle raged on all sides. Prince Murad's elephant was about to turn away, covered with wounds from arrows, spears, and battle-axes, but the rider ordered its legs to be chained together, so that escape should be impossible. Aurangzib, his cavalry hurled back by Dara's men, was giving like orders to his elephant-driver as he stood among the few squadrons left to him. "Take heart, my friends! There is a God! What hope have we in flight?"

Then one of the bravest of Dara's Rajputs wound a string of pearls round his head, and clad in yellow rode forth as a bridegroom, after the custom of his race, to seek death for a bride. Hurling his javelin against Murad's elephant, "What, dost thou dispute the throne with Dara Shukoh?" he cried, and shouted to the mahout to make the beast kneel down. An arrow from the Prince pierced him through the forehead, and he dropped dead. Another Rajput, "having washed his hands of life," hewed his way through the ranks of his enemies, sword in hand, cast himself beneath the elephant, and began to cut the girths which secured the howdah. He was cut to pieces, though Murad, in admiration for his daring, shouted that he was to be taken alive. The ground all about the feet of the Prince's elephant grew yellow as a field of saffron where the Rajputs fell, and his howdah "was stuck as thick with arrows as a porcupine with quills."

Beside Dara was a traitor, who was in secret Aurangzib's ally, and only waited for an opportunity of wrecking the elder prince's cause before he deserted it. In the supreme moment, when fortune was still wavering from side to side, this man whispered to Dara, "Now is your time! Dismount from your elephant, put yourself at the head of that squadron of cavalry, and ride down swiftly upon your brother Aurangzib. He has scarcely a man at his back, and you may take him easily."

Ever reckless, Dara sprang down, "without even waiting to put on his slippers." At that instant a rocket struck the howdah. The troops, who through that day had looked to the figure on the back of the tall Ceylon elephant as their standard, saw the howdah empty and broken, and believed him slain. They dispersed and fled in all directions.

Aurangzib flung himself upon the reeking ground, and returned thanks to the Giver of Victory. He then, after taking possession of Dara's tent, visited Prince Murad, who was covered with arrow wounds, and "wiped away the tears and blood from his brother's cheek with the sleeve of condolence."

The greater part of the imperial forces now turned to the rising sun. Dara, who had reached Agra with a handful of men, was too much bowed down with shame and remorse to see his father, although the Emperor sent for him. Taking his wife, son, and daughter, and as much as he could lay hands upon, in the shape of money and equipment, he stole out of the city that same night.

Aurangzib now marched upon Agra, and encamped outside the city. It was in vain that the Emperor sent letters, and when they were disregarded, sent Jahanara, with "words of kindness and reproach." "The answer she received was contrary to what she had wished, and she returned." Another letter from the Emperor followed, with the present of a sword bearing the auspicious name "Alamgir" ("World-Compeller"). Aurangzib accepted this as a good omen, and sent his son Prince Mohammad into Agra "to restore order in the city and to give peace to the people." This was done by attacking the palace. The dogged Moghul valour was a thing of the past, and Shah Jahan's musketeers were poor creatures who quaked with terror when their guns went off. There was a confused resistance, and a massacre, and the Emperor was a prisoner.

On the following day Aurangzib took possession

of Dara's house with all it contained, and shortly afterwards went in pursuit of the rightful owner, who was making his way towards the Punjab, gathering a new army about him on the road. With Aurangzib went Murad, who believed that his brother, caring nothing for the things of this world, had gone through all this trouble in order to proclaim him king at Delhi.

"This simple-minded prince had some good qualities," we are told, "but in the honesty of his heart and the trustfulness of his disposition he had never given heed to the saying that two kings cannot be contained in one kingdom. He was deluded by flattering promises, and by the presents of money which had been sent to him" (by Aurangzib), "but they were deposits or loans rather than gifts."

On the road to Delhi, Aurangzib told his brother that the auspicious day was approaching when the astrologers decreed that he should be proclaimed Emperor. A great feast should be made that all the army might rejoice; would Murad honour him by coming to a banquet in his tent, to pass away the hours until the planets should have reached the desired conjunction?

In his folly Murad rode to his brother's tent that night, accompanied by a faithful eunuch. Ere he entered one of his brother's officers passed and warned him of danger; the eunuch implored him to turn back to his own quarters. "None is braver than I," laughed Murad, as he ruffled in. At the entrance a *kazi* met him. "With your feet you have come here," he muttered, implying that some other agent than his own feet would take the prince thence. But Murad was "fey" that night, and mocked at warnings; and there was Aurangzib bowing down to the ground, all humility and devotion, keeping the flies from his face with a handkerchief, commanding dancing-girls and musicians to perform before him who was to be lord of Hindustan ere the morning broke.

To the entertainment succeeded a banquet; Murad, his cup filled at every moment by his brother, was soon overcome with wine. Then Aurangzib commanded that all should withdraw and leave the Emperor-elect to rest until the auspicious moment came. Only the eunuch remained, and he gently kneaded the feet of Murad, who lay in a drunken sleep on a couch.

As he kept watch, Aurangzib once more looked within the tent, and signed to him to come outside; scarcely had he stepped without the flap than he was seized by several men, and strangled before he could utter a sound.

The "White Snake" glided back and looked

through a loophole at the sleeper; Murad was alone, but he was armed with sword and dagger, and the brother had seen how well he could wield them. Aurangzib called his little boy, Muhammad Azam, a child of four years old. "If you can go into the tent and bring your uncle's sword away without waking him, see what a fine jewel for your turban I will give you!"

Delighted with this game, the child crept into the tent and came back with the sword.

"Now fetch me his dagger, and you shall have this other jewel too."

Again the child stole to the couch, and the dagger was borne away.

Lying in heavy sleep, Murad felt himself shaken by rough hands. This was not the way in which an emperor should be roused. He stared stupidly about him; the eunuch was gone, and six men stood over him, bearing fetters. Then he understood what had come to pass, and made no resistance, only groaning, "*This* is the word and oath sworn to me on the Koran."

Aurangzib had been overcome with horror at his brother's disobedience to the Prophet's edict against wine; never, he vowed, could he be guilty of the sin of putting such an unworthy son of Islam to rule over true believers. So Murad, stripped of all honour, was sent on an elephant to the citadel of Delhi, while Aurangzib, after laying hands on all his effects, was proclaimed Emperor. The "White Snake" had glided on, by twists and darts, until he lay upon the cushions of the Peacock Throne.

XIV.

THE CHILDREN OF SHAH JAHAN—1658-1682

"Twelve dervishes may sleep together under one blanket, but two kings cannot dwell together in one kingdom."—*Eastern Proverb.*

XIV.

THE CHILDREN OF SHAH JAHAN—1658-1682.

It was characteristic of the new Emperor that he began his reign by throwing unnecessary difficulties in the way of historians. Proclaimed in the garden of Shalimar, outside Delhi, immediately after making a prisoner of Prince Murad, in 1658, he chose not to put his name upon the coins or to ascend the throne with the usual ceremonies, until ten months later. Hence there is generally some uncertainty about the correct date of events in his reign. Another source of confusion, for which he apparently was not responsible, is that while he chose to call himself "Alamgir" ("World-Compeller"), from the Persian inscription on his father's sword, European writers have continued to call him "Aurangzib," as in the days when he was merely the third and least beloved of the Emperor's sons.

Whatever title he might usurp, there was much

to be done before he could sit at ease in his father's palace. Shah Jahan was safe under guard in the red fortress at Agra, and Princess Jahanara had demanded to share his captivity. Princess Roshanara was enjoying all the consideration due to her brother's ally and confidant. Murad had been removed from Delhi to the state prison at Gwalior. But Dara Shukoh was still at large. Almost the last act of Shah Jahan before he ceased to rule, had been to send five thousand horse and "some nobles and equipments" to join his favourite son, and Dara's son, Sulaiman Shukoh, was on his way to join the prince at Lahore. Shuja, with a strong army and a force of artillery, was advancing from Dacca, having been won over to Dara's side by the sight of the imminent danger in which all Aurangzib's brothers were placed.

The prospects looked black for the usurper; Dara had plundered the treasury at Lahore and was raising an army; if he succeeded, Mahabat Khan (son of Jahangir's rebellious general), who was viceroy at Kabul, was likely to join with him, and Kabul would be at his service either as a source from which to draw new levies, or as a safe retreat, whence at need it was easy to reach Persia.

Aurangzib faced the danger with the calm

with which he had withstood the frantic charge of the Rajputs on his chained elephant at Samugarh. A division was sent against Prince Sulaiman, who, losing heart, turned aside into the mountains round Srinagar. Here his followers deserted him, until, after wandering up and down for some time, only a few attendants remained. The Raja of Srinagar, coveting the gold and jewels that were still in his possession, prevailed upon him to enter a fort, where he was kept, nominally as a guest, but to all intents and purposes as a prisoner.

Aurangzib himself meanwhile had started in pursuit of Dara, whose newly raised army was already falling away from him. Dara, like all the sons of Timur, was no coward, but the "White Snake" seems to have exercised the paralysing influence of the serpent over him. On hearing that Aurangzib was approaching Lahore, he fled once more from this terrible brother who could neither be bribed nor cajoled, who was leading his army by forced marches, sleeping on the ground and faring like a common soldier, in order to work his ruin. Like Humayun in former days, he turned towards the deserts of the west, fearing their dangers less than his enemies.

There he was left to wander undisturbed

for a while; Aurangzib had first to check the advance of Shuja, and was content that thirst and sun and sand should do part of his work for him. The story is almost a repetition of Humayun's adventures, told with less detail. Dara, like Humayun, had taken his wife with him—the daughter of his uncle, that Parviz who had drunk himself to death in the Deccan. His followers deserted him; no carriers could be found for his baggage and treasure, part of which he was forced to abandon by the way. Vainly did he struggle through the great salt desert where the Indus drains by many mouths into the sea,—toiling through dense thorn-brakes and sandy wastes, losing all his baggage, daily seeing his men fall away or die from thirst and disease, while ever at his heels, nearer and nearer, came the horsemen of his brother.

Only a thousand followers were left to him when at length he reached Ahmadabad. A little flicker of hope came to cheer them for an instant; overtures of friendship were made by Maharaja Jaswant Sing of Marwar—the same Rajput prince who had had the gates of his castle slammed in his face by his wife. Having submitted to Aurangzib, the Rajput prince had fallen out with him on some question of precedence, and was ready to join Dara.

But Aurangzib, having just defeated Shuja in an action, the account of which reads like an echo of the battle at Samugarh, was free to give all his mind to his other brother. With his usual skill in diplomacy, he wrote with his own hand to the Maharaja, bestowing on him the rank and titles the refusal of which had been the reason for Jaswant's sudden revival of affection towards Dara. Jaswant—who, it must be said, was an unprincipled scoundrel such as has seldom disgraced Rajput history—at once broke off his alliance with the elder prince, and turned back to his own country.

Betrayed and deserted, Dara retired to a fortified position on the hills near Ajmir. For three long days he endured the cannonade of Aurangzib's artillery. On the fourth the Emperor's infantry worked round from the rear, and Dara, looking across his broken lines, saw his brother's standard waving from the summit of the hill.

In a frenzy of terror he fled, leaving his men to go on fighting, in ignorance that he had abandoned them. His son and daughter and some of the women of his harem went with him, out into the world.

The heat was terrible, the dust stifling, in the eight long spring days during which they rode to Ahmadabad. They were robbed by the Kolis of the hills, who, seeing a disorderly band in headlong flight, hung on their flanks, to plunder and cut off stragglers. They were robbed by the troop of horse who had accompanied them at first as a guard, and finding Dara's cause hopeless, dropped off, by twos and threes, some of the more unscrupulous laying hands on the treasure that the prince had brought with him. They were robbed by their own household, who, having been ordered to follow as quickly as possible with the women-servants and the baggage, seized what they could lay hands upon, stripped the women of their jewels, and made off for the desert.

Then Dara's wife, who had been wounded, seemed about to die; the Moghul women, like the men, had deteriorated from the hardy northern stock, and Nadira Begam could not endure the half of what her ancestress, Hamida, had survived. As they hurried on, by day and by night, scarcely daring to draw breath, they met a European, Maître François Bernier, physician and traveller, who was journeying on his own affairs to Delhi. He knew nothing of the disasters which had overtaken the prince, and was dismayed to find himself carried off with the fugitives, by order of Dara, who had no doctor in his party.

Dara Shukoh

At last they were within a march of Ahmadabad; they spent the night within a caravanserai —a poor place enough for royal travellers, but a welcome refuge, since its walls kept out the marauding Kolis. In the early morning, Bernier heard the wailing of women through the canvas screen on the other side of which the princesses were lodged. All night Nadira Begam and her daughter had been keeping up their hearts with the thought that a few hours would see them safe among friends within the walls of Ahmadabad: now a messenger had come from the city to say that the governor had declared for Aurangzib, and that Dara must fly at once if he cared for his life.

Stunned and like one half-dead, the prince came out among his followers, and strove to bind them to himself by entreaties and promises. Even Bernier wept as he saw the fugitives depart; four or five horsemen and two elephants were all that were left to the favourite son of Shah Jahan.

Back to Kachh they wandered, where Dara hoped for assistance from a zamindar,[1] whose daughter, in happier days, had been betrothed to the prince's son. But the zamindar had not even ordinary courtesy for the man upon whom he had fawned a few short months before, thinking to make his fortune with the prince's help. For two

[1] Landowner.

days Dara endeavoured to soften his heart; on the third, "with tearful eyes and burning heart," he resolved to proceed to Bhakkar. In Kachh he was joined by a small force, collected by a faithful adherent, Gul Muhammad; but as soon as they reached the Sind frontier, one of the two nobles who had accompanied him from Ajmir, "seeing how his evil fate still clung to him," went off to Delhi.

Dara, bewildered and irresolute, wandered from place to place. A friendly chieftain offered to escort him as far as Kandahar, on the way to Persia, but the fugitive would not resign all hope of regaining his crown.

In Kachh was a certain Afghan zamindar, Malik Jiwan, who had been condemned by Shah Jahan to be trampled to death under the feet of an elephant, and pardoned at Dara's intercession. He now sent to assure the prince of his fidelity, and came to the border of his territory to meet the exiles. Impetuous as ever, Dara consented to trust his life and the lives of all who were with him to this man's honour.

In a few hours, it was apparent to all that they were prisoners, not guests. Over Nadira Begam's mind brooded the horror of becoming the slave of Aurangzib, and she resolved rather to die. In vain did the servant in whom she confided dissuade her; in vain did he attempt to solve their difficulty by assassinating Malik Jiwan. His purpose was thwarted, and the Begam slew herself, with a last entreaty that her body might be taken to rest in the land that she would never see again. Then Dara broke down completely. Regardless of his own safety, he appointed Gul Muhammad, the one friend who had stood at his side through good and ill, to bear the corpse to Lahore with an escort of the few soldiers remaining to him. He himself, with only "a few domestic servants and useless eunuchs," would take the road to Persia, escorted by Malik Jiwan, after performing the ceremonies of mourning. Remonstrance was useless; he cared no longer what became of him.

Broken-hearted, worn out in body and in mind, alternately reckless and stupefied, he was an easy prey. "He might have been King of Hindustan if he had known how to control himself," one who knew and loved him wrote, when telling of his prosperity; adversity had come too suddenly for him to have learned better. Malik Jiwan sent word to Aurangzib that the prey was in the toils, and the Emperor despatched officers to bring Dara to his presence.

At Delhi, Aurangzib had taken his seat on the Peacock Throne with great ceremonial. The festivities were scarcely over when through the crowded streets was paraded a miserable elephant, without housings or trappings, covered with filth, on which sat a wretched figure dressed in the meanest clothes and loaded with chains. When the people recognised the prince, whom many of them had seen last standing at his father's right hand, there was universal lamentation, "men, women, and children wailing as if some mighty calamity had happened to themselves." As he sat, with fettered ankles, exposed to the glare of the sun, a faquir in the crowd cried, "O Dara, when you were master you always gave me alms; to-day I know well you have naught to give me." Dara took off the "dark dingy-coloured shawl" which had been put upon him, and threw it down. One of his guards took it away from the faquir, saying that a prisoner had no right to give alms. Bitter were the curses flung after him by the faquir, and echoed by the crowd, as the elephant was driven to the prison in Old Delhi appointed for the Emperor's brother. If one had been there to lead them, the crowds in the streets of Delhi that July day would have done something more than shriek and curse, and sway to and fro; as it was, though all wept, there was none to rescue the fallen prince.

Two days later Malik Jiwan was swaggering

through those same streets of Delhi, on his way to Court to receive the robe of honour and the titles that were to be the price of blood. He was recognised by some one in the crowd; word buzzed round that here was the man who had betrayed their prince. Forthwith the mob gathered round him, yelling the curses that only an Eastern tongue can speak; clods and stones flew through the air, wounding and killing his men; from the house-tops the women poured down ashes and indescribable abominations. Not one of the Afghans would have escaped alive, had not the *kotwal* with his guard come to the rescue, and protected Malik Jiwan by holding their shields over his head, so that bruised, battered, and covered with filth, he reached the palace gates.

It was evident that there would be no safety for Aurangzib so long as his elder brother lived. There was no difficulty in finding an accusation of heresy, concerning which the Emperor was as sensitive as any mediæval schoolman. Dara, like Akbar, had listened to Christian teachers, and loved to consort with Brahmans; he read the sacred books of Hindus, and had a Hindu sacred name engraved upon his rings. What more could be required? Mullahs and councillors pronounced him worthy of death, and the Princess Roshanara urged that he should be poisoned forthwith.

Whether in a momentary fit of compunction in a hope of gaining further pretext for what he was about to do, Aurangzib sent a message to his captive. "If I were in thy place, and thou in mine, what wouldst thou do with me?"

"Let the gates of the city answer thee!" was Dara's reply, "for each one should have seen a piece of thy carcase nailed there for the vultures and the kites."

After sending such an answer, Dara well knew that no hope was left for him. In his wanderings in Sind he had met a Carmelite monk, to whom he owned, "If there is any true faith in the world, I believe it to be that of the Catholics." He now entreated for a confessor, but none was allowed to come to him. As he walked up and down his prison one evening, repeating "Muhammad causes my death, but the Son of Mary is my salvation," his brother's messengers entered. He had no weapon but the knife with which he had been cutting lentils for his supper, and with this he defended himself until borne down to the ground.

Some men say that Aurangzib wept when his brother's head was set before him: some say that he struck at it with his sword, and mocked the fool who thought to have been master of Hindustan. An Englishman was there, who vowed that the Emperor cast the head to the ground and trampled upon it, and that "the head laughed a long *ha! ha! ha!* in the hearing of all."

The body, placed on an elephant, was once more carried about the streets of Delhi. "So, once alive and once dead, he was exposed to the eyes of all men, and many wept over his fate."

Shah Jahan sat at meat within the fort of Agra, Jahanara waiting upon him, when a messenger brought in a box, saying, "Your son, King Aurangzib, sends this to show he had not forgotten your Majesty." "Blessed be God that my son still remembers me!" cried the old man, and he bade them undo the wrappings. A head rolled out upon the table; Dara's father and sister once more beheld the face that they had loved.

Perhaps a little comfort came to them when Dara's daughter was brought to share their imprisonment. Sipihr Shukoh, Dara's young son, who had been taken prisoner with his father, was kept in the fort at Gwalior.

Now that Dara was removed, Aurangzib was free to take possession of the two most beautiful women of his harem. One, Udaipuri by name, was a Christian and a Georgian; coming of a stock that was accustomed to supply the Muslim with slaves, she submitted to her new master with such good grace that she is noted as the only woman for whom he ever showed anything approaching love.

The other was a public dancing-girl, whom Dara had loved and married, in spite of all obstacles. When Aurangzib claimed her, she made answer that she had belonged to Dara Shukoh; why should the Emperor desire her?

To which the Emperor returned answer that her long tresse had bound him as in a net. That night an officer brought him a packet wherein lay coil upon coil of perfumed hair.

Again the Emperor sent back word that it was the moon-like beauty of her face that had enthralled him.

Then the girl took a knife and gashed her face until it was a thing of horror. She wiped the blood from it with a cloth, and sent the cloth to the Emperor, in token that there was nothing left of that which he had desired. He troubled her no more, and in a little while she died of grief for her husband.

Dara was the only one of his family who was a serious danger to Aurangzib. A momentary anxiety was caused by the Emperor's eldest son, Muhammad Sultan, going over to Shuja in the course of a campaign against him in Bengal, but the foolish young man soon grew disgusted with

Gul Saffa, the Mistress of Dara Shukoh.

his uncle's cause, and came back to the imperial camp. Thence Aurangzib sent him to prison, where he spent the rest of his life. Shuja, finding that he could not hold Bengal against his brother, fled to Arakan, a district at that time inhabited by pirates, the offscourings of the Portuguese and other settlements, allied with half-castes, Malays, and refugees whose crimes had driven them from every other place. With "his personal effects, vessels of gold and silver, jewels, treasures, and other appendages of royalty," and some of his Khans and servants, he embarked on a boat and vanishes into the night. The clouds part afterwards for a moment to show him, penniless and wounded, fleeing over the mountains, with one woman and three followers; no one knew his end.

In the same year in which Prince Shuja disappeared for ever from Indian history, another figure comes forward once more. The Raja of Srinagar at length yielded to the pressure put upon him by Aurangzib, and surrendered Sulaiman Shukoh to the imperial envoys. Brought before his father's murderer in gilded chains, the son of Dara had one request to make. He was ready for death; let it strike him swiftly, with all his senses alive within him; let him not drink the poison that slew the mind and soul before the body.

For there is a deadly poison, compounded with the datura and the poppy, that, given daily in small quantities, will turn the victim into an evil thing, now mopping and chattering like an ape, now lethargic, playing with straws and dust, the body yet strong while the mind has gone. Even in our day there are criminals in India who make a practice of robbing travellers after mixing datura with their food or drink and thereby taking away their wits for a time. In the days of the Moghuls it was given to prisoners of state who, for one reason or another, it was not wise to kill outright.

Aurangzib's voice took its gentlest tones as he assured his brother's son of safety and kind treatment. Sulaiman was taken to Gwalior, where his younger brother had been confined ever since their father's death. The climate there is known to be unhealthy; perhaps there was something in the heavy blue mists that cling about the rock at dawn and sunset, which brought freedom to heart-weary captives. In a short time both the sons of Dara were dead, as well as the little son of Murad, who had been imprisoned with his father.

The climate of Gwalior, however, could not be held responsible for the death of Murad himself. A faithful servant, who had lived at the foot of the rock, watching for an opportunity of rescuing his master, contrived a plan for fastening a rope-ladder to the ramparts at a given hour of the night. Murad, a fool to the last, must needs take farewell of a woman who had shared his captivity, before escaping; she, a greater fool than her lord, or perhaps a traitor, lamented so loudly that the guard took alarm, and after flashing their torches up and down, discovered the ladder. Upon which Prince Murad was executed after a mock trial.

Meanwhile the poor old man in the fortress at Agra was dragging out the remnant of his days. He continually demanded to see the Emperor, but Aurangzib always refused, because "under the influence of destiny his father lost all self-control." There had been an angry controversy over the jewels and pearls left behind in the palace of Dara; Shah Jahan at first refused to yield his son's treasures, and it was only "after much contention, perquisition, and demanding" that he surrendered them to Aurangzib with a letter of forgiveness—written under compulsion.

Except for giving his father liberty, Aurangzib treated him with every consideration. Presents of all kinds were sent to him; his cooks were the best that could be found. If he needed to be amused, dancing-girls and musicians were at his service. If he were seized with a fit of senile piety, holy men were there who could read and expound the Koran.

Towards the end of his life Shah Jahan was seized with a desire to see once more the buildings that he had raised, and made entreaty to be allowed to leave the fort for this purpose. Told that his request was granted, he burst into the unavailing fury of helpless old age when he found that he was expected to embark upon a war vessel and view his work from the river. Rather than that, he would never set foot outside his prison. So in January 1666, while the good people of London were returning to homes swept free of the plague, he was borne down to the little white pavilion overlooking the river, and there, his dying eyes fixed on the shadowy dome of the Taj, he passed away from a world that had grown very drear and empty since the time when he and the wife of his youth had faced it together. Before the end—so says one story—he sent his forgiveness to his son, at the instance of the two holy men who had ministered to him.

After her father's death Princess Jahanara demanded to be released. When she left Agra men did not look for her to live long; Aurangzib and Roshanara would be certain to poison her.

But she disappointed expectations by surviving Roshanara for many years. Aurangzib granted her a house and the title of Shah Begam (Crown Princess). Visitors to the mausoleum of the saint

Nizam-ad-din-Aulia, near Delhi, may see her tomb in the courtyard that surrounds the shrine—"a casket-shaped monument, hollow at the top and open to the sky." In the hollow a few blades of grass struggle through the earth; on a narrow slab of marble at one end is the inscription written by herself: "Let nothing but the green conceal my grave! The grass is the best covering for the tombs of the poor in spirit. The humble, the transitory Jahanara, disciple of the holy men of Chist, the daughter of the Emperor Shah Jahan."

XV.

THE MOUNTAIN RAT—1627-1680

XV.

THE MOUNTAIN RAT—1627-1680.

THERE is probably no country in the world better fitted to resist invasion than the Konkan, a district lying between the Deccan and the Arabian Sea. On the east rise the Ghauts, with black basaltic rocks where scarcely a shrub can find root, their sides clothed with trees and brushwood. For six months of the year almost perpetual rain falls on the forests and on the deep valleys choked with vegetation that lead westwards to the strip of fertile land along the coast, where the mountain torrents wander through mangrove swamps to the sea. Wild beasts lurk in the forests and ravines; and, in the days of Aurangzib, wild men, more dangerous than the beasts, made their homes among the rocks.

The Marathas, a sturdy, dark-skinned race, had lived for many generations in their villages, tilling the land, their existence almost forgotten by the rest of India, remembered by the Mahommedan rulers of the Deccan kingdoms when it was a question of collecting tribute or of gathering an army. As light cavalry they had few equals; the little sturdy horses and the little wiry men could climb or scramble anywhere, and find food where others would starve; moreover, they had no objection to fighting against each other if their superiors happened to be at war.

It happened that in the year 1599, a certain Rao or chieftain who was esteemed to be of greatest rank and importance among them had invited friends and neighbours to his house to celebrate the Holi festival. Among the guests was Maloji Bhosla, who came of a family with no pretensions to high rank, and owed his advancement in life to the patronage of the chieftain. With him had come his little boy, Shahji, a child of about five years old, who played with the host's little daughter.

"Wilt thou take this boy as thy husband, child?" laughed the Rao, as the children pelted one another with red, imitating their elders.[1] "They are a fine pair," he added, looking round him.

All laughed obsequiously at the jest, except

[1] This is one of the amusements of the *Holi* festival.

Maloji, who sprang quickly to his feet. "Bear witness all!" he cried, "the Rao has this day made a contract of marriage with me."

Some of the company laughed assent, but the host glowered wrathfully; the jest was going too far. His vexation was greater still next day, when Maloji refused an invitation to dine with him unless he acknowledged Shahji as his future son-in-law, and his wife's fury knew no bounds. A pretty joke, indeed, to match his daughter, even in sport, with the son of a mere nobody,—for what were the Bhoslas but nobodies, though they might pretend—like many of their betters—to a Rajput descent? So Maloji went home, discomfited for the moment; but he never lost sight of his object.

In a moribund kingdom, where wealth was the only thing regarded, men might laugh and whisper to each other when, after an interval of retirement, Maloji reappeared with great wealth, and told an edifying story of an apparition of Bhavani—the goddess most revered by Marathas—and a hidden treasure; but it cleared the way to office and title, and the son of a petty Raja and commander of five thousand horse was no longer unworthy of the Rao's daughter.

The child of their marriage was Sivaji, the hero of Maratha ballad and story, who was born in

1627. His childhood was spent at Poona, under the care of his mother, who troubled herself very little about Shahji after he had taken another wife. Beautiful, clever, and a religious enthusiast, it was she who formed the boy's mind long before he had learned to bend a bow, to hurl a spear, or wield sword and dagger—the only lore imparted to a Maratha, who regarded books and pens as beneath the notice of a chieftain's son. To the end of his life, Sivaji could not write his own name; but his memory was stored with the legends of the Mahabharata and Ramayana, and his mother taught him to dream of a time when the Marathas should drive the cow-slaying Toorks before them, as Rana had driven the ogres. She herself was the favoured of the gods, visited in dream and trance by the "Great Mother"—Bhavani—who foretold the coming of a champion to avenge desecrated shrines and slaughtered cattle; that champion should be her son.

Roaming about hill and glen at his will, hunting, or—so it was said—taking part with gangs of robbers, Sivaji knew the Konkan and its inhabitants as well as his father's house before his beard was grown. At the age of twenty, by some unknown means, he was master of a hill-fort; a little later we find him taking possession of his father's fief of Poona, and declining to send any more of the revenue to its rightful owner, because "the expenses of that poor country had increased."

About this time, the commandant of another hill-fort died, and his three sons quarrelled as to who should succeed him in his fief. Neither had any right to it without the sanction of the King of Bijapur, of whom Shahji and Sivaji were also the nominal vassals; but the king, who was raising those palaces and tombs which are still the wonder of the few who turn aside from the beaten track to visit his deserted capital, never troubled himself about so remote and valueless a part of his dominions as the western hills. Sivaji, called upon to arbitrate between the brothers, secretly urged the two younger to enforce their claim with the strong hand, and offered them the help of his band of marauders. By next morning he and his men held the fort, the eldest brother was a prisoner, and the other two, with the garrison, helpless to resist. As they chafed in rage and shame, he called upon them to forget their injuries, and to stand with him; Bhavani had chosen him to break the yoke of the "Toork"; he had seized the fort, not for his own aggrandisement, but as a move in the game. All three, carried away by his words, vowed to be his men from henceforth, and kept their vow.

Thus, by stratagem, bribery, or assault, Sivaji

won fortress after fortress. Once, like Thomas Binnock at Linlithgow, he and his men came to the gates of a fort with bundles of grass, disguised as peaceful villagers, and were admitted. The garrisons were miserably weak, the commandants treacherous or incapable, and he found it little trouble to win them. Quietly, almost unnoticed, he gathered strength thus for two years; then, in 1648, hearing that a convoy of royal treasure was on the way to Bijapur, he swooped down with three hundred horse, dispersed the escort, and carried the booty to his main stronghold at Rajgarh. Almost simultaneously with this came the news that his forces had occupied the whole of the northern Konkan.

This was too much even for the *fainéant* King of Bijapur; Shahji was arrested, and in spite of his protests that he had no control over his son, and would be thankful to see his Majesty's troops teaching him a lesson, he was flung into a dungeon; the door was built up, leaving an opening so small that a single stone could fill it. "Unless your son submits," swore the king, "that stone shall be rolled into its place, and never moved again."

If Muhammad Adil Shah hoped by threatening the father's life to bring the son to his feet, he was mistaken. Sivaji turned to Shah Jahan—

with whose territories and subjects he had ostentatiously forborne to meddle—and offered to become the Emperor's man, if assured of protection for himself and his father. The bait was taken; the outlaw became a commander of five thousand, and a little pressure upon the King of Bijapur brought Shahji from the dungeon, although for the next four years he was retained as hostage for his son's behavour. In this interval Sivaji dutifully forbore to harry Bijapur territory more than was reasonable, and staved off any demands upon his services from Delhi by trumping up various claims which must be settled before he could act.

At the end of four years Shahji was released, and the first use he made of his liberty was to write to Sivaji: "If you are my son, punish Baji Rao,"—a Maratha who had gained possession of some of Shahji's lands during his imprisonment. His son obeyed this injunction, at a convenient season, by slaughtering the offender with most of his kin and followers, and setting his village in flames. For the present he had business of his own which required all his attention: a Hindu raja who refused to join him in rebellion against Bijapur must be assassinated, and his territories annexed in the confusion which followed; there were forts to be surprised, and forts to be built. In the middle of all this activity, he heard that Prince Aurangzib had come to the Deccan as Viceroy for Shah Jahan, and was about to make war upon Bijapur.

Here was a golden opportunity of obtaining indemnity for the past; in a little while Sivaji had not only obtained Aurangzib's permission to keep all he had taken from Bijapur, but was encouraged to continue his ravages upon that kingdom.

Unluckily, the greed for plunder which had grown in late years with what it fed upon could not be repressed, even for the sake of more solid advantages in the future; it was not in Sivaji or his men to refrain when there came an exceptional opportunity of carrying off silver, horses, elephants, and rich clothes from the Moghuls at Juner and Ahmadnagar. Aurangzib's successes against Bijapur, however, soon reduced Sivaji to a condition of penitence that no doubt, for the time, was genuine. Called from the Deccan by Shah Jahan's illness, the Moghul prince found it convenient to forgive until there should be a chance of punishing. For the next few years he was too busy settling himself upon his father's throne to give much time to the Deccan, and Sivaji could continue his industries, undisturbed by the Moghul army.

"Whenever he heard of a prosperous town or district, he plundered it, and took possession of it."

In the meanwhile the old King of Bijapur was dead, and the advisers of his young son decided that it was absolutely necessary to crush the Marathas, who had become an intolerable nuisance. An expedition was sent out, under command of Afzul Khan, a Muslim nobleman, who vowed to bring the rebel leader in chains to crawl before the throne.

As the army drew nearer, Sivaji, who had retreated to the hill-fort of Pertabgarh, seemed overcome with terror. From his eyrie he sent piteous messages to Afzul, imploring the envoy to protect him from the king's anger, offering to surrender every inch of ground that he had taken. Who was he, a worm and a slave, that he should venture to oppose the Khan who was chief of the warriors of the king? Let him only be assured of forgiveness, and he would submit.

A Brahman in Afzul's suite was sent to the village below Pertabgarh to confer with Sivaji, who came down to meet him. The Maratha's tone was humble, but less abject than before; if he might hold his conquests as a fief from Bijapur, he would see to it that no other rebel should trouble his lord, so long as he could mount horse.

As the Brahman sat that night in the quarters assigned to him, a man stole into the room. It was Sivaji, who came to declare himself the avenger appointed by "the Mother" to drive out the cow-slaying infidel; would one of the "twice-born" hearken to her call? Riches and honour, and a village for him and his descendants, should be his reward.

The Brahman hearkened, either to the call of religion or of avarice. Before the two parted the snare was devised.

It was on an October morning of 1659 that Afzul Khan was borne in his palanquin to the appointed spot—a level clearing below the fort of Pertabgarh—where he was to meet Sivaji. Fifteen hundred of his troops came with him, but were ordered to halt at "the distance of a long arrow-shot." The envoy, "whom the angel of doom had led by the collar to the place," had waited impatiently for some little time before Sivaji was seen descending from the fort. Low of stature, mean in appearance, huddled in a quilted silk cloak lined with red, a padded silk cap half concealing his features, he crept forward, hesitating at every step, pouring out deprecations and entreaties, "with limbs trembling and crouching."

Afzul Khan, who at his prayer had signed to the armed men and bearers standing round his palanquin to move farther off, stood awaiting his approach, a stately figure, clad in muslin, and armed only with his sword as had been agreed between them. Weeping violently, the Maratha flung himself at the feet of the envoy, who raised him, in order to "place the hand of kindness on his back and embrace him."

At that moment the attendants saw the Maratha's long arms flung about their master, and saw the Khan stagger helplessly to and fro. "Treachery! murder!" he cried, clapping his hand to his sword, till a thrust from Sivaji's dagger brought him down. The blast of a horn sounded close beside them; from rock and brushwood, thicket and tree, sprang armed men. The bearers, faithful to the end, lifted the dying Khan into the palanquin, while his guards made ineffectual resistance; Sivaji drew the sword which, as the Marathas believed, Bhavani herself had charmed, and smote off his victim's head.

While this was passing, the main body of Sivaji's troops had fallen upon the Bijapur troops from all sides. Many were slain ere they could draw weapon; all were plundered; those who submitted to Sivaji's orders were spared, and some of these took service with him. The ladies of Afzul Khan's family, and his son, bribed one of Sivaji's officers to take them across the hills into a place of safety; when this came to Sivaji's ears, the officer was executed at once.

The Brahman received his promised reward; well had he and Sivaji arranged their plot. In the eyes of a Maratha, who believed himself Bhavani's chosen warrior, such treachery was meritorious, and the slaughter of the envoy was an act of devotion. Sivaji, before descending to the tryst, his purpose fixed for murder under trust, had laid his head at his mother's feet and asked her blessing; the sword—a beautiful Genoese blade—was worshipped at Satara "because the spirit of Bhavani resided in it." With it are still preserved "the tiger's claws"—three crooked steel blades fitted to the fingers by two rings, and concealed in the closed hand—which he thrust into Afzul Khan's body when embracing him.

After this success, the Marathas overran the country, levying contributions from the towns, and plundering up to the gates of Bijapur, until checked by the advance of another and stronger army. In the intervals of his work upon land, he fitted out a fleet whose exploits surpassed even those of the Portuguese, hitherto notorious for piracy. When at length a truce was patched up with Bijapur, through the mediation of Shahji —playing, for once, the part of an advocate of law and order—the rebel was master of the whole of the Konkan, and had an army of fifty thousand foot and seven thousand horse to keep it.

While Sivaji was settling his differences with Bijapur, the Moghul forces, under Shayista Khan, the brother of Aurangzib's mother, had entered, within the bounds of what he considered his territory. An attempt to drive them out ended in the discomfiture of the Marathas. Shayista Khan, after taking several forts and strong places, marched in triumph into Poona, and lodged in a house belonging to Sivaji. Knowing the talent of that "hell-dog" for surprises, he ordered that no one, armed or unarmed, should be allowed to enter the city or the lines of the army without a pass, and that no Maratha horseman should be enlisted in his army.

On one particular day there was an unsual number of strangers in the streets of Poona. In the morning a procession of country folk—all displaying passes from the *kotwal*—marched along, with song and jest, and discordant music of drum and pipe, bringing a veiled bride to the house of her bridegroom. Later on came a dismal array—

a number of armed men in charge of some Maratha prisoners who, said they, had been captured at one of the outposts. Bareheaded and pinioned, the captives were dragged along by ropes, to the accompaniment of abuse and reviling from their guards.

If any of the good people who stared and laughed or cursed, in accordance with their sympathies, had chanced to follow either procession, they would have seen the wedding party and the prisoners meet in a secluded place within the city walls and arm themselves, the bride strip off her veil, and be revealed as a sturdy Maratha lad, and one of her attendants displaying the sword charmed by the "Great Mother."

At midnight they came to the house where Shayista Khan slept, assured of safety after all the precautions he had taken. Sivaji, having lived there as a boy, knew that in the cook-house there was a window filled with mud and bricks which had opened upon the women's quarters. It was Ramazan, the month of fast, and some of the cooks were at work preparing the food which might be eaten only during the hours of darkness, while the others slept. The sleepers never woke again; the others, for the most part, were cut down ere they realised that any one was in the room, although there were one or two cries, and a slight scuffling which aroused a servant who slept in a room close by.

"Some one is trying to break into the house," he reported to his master.

"Son of an owl!" said Shayista Khan, whose temper, like that of all good Muslims, was not amiable during Ramazan, "the cooks are early at their work."

At this point the shrieks of some of the maid-servants informed him that "some one was making a big hole in the wall."

As the Khan sprang up and seized his weapons, the place seemed to be filled with Marathas; two fell by the Khan's hand, two more plunged by accident into a reservoir of water, and gave him a moment's space to let himself from a window and escape, with the loss of one of his thumbs. Marathas were in the guard-house, killing every one whom they found there, asleep or waking, with the comment, "This is how they keep watch"; Marathas were at the door, where Shayista's son was slain, resisting bravely. Two of the Khan's women were killed in the fray, "and one of them was so cut about that her remains were collected in a basket," says the Muslim historian, with his usual love of gruesome detail. Then, without waiting to plunder, Sivaji and his men retreated to the hill-fort whence they came, "amidst a blaze of torches which made his triumph visible from every part of the Moghul camp."[1]

His next move was to surprise the town of Surat, where he thought to plunder the merchants, native and foreign, unmolested. He had not reckoned, however, with Sir George Oxinden, the head of the English factory, who prepared for defence, and in reply to requisitions and menaces, "still bid him keep his people out of the reach of our guns, else we would shoot them,"—and was as good as his word. A threat to raze the factory to the ground and cut off the head of a luckless Mr Anthony Smith, taken prisoner by the way, merely brought a request that "the grand rebel of the Deccan" would "save the labour of his servants running to and fro on messages, and come himself with all his army."

So the English factory was unhurt, when the approach of the Moghul army forced Sivaji to retreat with a booty worth many hundred thousand pounds, having burned and destroyed to an equal amount. It was a proud moment for Oxinden; the townspeople, many of whom had taken refuge in the factory, "cried out in thousands" for the Emperor to reward the English "that had by their courage preserved them when those

[1] Grant Duff.

to whom they were entrusted, as the governor, &c., dared not show his head." When Oxinden laid down his pistol before the commander of the relieving army, saying that he now left the care and protection of the city to the Emperor's forces —"which was exceedingly well taken,"—he was offered a robe of honour, a horse and a sword. There was a touch perhaps of sarcasm in Sir George's answer that these were things becoming a soldier, "but we were merchants, and expected favour in our trade." He had what he asked for, —the English were exempted for ever from part of the customs duties exacted from other nations. A monument—forty feet high, with two domes, supported on massive pillars—still towers over the English cemetery at Surat, erected to himself and Christopher Oxinden, "most brotherly of brothers."

There were more forays by sea and land, before Aurangzib sent an army with instructions to bring the Marathas to order. The Emperor's policy was to weaken the Deccan kingdoms, one by one, until they fell into his hands, and Sivaji was too useful in playing his game to be utterly wiped out; at the same time Sivaji had taken of late to stopping the ships full of pilgrims bound from Mecca from the western coast, and this was more than Aurangzib's piety could endure.

All seemed to go well, in spite of the Marathas' "seizure of the roads and difficult passes, and firing of the jungles full of trees," which severely tried the nerve of the Moghuls. Sivaji, blockaded in Rajgarh, surrendered upon terms, promising to deliver twenty-three out of the thirty-five forts he possessed, and when called upon, to serve in the imperial army. Shortly afterwards, "that evil malicious fellow," as the contemporary Muslim historian calls him, was summoned to Court. The Raja at whose name the Deccan quaked, found himself a nobody. Aurangzib would take no pains to conciliate the low-born upstart whom he contemptuously called "the mountain rat"; when he arrived two nobles of inferor rank were sent to meet him; when he came to the Audience Hall to present his offering, he was made to stand among the "commanders of 5000," far from the throne; and when his rage and mortification found vent in words none too respectful to the presence in which he stood, he was told that the Emperor in future would not receive him.

When Sivaji demanded to be allowed to return home, he could get no definite answer—except such as might be inferred from the *kotwal* placing a guard round his house who followed him wherever he went. Taking another tone, he bewailed that the innocent followers who had accompanied him should be condemned to languish in the evil climate of Delhi and Agra because he had offended the Emperor, and forthwith passports were sent for every one except himself and his son Sambaji.

The Maratha raja now seemed in desperate case, and he took to his bed, with groans and sighs, complaining of internal pains. No one believed in the reality of his illness, but, confident that the rat was in the trap, they paid little attention when, professing to be cured, he sent presents to attendants, physicians, Brahmans, and the poor. In the East sweetmeats form an invariable part of such offerings, and his guards never troubled to examine the huge paper-covered baskets of confectionery daily sent to the holy men of the neighbourhood. To them it seemed natural enough that one in imminent peril of losing his head should do his utmost to conciliate the spiritual powers.

One day a spy came into Agra with the intelligence that Sivaji was once more at large. The *kotwal* posted off to make inquiries, and found his guards still round the house; they went within, and reported that the Raja was lying asleep on a couch; his face was covered with a muslin scarf, but they could swear to the gold ring on his hand.

Back went the *kotwal*, and had scarcely re-assured his official superiors, when another spy came in who swore that Sivaji had escaped, and was by now a hundred miles away. It was true enough, as the *kotwal* discovered when he returned, crestfallen, to the Raja's house. The sleeping man was one of Sivaji's attendants, and Sivaji and his son had been carried out in two baskets, which the guards had thought to be sweetmeats for the Brahmans of Mathura. At a place outside Agra swift horses were waiting; Sivaji took the boy in front of him, and rode at topmost speed to Mathura.

There he and forty or fifty of his Marathas shaved off beard and whiskers, smeared their faces with ashes, and otherwise disguised themselves as Hindu faquirs. They hid their jewels and gold mohurs in hollow walking-sticks, or in their mouths, or sewed them in old slippers, and started for Benares, by way of Allahabad.

After some time they reached a certain place[1] where the alarm already had been given that Sivaji had escaped from Agra. Seeing this large

[1] The name of it is not given by Khafi Khan, who tells the story.

party of Hindus enter the town, the governor ordered all to be put in prison until he had ascertained who they were. For a night and a day they were kept in ward; on the second night one of them demanded to speak with the governor in private. "I am Sivaji," he whispered, when the two were alone; "my life is in your hands. With me I have two gems, a diamond and a ruby, of great value, and more than a lakh of rupees. Send me and my head to Agra —you must send jewels and money also; here am I, and here is my head; keep your hand from me in this strait, and the Emperor will know nothing of the jewels."

Next morning, after a few inquiries for form's sake, the governor released all the prisoners, and Sivaji went on his way to Allahabad, the poorer by a diamond and a ruby.

"Har, har, Mahadeo! the fire is on the hills!" The Maratha war-cry pealed from rock, and thicket, and ravine, when the word flew through the Deccan that Sivaji had returned to his fortress of Rajgarh after nine months' absence. Once more his hordes swarmed through the country; and once more Aurangzib was obliged to purchase peace by concessions.

In the interval of quiet which followed—broken,

of course, by raids upon Bijapur and Golkonda —Sivaji organised his army and his government, so as to be ready for the next opportunity.

This was not long in coming; in 1671 he was again at the gates of Surat, and being unopposed, except by the English, who defended their factory as before, was able to spend three days very pleasantly in sacking the city without hurrying. The province of Khandesh was plundered, and the trembling headmen of the villages were forced to sign an agreement to pay to Sivaji for the future one-fourth of the revenue due to government,—the beginning of the tribute which the Marathas for many years were wont to levy from Moghul territory.

Bijapur, Golkonda, and Delhi looked on helplessly at the outlaw, who was solemnly enthroned at Rajgarh, as "His Majesty the Raja Siva, Lord of the Royal Umbrella," and sanctified his depredations by being weighed against sacks of gold,[1] which were distributed among the Brahmans. Whatever move his adversaries might make of repression or conciliation, it invariably turned to their discomfiture and the advantage of the Marathas. For fourteen years after his escape

[1] Dr Fryer, an English witness, says he only weighed about ten stone, which bears out the tradition of his small size.

from Agra he continued to lead the same sort of existence, never risking a pitched battle if he could help it, unwearied in skirmish or raid. His light-armed bands had spread as far south as Madras and Tanjore, levying blackmail at every step of the way, before a swelling in the knee-joint brought on fever which put an end to his forays in 1680. In less than fifty-three years of life he had contrived to do such lasting damage as few are privileged to achieve.

An attempt has been made to cast a glamour about him and his hordes, as patriots, deliverers of their country from foreign rule, devoted heroes who faced desperate odds. After a dispassionate survey no glamour remains. Sivaji was a typical Maratha of the best kind—that is to say, he was as unlike the Rajputs from whom he claimed descent as the South African Boer from the good Lord James of Douglas. Never, unless they were driven to it, did the Marathas fight a pitched battle in open field; the joy of fighting, which made the Rajput deck himself with the bridal coronet, the desperate valour which heaped the plain of Samugarh with yellow robes till it looked like a meadow of saffron, was incomprehensible to the wolves of the Deccan. They fought, not for a point of honour, or because they enjoyed fighting, but in a commercial spirit, for the sake of what they could get; their word for "to conquer in battle" means simply "to spoil an enemy." The Rajput was indolent, when not roused by pride or the thirst for battle; the Maratha was untiringly energetic as long as he had anything to gain, but would sacrifice nothing for pride or scruple.

This must be said for Sivaji, that while he lived his followers were forbidden to plunder mosques or women; after his death his son pursued a different policy. Moreover, he was seldom deliberately cruel, unless he suspected his prisoners of concealing their wealth. Mr Anthony Smith witnessed how at Surat "the rogue" in one day "cut off more than twenty-six hands and as many heads; whoever was taken and brought before him that could not redeem himself, lost either his hand or his head." But this was unusual severity, and may have been intended to impress Mr Smith; or Mr Smith may have exaggerated his dangers in order to impress his brother merchants, who had declined to yield the English factory in order to save him from the Raja's vengeance. He was no heroic figure, this slayer of an unarmed man who had sworn to intercede for him; at the same time Hindustan and the Deccan had reason to mourn when, in the words of the Moghul historian, "the infidel went to hell," and the control of his swarms of freebooters passed into hands less merciful and less capable than his.[1]

[1] See Meadows Taylor's romance 'Tara' for the story of Sivaji's murder of Afzul Khan, told by a sympathiser with the Marathas.

XVI.

THE GREAT PURITAN OF INDIA—1658–1707

"Be it known to the readers of this work that this humble slave of the Almighty is going to describe in a correct manner the excellent character, the worthy habits, and the refined morals of this most virtuous monarch, Aurangzib Alamgir.

"Under the management and care of this virtuous monarch, the country of Hindustan teems with population and culture."

—*Mir-at-i-Alam of Bakhtawar Khan.*

XVI.

THE GREAT PURITAN OF INDIA—1658–1707.

SIVAJI was not the only thorn in the side of the Emperor of Hindustan.

To this day the Hindu regards Aurangzib as the middle-class English Protestant regards Philip II. of Spain—as a monster of cruelty and duplicity, who concealed some sinister purpose behind the simplest action. The Muslim considers him a saint who displayed upon a throne the austere virtues of primitive Islam.

The impartial observer, struggling to read between the lines, sees one who, having committed nearly every crime under the sun to obtain a throne, imperilled himself and it by too rigid an adherence to the paths of virtue. He would murder brothers and nephews without an atom of compunction; he could not endure that harmless and law-abiding subjects should bow down to idols in the temples where their forefathers worshipped. He would keep his own sons in captivity upon suspicion; his tenderness to other evil-doers was such that corruption and oppression flourished unchecked throughout his dominions. His blunders, committed from religious motives, had far worse consequences for himself and his successors than his crimes.

No doubt he could have justified every step that led him to the Peacock Throne. The sensuality of his father, the heresy and profligacy of his brothers, were ample reason for setting them aside. He saw how luxury and ease had corrupted the old Muslim spirit; how the descendants of the men who had fought for Islam were leaning to Shia heresy or Hindu idolatry, or to a careless indifference to all religions; and he resolved to bring them back to the simplicity and earnestness of the old time.

It was in vain—as every attempt to set back the clock must be, even when made with cleaner hands than those of Shah Jahan's son. If he could have put a new heart into his idle, self-indulgent courtiers, his effeminate warriors, he could not have undone the work of the Indian climate upon a Northern race. It was in vain that he renounced all worldly pleasure, and led the life of an ascetic, eating no meat, drinking nothing but water, reading the Friday prayers in the mosque, keeping fasts and vigils, learning the whole of the Koran by heart, and making copies of it with his own hand for the cities of Mecca and Medina. It was in vain that, in accordance with the Prophet's injunction that every Muslim should work for his bread, he spent his leisure time in making skull-caps, which he sold to the Court. It was in vain that he "gave a liberal education to his fortunate and noble children," and made the ladies of his household learn "the fundamental and necessary tenets of religion, and devote their time to the adoration and worship of the Deity, to reading the sacred Koran, and performing virtuous and pious acts."

"Every plan that he formed came to little good," we are told; "every enterprise failed." One of his first acts was to employ the treasure of Dara Shukoh in building a great mosque at Lahore—still standing, although sorely damaged by Sikhs and earthquakes; for many years no Muslim would set foot in the accursed place, and even now it is little frequented.

In order to begin his reign with an act of clemency, he remitted many of the most oppressive taxes by which Shah Jahan's magnificence had been maintained, such as the toll collected on every highway, frontier, and ferry, the house-tax paid by every tradesman, and the tithe of corn. But as the historian laments, "the avaricious propensities of men prevailed"; all over the kingdom, and especially in the outlying districts, the revenue officers continued to collect most of these taxes, and even to increase them, putting the sums thus obtained into their own pockets, until goods and merchandise, between the times of leaving factory or port and reaching their destination, had paid double their cost price in tolls. The treasury was nearly empty, and Aurangzib, in the latter years of his reign, had not wherewithal to pay his soldiers their arrears, while the wretched peasantry, artisans, and merchants were ground down by exactions on all sides; and even when they had succeeded in gaining something more than a bare subsistence, durst not let any sign of it appear in their way of living.

The arts which had developed under his predecessors found no encouragement from Aurangzib, who disfigured some of the most beautiful carvings at Fatehpur-Sikri, because they represented human figures, which was contrary to the Law of the Prophet. The minstrels and singers attached to the Court "were made ashamed of their occupation," and stern edicts issued against singing and dancing. All poetry was discountenanced, except such as contained a moral. Astrologers were forbidden to continue their trade. Former emperors had carefully supervised the writing of their annals by competent persons; but "after the expiration of ten years, authors were forbidden to write the events of this just and righteous Emperor's reign."

All his predecessors of the house of Timur had been accustomed daily to show themselves to the people from a window in the palace at Agra or Delhi looking towards the Jumna. Not only the courtiers, but thousands of men and women of all classes gathered there daily, and many of them tasted no food till they had seen the Emperor. As Aurangzib stood one day at this window, he saw beneath him a number of singers and minstrels who bore a bier, while public wailers uttered their shrill cries. "What does this mean?" he asked. "What corpse have you there?"

"The corpse of Music, sire," answered the minstrels; "he is slain, and we carry him to his burial."

"'Tis well," answered the Emperor, turning away; "look to it that you bury him deeply, so that never a sound from him comes to my ears."

When the crowds gathered beneath the window next day, they were dispersed by the royal guards; the Emperor had made up his mind that this daily showing of himself to the people was "among the forbidden and unlawful practices," and the window was to be walled up.

Even Jahangir, in his worst bouts of drunkenness, had not dared to remit the practice for more than a day at a time. Under a despotic government this was an easy way of keeping the people contented. So long as they had a distant glimpse of gold and diamonds, all classes were assured that they had an Emperor who was ready to hear them if they cried to him; henceforth they were cut off from the fountainhead of justice, and felt that their Emperor was nothing to them as they were to him.

If the throne could have been filled by a man of sufficient capacity to check the official depredations which were ruining commerce and agriculture, and sufficient common-sense to leave alone most other things and people—especially the Deccan—the Empire might have continued to prosper for many years. Unfortunately, to leave alone was a virtue of which Aurangzib was incapable; his thirst for power led him to waste treasure and men in making conquests which his successors could never hope to retain, and his religious bigotry created incessant strife within his own border. To all appearance, at the time of his death, he was the greatest and most powerful Emperor who had ever ruled Hindustan; but the very foundations of his empire were rotting to pieces, while he stretched its limits farther and farther.

One of his first actions was to destroy temples at Mathura and Benares, and bury the images beneath the steps of the mosque at Agra, in the style of Mahmud the Idol-breaker. Some who have penetrated as far as outcasts may into the holy place at Benares, standing among stench and filth and unspeakable abominations, their whole being struggling in revolt against the presence of evil, have looked up to the towers of the mosque that he built, with a grateful remembrance of "the great Puritan of India."

An insurrection of devotees was soon put down, and the poll-tax which Akbar had remitted was levied once more upon all of his subjects who were not Muslims. In vain did the Hindus throng about the palace; the window was closed, and their cries and murmurings could not penetrate the walls. Next Friday the Emperor's road to the mosque was blocked by resentful crowds; finding that they would not stand aside at his bidding, he ordered his guards to charge them, and many were trampled to death or injured by the elephants.

The people were terrorised for the moment; a few months later, in the midst of universal disaffection and discontent, Raja Jaswant Singh—who has already appeared several times in this story, and never with any credit—set spark to powder by dying at Kabul, whither he had been sent by Aurangzib. The Emperor thought this a good opportunity for getting the little heir of Marwar into his hands, and when the widowed Rani and her son passed by Delhi on their way homewards, their encampment was surrounded by the Emperor's soldiers.

This was an opportunity for showing the mettle of the Rajputs. The Rani was disguised as a slave, the baby Raja hidden, like Sivaji, at the bottom of a basket of sweetmeats, and hurried away with the women and children of inferior rank. The Emperor demanded that mother and child should be surrendered forthwith, and the Rajput chiefs made answer that they would rather shed the last drop of their blood. The surviving women of Jaswant's family were "sent to inhabit heaven" as the enemy attacked the camp, and the warriors, knowing that every moment gained saw their Raja farther away from Delhi, mounted their steeds, joyously crying, "Let us swim in the ocean of fight!"

When the imperial troops at length made their way into the camp, over the dead bodies of its defenders, they found there a woman and a child dressed in princely garments, whom they brought to the Emperor. When the supposed Rani was discovered to be a servant, and the child a boy of the Raja's age, Aurangzib, instead of throwing them into prison, treated the captives with every respect, as if they had been what he hoped to find. His shrewdness perceived that a pretender to Marwar might be a useful tool, though the rightful heir had escaped him.

The result, of course, was war between Delhi and all the Rajput states excepting Amber, for the Rajputs refused to believe that the real heir was in captivity at the Moghul Court, and were, moreover, as obstinately convinced that the child's father and elder brother had met their death through the Emperor's contrivance. It was war to the death; the Moghul troops cut off all supplies from the country, ravaged the lands, burned the villages, hewed down the trees, and carried off the women and children; the Rajputs, in their lurking-places amid the Aravali hills, might be starved, but they could not be subdued. Prince Akbar,

Aurangzib's third son, decoyed into one of the mountain passes, owed his life to Rajput generosity, and between admiration for their valour and horror at his father's cold-blooded cruelty, was afterwards won to their side. When the news came that he was marching against his father with seventy thousand men, Aurangzib, calm as in the days when he confronted the allied forces of two brothers, used diplomacy to such good effect that the deserters returned to him by thousands, and Akbar durst not risk an engagement. Under escort of five hundred Rajputs, the Prince hurried across country to the Deccan, whence he took ship for Persia. Aurangzib for once lost self-control hearing that his son had escaped; "rage so far got the better of his religion," as a Rajput historian tells us, "that he threw the Koran at the head of the Almighty."

Akbar's flight did not end the war, which continued with increased bitterness on either side, the Rajputs, who had learned some lessons from their persecutors, plundering mosques, burning Korans, and insulting mullahs. Then news came from the Deccan which made the Emperor anxious for peace at any price, and a truce was arranged with Udaipur, the chief Rajput state, on honourable terms. It was not kept for long; Marwar and other states remained in revolt, and it was not in human nature for the Rana to hold aloof while all his western neighbours were at war with the "Toork." Henceforth there could be no friendship between Rajput and Moghul. With his zeal for religion, and his thirst for universal dominion, Aurangzib had dealt a fatal blow to his empire; now that the Moghul stock had become degenerate, the only soldiers capable of facing the Maratha swarms were the Rajputs, who from henceforth would never fight his battles, and, if not at open war with him, would hold aloof while others attacked. The situation has been summed up in one sentence: "Aurangzib had to fight his southern foes with the loss of his right arm."[1]

One arm, however, was enough for Bijapur and Golkonda. Cringing where they should have been bold, defiant when submission was the only safe policy, "the foolish amirs of the Deccan" had to pay the price of their folly. In 1685, Aurangzib came to Bijapur to conduct the siege in person, taking up his quarters in the great mausoleum of Sultan Ibrahim II. In the following year the city yielded, and the king and chief nobles were brought before the Emperor, bound with silver chains.

It was now the turn of Golkonda; for many years "it had secretly subsidised Bijapur to enable

[1] By S. Lane Poole.

it to defend itself against the Moghuls, and at the same time bribed the imperial officers to attack Bijapur rather than itself." Its king, Abu-l-Hasan, hearing that the Emperor was going on pilgrimage to a shrine at Gulbarga, guessed where that pilgrimage would end, and vainly sent entreaty and submission. Then a flicker of courage came to him and his nobles, and, finding that nothing could save them, they prepared to end the story better than they had begun it.

"Day by day, and week by week, the approaches were pushed forward; the fighting was desperate, and many were killed on both sides." The besieged, well supplied with ammunition, kept up an incessant hail of cannon-balls, bullets, and rockets from their walls. Aurangzib himself, "after observing the rite of purification," sewed the seams of the first sandbag that the besiegers flung into the moat. Sambaji, son of Sivaji, had come to the help of Golkonda when it was too late to save, and his light-armed troops harried the Moghuls incessantly, laying waste the country and carrying off supplies of grain. Plague broke out in the besiegers' camp, and many died or deserted.

After three months' suffering, the Moghuls attempted to scale the ramparts by night; a few reached the summit, and one of the Emperor's servants rushed off to report success. Aurangzib

Aurangzib.

commanded the drums of victory to be beaten, and ordered out his royal equipage and state dress. Unhappily, none of the storming-party returned to share these rejoicings, for every one of them had been slain by the garrison, whom a faithful dog had roused. Next day the dog was decorated with a gold collar, by Abu-l-Hasan's order.

So desperate was the plight of the Moghuls that Abu-l-Hasan, after showing some of his prisoners his stores of corn and treasure, offered the Emperor a sum of money to depart, "so that any further slaughter of Muslims might be prevented." In any case he was ready to supply them with grain. "Let Abu-l-Hasan come to me with clasped hands, as a suppliant, or else let him be bound before me," answered the Emperor; "I will then consider what mercy I can show him." And there and then he ordered fifty thousand bags of cotton from Berar to fill the moat.

Mines and countermines blew besiegers and besieged into the air, while Aurangzib quietly sapped at the foundations in his own way. One by one all the nobles of Golkonda were bribed to come over to him, and only Abd-ar-Razzak Lari and Abdullah Khan remained faithful. At length Abdullah yielded to persuasion, and agreed to open one of the gates of the city to the Moghul troops.

No bribe could avail with Abd-ar-Razzak; Shia heretic though he was, Khafi Khan is wrought to admire "the ungracious faithful fellow" whc, "in the most insolent manner, exhibited the Emperor's letter to the men in his bastion and tore it to pieces in their presence," sending a message by the spy who had brought it "that he would fight to the death, like the horsemen who fought with Imam Husain at Kerbela."

In the last watch of a September night, a cry rose at one of the city gates; the enemy had entered. Abd-ar-Razzak heard the shout of victory, and flung himself on a barebacked horse, sword in one hand and shield in the other. Down to the gate he thundered, with ten or twelve followers at his heels; they were soon dispersed, and he fought on alone, "like a drop of water falling into the sea, or an atom of dust struggling in the rays of the sun," shouting that he would fight to the death for Abu-l-Hasan. At every step, one of the thousand swords bristling around him thrust or gashed, so that "he was covered with wounds from the crown of his head to the nails of his feet. But his time was not yet come, and he fought his way to the gate of the citadel without being brought down." Unable any longer to guide his horse—like himself, a mass of wounds, and reeling as it went—he gave it the reins, and it bore him to a garden near the citadel, and halted under a cocoa-tree. With a last effort, clutching at the tree, he dismounted, and lay as one dead beneath its shade.

Roused by the shouts and cries in the city, the king knew that all was over. He went into the harem to bid farewell to the women, and ask their pardon; then he took his seat upon the throne "and watched for the coming of his unbidden guests." When the dinner-hour came he ordered food to be served, as usual; and when the Moghul officers entered his audience chamber, he received them with perfect self-control and dignity, saluting each one, and speaking to them "with warmth and elegance."

While he waited in the Moghul camp until he should be sent to honourable imprisonment in the fort at Daulatabad with the King of Bijapur, it chanced that a musician was playing various Hindu airs in his presence. One of them pleased the king so much that he exclaimed, "If I but had a lakh of rupees, I would give it all to that man!" The speech was reported to Aurangzib, who immediately sent the money, that the captive might enjoy the pleasure of giving.

The day after the city had been captured, a

party of Moghul soldiers passed through the garden near the citadel, and saw a wounded horse standing beneath a cocoa-tree. Going up to it, they found a senseless man upon the ground; twelve wounds were on his face, which was no longer recognisable, and only by his dress and his horse did they know that Abd-ar-Razzak lay there. Touched with pity in spite of themselves, finding that he still breathed, they carried him to a house, and laid him upon a bedstead. There his servants came and dressed his wounds, and two of Aurangzib's Khans disputed what should be done with him: one would have cut off his head forthwith, and hung it over the gate; the other considered that such conduct "was far from being humane." While they wrangled, two surgeons, a European and a Hindu, came on the scene, sent by the Emperor to attend Abd-ar-Razzak. After counting seventy wounds they gave up counting in despair; "the cuts upon his body seemed as numerous as the stars."

"If Abu-l-Hasan had possessed only one more servant as true as this man, it would have taken much longer to enter the fortress," said Aurangzib, who had daily reports brought him of Abd-ar-Razzak's condition.

At the end of sixteen days the patient opened one eye, and, in defiance of the doctors, expressed a hope of recovery. The Emperor sent a gracious message, promising honours as well as pardon for himself and his sons. "If it should please the Almighty to grant me a second life, I am not likely to be fit for service again," was the answer, "and if I were, I feel that no one who has eaten the salt of Abu-l-Hasan and thriven on his bounty can ever take service with the Emperor."

"On hearing these words a cloud was seen to pass over the face of his Majesty, but he kindly said, 'When he is better let me know.'"

Every device was tried to gain "this devoted and peerless hero," as Khafi Khan cannot help styling him, but in the end Aurangzib was forced to recognise that there were men whom the gold of Delhi could not buy. Abd-ar-Razzak's sons came to Court, and were rewarded with commands and fiefs; the old warrior himself journeyed to Mecca, where he had vowed to spend in prayer the "second life" that had been given to him.

The Mahommedan kingdoms of the Deccan had come to an end; the stately palaces had fallen, and nothing remained but to drive out the rats who swarmed in the ruins. It seemed a trifling matter when Aurangzib began it; it was to last him till the end of a long life.

For the Moghul army, brave and imposing in

appearance, with its bejewelled warriors, its steeds caparisoned with satin and velvet, its kettle-drums and yak-tail standards, was nothing more than a show. The nobles, completely demoralised by luxury and the Indian climate, made their campaigns in palanquins, their full petticoats standing out round their bodies, scarcely able to move beneath the burden of wadded coats and chain-armour. They would not journey a single stage without all the state and superfluities to which they were accustomed in Delhi or Agra, and the train of camp-followers amounted to ten times the number of fighting men. It was useless for Aurangzib to set them an example, controlling every movement of the army, facing hardships, at long past seventy years of age, as gallantly as when he led his father's troops to the North-West. Austere as he was, he must bring canopies and silken tents, menageries and mosques, halls of audience, and Persian carpets, since the Emperor of Hindustan could not make a campaign in other wise, and his Court imitated his magnificence. It was of no avail to issue an edict that no officer was to bring wife, family, or property into the field; "in the marches and campaigns such orders could not be enforced without resorting to punishment," and Aurangzib would never punish any more than he would trust.

As for the rank and file of the army, it was even worse than the leaders. Many of the soldiers were household slaves, thrust into the ranks by the amirs in order to fill up the gaps in the muster-roll, and their pay was always in arrears. Sullen, unwilling, perpetually on the verge of mutiny, the unwieldy army dragged itself from place to place, everywhere meeting with disaster, till the cry was wrung from the Emperor's heart, "Of what use to go on fighting when everything goes against us?"

What, indeed, could such an army do against men who lived upon dry bread and onions, slept upon the bare ground, with their horse's bridles twisted round their right arms, and carried all their field equipment in two cotton bags hung from their saddles? Grooms and cooks could have done nothing for them, and Sivaji had punished with death any man who dared to bring a woman into the field.

The fall of Bijapur and Golkonda had added greatly to the numbers of the Maratha forces; every masterless man, every soldier who had served the two kings, was welcome to join them if he could by any means provide himself with a horse and a spear. They hung upon the flanks of the Moghuls as a pack of wolves upon a herd of bulls, harassing them incessantly, cutting off stragglers, plundering and robbing. If the Moghuls pulled themselves together to charge the pack, it broke asunder and streamed away again in all directions, taking cover among woods and rocks. "In that country where," as the Muslims bewailed, "all the hills rise to the sky, and the jungles are full of trees and bushes," the heavily-armed Moghuls floundered and toiled, but could never overtake them. Then growing bolder, on one or two occasions when they were certain of having an overwhelming superiority in numbers, the Marathas openly joined battle, and put the men of Delhi to flight.

Sambaji, son of Sivaji, led them for a few years after his father's death; no man was safe from his cruelty, no woman—even of his race—safe from his lust, and he allowed his followers corresponding latitude. What they lost in discipline, however, was more than atoned for by the increase in the numbers that mustered at the cry, "Har! har! Mahadeo!"

Captured by Aurangzib's troops—he had been warned of his danger, but had refused to believe it and cut out the tongues of those who warned him,—Sambaji was put to a cruel death, amid the rejoicings of all classes, "from chaste matrons to miserable men," who could not sleep for delight when they heard that he was a prisoner. Ram

Raja, his brother, continued the strife; when he died men thought that the star of the Marathas had sunk for ever; Ram had left only widows and infants behind him, Sambaji's son Sahu was a prisoner with the Moghuls. Then Ram's elder wife, Tara Bai ("the Star Lady"), made her three-year-old son successor to his father, took the government into her own hands, and won the hearts of all her officers. Her men ravaged imperial territory, carried out an elaborate system of blackmail, by which every province paid toll to them, and spread their devastations to Ahmadabad and Malwa. They plundered caravans within twenty miles of the imperial camp; they kept many of the Moghul district officers in their pay; they would boldly join their countrymen in the Moghul army in riot and feast, and mock at the Emperor and his faith.

Nominally lord of all India, from Kabul to Trichinopoly, Aurangzib was unable to keep any of it in peace. During the twenty years in which he had been campaigning in the Deccan, Hindustan had broken out of hand; the Jats—the lawless tribes whom we first met harassing the retreat of Mahmud of Ghazni—rose in insurrection near Agra; the Rajputs were never at rest. His insistence upon keeping all the threads in his own hands resulted in his never having the time to disentangle them, never having the resolution to trust them to other fingers. The finances of the Empire were in hopeless disorder. When the troops murmured for their arrears of pay, he told them that if they did not like his service they were welcome to leave it. Mutinies were always breaking out, and could scarcely be appeased by wringing some advances from the unhappy cultivators, who, bled by imperial tax-collector and Maratha freebooter, left off agriculture and became freebooters in their turn, for want of employment. Plague and famine came to destroy what war and pillage had left, and heavy floods put the last touches to the universal misery.

It must not be forgotten that the Moghuls were aliens in the land they ruled almost as much as are the English to-day. To maintain authority, it was absolutely necessary that both army and civil service should be strong and efficient. Between mistaken scruples and mistaken kindness, Aurangzib had allowed both to go to ruin, unchecked. His revenue officers and administrators did as they pleased, knowing well that even if their crimes were found out, the Emperor would not punish them; the army was deficient in numbers, since few amirs troubled themselves to keep up their levies to the full standard, and entirely lacking in morale. It was impossible to hold India in hand under such conditions.

In 1705 Aurangzib was so ill as to inspire the worst misgivings among his retinue, who feared that if he were to die "not a soul would escape from that land of mountains and raging infidels." He led what was left of his army back to Ahmadnagar, still keeping the fixed smile that men were used to see upon his face, and at nearly ninety showing none of the infirmities of age beyond a slight deafness, and reading his correspondence without spectacles. There was none to stand at his side; ever suspicious, ever playing off one man against another, in all his life he had trusted no human being fully; and, knowing themselves suspected and spied upon, his amirs had never given him heart-whole service. His eldest son was a captive, his third an exile in a strange land. Another son he had imprisoned for seven years, in some jealous misgiving; another went in such terror that he never received a letter from his father without turning pale. Only the youngest, Kam-Baksh, seemed to be regarded in these latter days with some sort of tenderness by the lonely old man, who could never forget how Shah Jahan had lost his throne.

Fever attacked the Emperor, and it was evident

that the end was near. He wrote farewell letters to the sons whom he durst not have with him, since they had already begun to show jealousy of each other. "Old age is arrived; weakness subdues me, and strength has forsaken all my members. The instant which has passed in power hath left only sorrow behind it. I have not been the guardian and protector of the empire. My time has been passed vainly. . . . I have a dread for my salvation and with what torments I may be punished. The Begam" (his daughter) "appears afflicted, but God is the only judge of hearts. The foolish thoughts of women produce nothing but disappointment. Farewell! farewell! farewell!"

"I carry with me the fruits of my sins and imperfections," he wrote to Kam-Baksh. . . . "Wherever I look I see nothing but God. The breath which rose is gone, and has left not even hope behind it." . . . At the close comes the plea that many a parent has had to urge: "I am going; whatever good or evil I have done, it was for you."

It was on Friday, March 4, 1707, after a reign of nearly fifty years, that the Emperor Aurangzib went to face the judgment that he dreaded, his stiffening fingers clutching at his beads, his bloodless lips gasping prayers to the last moment of life. As the soul parted from the body a fearful tempest arose; the sky was darkened, as at midnight, trees and tents were hurled in all directions by the wind. It might have seemed that the Genius of the House of Timur fled away upon the blast, never to return again.

XVII.

THE SONS OF THE SWORD—1469-1764

"He is of the Khalsa
Who protects the poor,
Who combats evil,
Who remembers God,
. . . .
Who is wholly unfettered,
Who mounts the war-horse,
Who is ever waging battle,
Who slays the Toorks,
Who extends the faith,
And who gives his head with what is upon it.
. . . .
At the doorway of a Sikh shall wait elephants caparisoned,
And horsemen with spears, and there shall be music over
his gateway.
When myriads of matches burn together,
Then shall the Khalsa conquer East and West."

—*The Rules of Guru Govind.*

XVII.

THE SONS OF THE SWORD—1469-1764.

AKBAR had striven, and striven in vain, to reconcile the different races and castes within his empire in a worship of One God. In the evil days, when his empire was falling to pieces, there indeed arose a brotherhood open to all castes and all degrees — but it was a brotherhood of the sword.

In the latter half of the fifteenth century a number of pilgrims, having accomplished the last stage of their journey to Mecca, lay down to rest, their heads turned towards the Kaaba, as befitted all orthodox Muslims. One of the guardians of the Holy Place, going up and down between the rows of sleepers, saw among them a man in blue clothing, who, shameful to tell, lay with his feet where his head should have been.

In a spasm of pious horror, the guardian kicked him soundly.

"Ho! what infidel have we here that dishonours

the House of the Lord? See how he turns his feet towards it!"

"Nay," answered the pilgrim, "is there a place on earth to which I may turn my feet where the Lord is not?"

The guardian was in no mood for argument. Still snorting with fury, while the other pilgrims sat up, rubbed their eyes, and made pious or profane ejaculation, he seized the offender by the leg, and dragged him forcibly into the conventional position for a True Believer, when sleeping.

Then lo! in the sight of all men, the Holy Place itself turned until once more it stood at the strange pilgrim's feet; for the man in blue clothing was Baba Nanak, the Guru, on whose name the Sikhs call unto this day.

Baba Nanak, the son of a grain merchant at Lahore, after the pattern of Prince Siddhartha and St Francis of Assisi, left his father's house, and wandered into the world with "Lady Poverty" for his companion. Over the length and breadth of India did he travel, through Persia, and to Mecca, everywhere seeking out holy men and priests of every religion, that from them he might learn "the way." He read the sacred books of Brahman and Mullah, he meditated in solitude, he worshipped at shrine after shrine;

but what he sought was not to be found in the Vedas or the Koran.

At length illumination came upon him. God is One, the Timeless, the Giver of Grace, the Truth, Who was before the world began, the First and the Last, without Whom none may find salvation. Before Him race and caste are nothing, and each man will be judged by his own actions. "God has said, no man shall be saved, except he has performed good works. The Almighty will not ask him to what tribe or persuasion he belongs. He will only ask him what has he done."

"One God, One Way," was Nanak's cry from henceforth; and in a land where the most trivial act is hedged about with restrictions, where for centuries men have sought to win heaven by accumulating penance upon penance, he taught that to find salvation it was not necessary to forsake the ordinary duties of mankind, or to hold apart from other men. He set the example by going back to his own home, and living with the wife and children whom he had forsaken when he went out to find "the way." He refused to wear the sacred thread of the Hindus. "Make mercy thy cotton, contentment its thread, continence its knot, and truth its twist," he said to a Brahman disciple; and to a Mahommedan his counsel was, "Make kindness thy mosque, sincerity thy prayer-carpet, the will of God thy rosary."

Out of respect to the prejudices of others, he would not insist upon his followers eating either the ox or the swine, and he praised those who should abstain altogether from animal food. But to all he gave the warning, "Eat and clothe thyself, and thou may'st be happy; but without fear and faith there is no salvation." He condemned suttee and the murder of female children, and forbade the image-worship of the Hindus as sternly as the devotion to saints practised by both Hindus and Muslims. "Worship not another than God; bow not to the dead."

Legend has gathered about him so closely that it is scarcely possible to disentangle the true from the false. One story says that it was he who summoned Babar and the Moghuls into Hindustan, to drive out the cruel Afghans who oppressed the people. It may be true that he met Babar during the brief interval when the Emperor was trying to put his conquests in order, even though he may not have foretold that Babar and he should each found a dynasty of ten sovereigns.

He died at the age of seventy, appointing one of his disciples as "Guru" or teacher, since of his two sons, one, in disregard of his father's teaching, had become an ascetic, the other was given over to pleasure. But the Sikhs believed that his spirit became incarnate in the body of the nine Gurus who followed him. "Nanak thus put on other habiliments, as one lamp is lighted at another."

Ram Das, the third successor to Nanak, was one of the holy men whom Akbar "heard gladly," and to him was granted a piece of land to the north of Lahore. Here he made a tank, "the Pool of the Water of Life," wherein still stands the Golden Temple, the holy place that is to the Sikhs what Mecca is to the Mahommedan, or Benares to the Hindu. In the pool the Sikhs—who are baptised into their religion by water—bathe before they pass into the temple enriched with spoils from Moghul tomb and palace, where the white-robed high priest reads the "Granth" or sacred book, and receives their offerings. Fans wave to and fro above the "Granth," embroidered coverings enwrap it; when it is carried in procession jewelled canopies are borne over it, and brooms of peacock feathers sweep the dust of the worshippers from the temple floor.

All these splendours date from long after the time of Ram Das, in whose day the Sikhs were a small and obscure sect, of no wealth or importance. It was his son, Arjun, who made Amritsar their holy city, and first compiled the "Granth." Under his rule the Sikhs increased and prospered, acquiring a great reputation in foreign countries as traders, and paying a fixed tax or tithe to the Guru.

There was a certain official administering the finances of the Lahore province under the Emperor Jahangir, who sought a husband for his daughter. Someone suggested that he might do worse than take the son of Arjun. "Shall I give my daughter to a beggar's son?" he objected. "Arjun is wealthy," urged the match-maker. "That may be," answered the official, "but he receives alms from other men."

Some busybody repeated this speech to Arjun, and when the official—who in the meantime had been considering the matter more carefully—sent a formal proposal for a marriage between the children, the Guru would not hear of any such thing. Never, he vowed, should his son marry the daughter of a man who had called him a beggar.

The official, insulted in his turn, avenged himself by slandering Arjun to Jahangir. The Emperor, engaged just then in impaling seven hundred of the men who had been concerned in his son Khusru's rebellion, was told that the Sikh Guru had prayed for the Prince's success. Arjun was summoned before his Majesty, fined, and imprisoned. The Sikh stories tell that even though he had justified himself to the Emperor, his enemy still held him in ward, and threatened to bring other accusations against him. On the morning of the day on which he was to be brought for a second time before Jahangir, he asked leave to bathe in the river Ravi. His guards watched him wading out into the shallow stream, till suddenly he vanished. Whether he had let himself sink beneath the waters, or whether, as his disciples believed, he was miraculously rapt from them, no human eye ever beheld him again.

For many years he had been childless. Then his wife remembered that a very old man, the last of those who had followed Nanak, still survived. Dressed in her richest *sari*, she bowed before him, and laid offerings worthy of a princess at his feet, imploring him to bless her so that she might bear a son. But the old man turned away his head, and made no answer.

She came again, and this time she brought no train of servants, but entered his presence alone. Her feet were bare, her *sari* was that of a peasant woman, and on her head she bore the offerings of food that the poorest bring. Then the old man smiled upon her. "A son shalt thou bear who shall be lord of grace and power, and from him shall spring all the Gurus who are to come after him."

This son, Har Govind, only eleven years old at the time of his father's death, was soon at work organising the Sikhs into a military caste. He led them to battle against their enemies, or those of the empire, wearing two swords in his girdle, one—so he said—to avenge his father's death, one to stay the false miracles of Mahommedanism. This did not prevent him from serving Jahangir for many years; and in spite of differences of opinion after that Emperor's death, which brought him and his followers into collision with the troops of Delhi, he died in peace.

Two of his descendants succeeded him, who did nothing worthy of remembrance. Then came the turn of his younger son, Teg Bahadur, who had the misfortune to draw upon himself the unfavourable notice of Aurangzib. The Sikhs maintain that he was living the life of a saint and an apostle, and that he was foully slandered by a jealous nephew who had looked to be acknowledged as the Guru in his stead. Other authorities represent him as leading the life of a Robin Hood in the deserts near the Sutlej, levying contributions from rich Hindus, which he shared with the peasantry, who regarded him with not unnatural affection.

Saint or robber, Teg Bahadur received a summons to Delhi which he might not disregard, for the sake of his followers, who must all perish were he to resist. He had always refused to wear the sword of Har Govind, saying that he was not worthy; he now bound it upon his young son, another Govind. "I go to death; see to it that my body is not left for dogs and vultures to tear, and avenge me when the time shall come."

At Delhi he was thrown into prison, whence they brought him before Aurangzib, who bade him work some miracle if power were indeed given him from heaven. Now miracles were forbidden to the Guru. "Fight with no weapon save the sword of God," Nanak had enjoined them; "a holy teacher hath no means save the purity of his doctrine." Teg Bahadur made answer that the duty of man was to pray to the Lord; he could do no more.

The Emperor condemned him to die, on the pretext that he had been seen standing on the roof of his prison in the fort, gazing towards the rooms where the royal harem dwelt.

"O Emperor!" cried the Guru, "I was on the top storey of my prison, but I looked not at thy private apartments or at thy queens. I was looking towards the white men who shall come from overseas to tear down thy *purdahs* and destroy thine empire."

This was in 1675. Nearly two hundred years afterwards, when Nicholson led Sikhs to the assault of Delhi, they chanted Teg Bahadur's prophecy as they charged.

A Sikh legend tells how, at the last, when brought forth to execution, Teg Bahadur confessed to the Emperor that though he might not work miracles, he knew of a charm that could save from death. Let him write it on a piece of paper, and fasten it about his neck, and the sword of the executioner could not harm him. Emperor and court watched while he traced a few words on paper and while the sword flashed in the air,—when, to their surprise and disappointment, the Guru's head and body rolled apart. One of them picked up the paper and opened it; within was written, "My head I gave, my secret I gave not."[1]

His body, exposed in the streets of Delhi, was stolen thence by some of his followers, belonging to the sweepers, whose touch is pollution to the other castes of Hindus. For the next twenty years nothing was heard of his son.

In the wastes and solitudes where he hunted

[1] In the original there is a play upon the words "Sir," a head, and "Sirr," a secret.

the wild beasts, enlightenment came upon Govind; he chastened his body with fasting and penance, he gave his soul to contemplation, he made sacrifice like the heroes of olden time, and the "Great Mother," Bhavani, appeared amid the smoke of the burnt-offering, and touched his sword, in token that victory and power were given unto him.

Then he gathered the Sikhs about him, and gave them the new law. The way of salvation was open to all—as Nanak had declared, two hundred years before—and the bond of union was to be the sword. All caste was to be forgotten; all the disciples should bathe in the sacred pool, and eat together of the sacred food which made them of the "Khalsa"—the elect. Their hair should be unshorn, they should bear steel about them, and their garments should be blue in colour. No longer were they to be called "Sikhs" or "disciples," for each of them from the hour of his baptism into the faith became "Sing," or "a lion"—a warrior vowed to arms, to slay the "Toorks."

The appeal was answered; some few disciples were of such high caste that they would not consent to be brought down to a level with *sudras* and sweepers; the rest accepted the new law, and many more joined them. It is proof that "the brotherhood of the sword" binds more closely than ties of race, creed, or position, that one hundred and fifty years after Guru Govind's initiation, Mountstuart Elphinstone could write that "the Sikhs have now as distinct a national character as any of the original races in India."

Govind and his followers now began a series of small campaigns, as the foes or allies of the various hill chiefs in their neighbourhood. Then Aurangzib, taking alarm at their success, and perhaps fearing that another Sivaji had arisen in the north, sent an army against them. "The Khalsa" was not yet strong enough to face the troops of Delhi; Govind might condemn all who deserted him to suffer in this life and the next, but spiritual weapons were not so terrible as the Moghul artillery. Day after day saw the gaps in their ranks widen, till only forty men were left with him. He sent away his mother, his wives, and his two youngest boys, who escaped to Sirhind; there they were betrayed to the Moghuls, who slew the lads in cold blood.

Govind had taken refuge in a fort with his elder sons, and the two-score men who still remained faithful. The Moghuls closed upon them; both the young men and most of the garrison were slain, and Govind, who had vainly exposed himself everywhere, fled again, under cover of a dark night. Aided by kindly Muslims, whom he had befriended in former days, he escaped, disguised in the blue dress of a Pir, into the broken country near Bhatinda, whither the Moghul troops did not trouble to follow him. Some will have it that the Sikhs wear blue clothes in memory of this flight of their last Guru.

In the inevitable struggle for the throne which followed the death of Aurangzib, Bahadur Shah, who had overcome two of his brothers, and taken what was left of the empire to himself, summoned Govind to his aid, and gave him a military command. Once again the Sikh war-cry of "Wah! Guru!" was heard, and the "Khalsa" gathered together. But Govind would lead them no more; Nanak's prophecy of "ten kings" was about to be fulfilled. In a fit of passion he had slain a Pathan horse-dealer with whom he was quarrelling over the payment due for some horses. Remorse came too late to the childless man, whose slain father was still unavenged. He was ever in the company of the dealer's sons, playing games of skill with them, harping continually upon the duty of revenge, as if he sought death at their hands. Their mother, too, whetted her tongue upon the sons who had not the courage to take blood for blood, and at last, while Govind slept, the young men crept up to him, unperceived, and stabbed him where he lay.

The Guru started up; his men hurried in from all sides and seized the Pathans, who smiled scornfully; they had avenged their father, and could face death unmoved. "Loose them!" commanded Govind; "harm them not; they have done well."

"Who shall show us the way when thou art gone?" wept his disciples. "Who shall lead us to victory? Thou hast no son to stand in thy stead."

"Be of good cheer," answered the dying man, "the Ten are no more, and I go to deliver the 'Khalsa' to Him who continueth. He who wishes to behold the Guru, let him search the Granth; he who wishes to behold the Guru shall behold him in the 'Khalsa.' Be strong, be faithful; behold, wherever five Sikhs are gathered together, there will I be in the midst of them."

It was on the banks of the river Godavery, in the Deccan, at the end of the year 1708, that Govind died, and since that time no other Guru has arisen among the Sikhs.

To the north-west sped Banda, whom the dead man had appointed to lead the "Khalsa" in war, and displayed the arrows of Govind to the Sikhs who mustered at his call. Here was pledge and token of victory; let them avenge the slaughtered sons of their Guru upon the accursed "Toork." Then followed eight years of reprisals from either side. Like a swarm of locusts the Sikhs swept down upon the province of Sirhind, and spread through the country to the east of the Sutlej and the Jumna, destroying mosques, slaughtering mullahs, massacring and plundering wherever they went. In the town of Sirhind fearful vengence was taken—men, women, and children were butchered, even the dead were not allowed to rest, but were torn from their graves and flung to the jackal and the vulture. For many generations afterwards no faithful Sikh would go by the place where Sirhind had once stood without bringing away a brick, so that nothing might remain to tell where Govind's sons had been murdered.

A temporary repulse drove them back to their headquarters upon the upper waters of the Sutlej, between Lodiana and the mountains; thence, in a little while, they broke forth again, and were laying waste all the country between Lahore and Delhi. Bahadur Shah, the Emperor, himself came against them, and forced them to leave the open country. Banda and his men retreated like savage dogs, biting fiercely at every step of the way, and took refuge in a fort. Here, while the legions of Delhi hemmed them closer and closer, they endured the last extremity of famine, until so many had died of starvation that they could hold out no longer. Then the survivors came forth, sword in hand; some fell, after slaying numbers of the enemy; a few cut their way through the lines, and escaped.

There was one among them who by dress and appearance seemed to be their leader; he was captured by the Moghuls, and brought before the Emperor. Great was the wrath of all when he was found to be, not Banda, but a Hindu convert who had taken his place; the real Banda had been among the few who escaped.

Bahadur Shah had neither the grace to forgive nor the courage to punish outright; he would not take the life of the brave Sikh, but he ordered him to be shut up in an iron cage and sent to Delhi.

Banda lost no time in making himself felt, and for a while there was none to stay him; Bahadur Shah had died at Lahore, and his sons must needs go through the usual civil war in order to establish the succession. Sirhind was again plundered, and the Punjab suffered much before an army under the governor of Kashmir defeated the Sikhs, and sent them back once more towards the hills.

Shut up in the strong fort he had built for himself between the Ravi and the Beas, Banda and his men again endured all the horrors of slow starvation, and this time there was no escape. Some were killed at once upon surrender; Banda and seven hundred and forty men were sent to Delhi, and paraded through the streets, mounted upon camels, and dressed in black sheep-skins, with the wool outside. The smooth-faced people of the city cursed the shaggy ruffians, with their flowing hair and long beards parted in the middle and brushed over their ears, after the fashion of the Sikhs. One old woman saw among them the man who had assassinated her son, the governor of Sirhind; seizing a stone, she flung it down with so true an aim, that it crashed upon the Sikh's skull, and he fell dead.

Every day a hundred of the prisoners were executed—all, we are told, disputing who should be the first to go; on the eighth day, Banda himself was exposed in an iron cage, and put to death with fearful tortures. Every living thing belonging to him, from his son to his cat, was slain with him.

For a while the "Khalsa" seemed to have come to an end; with a price set on the head of every

Sikh, those who would not conform must hide in the jungles or the hills.

For a generation other creeds and races tore the empire of Akbar asunder, the Marathas advancing to the very gates of Delhi, the Afghans seizing upon Kandahar. Then Nadir Shah, the Persian, entered Delhi, and for two months pillaged, murdered, and tortured at his will. In the anarchy that followed, the Sikhs—who until then had been earning a precarious, and what might almost have been considered an honest, livelihood as petty robbers—gathered together in bands and plundered with strict impartiality the stragglers from his army and the fugitives from Delhi. For the first time in many years they dared to visit Amritsar in open day and bathe in the Water of Life.

The empire lay in the death throes, and foe after foe cut a portion from the quivering body. Ahmad Shah, the Afghan ruler of Kandahar, now turned southwards and attacked Delhi. The old days when the men of the hills came down through the northern gates, in wave upon wave of invasion, to ravage the fat plains of Hindustan, had returned again; four times did he come with a host of spoilers at his back. The third time he seized Delhi, and repeated the weary round of pillage, torture, and violence.

It was the opportunity of the Sikhs, who for some time had been seizing upon one territory and another, as chance favoured them, often driven back and forced to disperse, but collecting again, with invincible obstinacy, so soon as the immediate pressure was relaxed. They occupied Lahore, and used the Moghul mint to strike a rupee "coined by the grace of the Khalsa." Then for a little while the Marathas were paramount; the Sikhs must leave Lahore. Then Ahmad Shah crossed the Indus for the fourth time, and beat the wolves of the Deccan at Panipat (1761). On his way back to Kandahar, to appease the religious enthusiasm of his army, he destroyed the temples which the Sikhs had lately rebuilt at Amritsar, bathing their foundations in bullocks' blood, slaughtering cows in the sacred pool, and washing out the desecrated mosques with the blood of slain Sikhs.

He went, and while India lay inert and helpless, Maratha and Moghul incapable of further effort, the Sikhs rallied, and were up and doing. They plundered a Pathan colony, they slew a Khan who had offended them, they marched once more to Sirhind, where the Afghan governor came out to meet them in 1763. After their victory, men told how the Sikh horsemen scattered apart, and rode day and night through the plains between the Sutlej and the Jumna, each flinging his belt, his sword sheath, his scarf into the villages that he passed, as a sign that he had taken possession, until all were nearly stripped naked before their wild ride had come to an end. The town of Sirhind itself was made a desolation for ever.

In the next year they were masters of Lahore, with their chained Afghan captives washing the foundations of the mosques in the blood of swine. At Amritsar they held a solemn assembly, and struck coins with the inscription, "Grace, power, and victory without pause, Guru Govind Sing obtained from Nanak."

A hundred and forty years later the Sikhs had gathered at the Durbar of 1903, to acclaim the ruler of the white race whose coming Teg Bahadur had foretold. They came together to worship at the shrine erected in memory of their murdered Guru; they made prayers and offerings; and they saluted their "Granth" with the cry of "God save the King."

XVIII.

THE DEATH-THROES OF AN EMPIRE—1707-1761

"The country was torn to pieces with civil wars, and groaned under every species of domestic confusion. Villainy was practised in every form; all law and religion were trodden under foot; the bonds of private friendship and connections, as well as of society and government, were broken; and every individual, as if amidst a forest of wild beasts, could rely upon nothing but the strength of his own arm."—A. Dow (referring to India in 1754).

XVIII.

THE DEATH-THROES OF AN EMPIRE—1707-1761.

THE last agonies of a dying empire, when the decay has been brought on by its own folly, stupidity, and selfishness, are as painful to dwell upon as the last agonies of a human being in like case. The events of the next fifty years must be passed over as briefly as possible; were they told in detail, scarcely a human being could endure the record of misery, crime, anarchy, cowardice, and selfishness beyond belief, and cruelties which can hardly be named.

A transient gleam of brightness came in the short reign of Aurangzib's son, Bahadur Shah. With Rajputana in revolt, the Sikhs overrunning the Punjab, the Marathas terrorising the Deccan, and the Jats breaking loose near Agra, and hampered, moreover, by having to fight two of his brothers before attending to the rest of the empire, he did the utmost that man could do against such odds. When once the princes' insurrection had been put down, he pardoned all the chiefs who had taken part with them, and bound them to himself with favour and honours. He released Sahu, the son of Sambaji, who had been a prisoner at the Moghul Court since the time of his father's execution, and sent him to keep the Marathas in such order as was consistent with their nature. He made a peace with the Rajputs, by which Udaipur and Jodhpur were rendered independent in all but the name; and then he went against the Sikhs, who had proved more than a match for his generals. But he was an old man — nearly seventy years of age—and he had not made much impression upon them when death overtook him in 1712.

"Great confusion immediately followed in the royal camp, and loud cries were heard on every side. The amirs and officials left the royal tents in the darkness of the night, and went off to join the young princes. Many persons of no party, and followers of the camp, unmindful of what fate had in store for them, were greatly alarmed, and went off to the city with their families. Ruffians and vagabonds began to lay their hands upon the goods of many. Several persons were to be seen seeking refuge in one little shop. Friends and relations were unable to answer the calls made upon them. Great disturbances rose in the armies of the princes, and none of the great men had any hope of saving their lives. The soldiers loudly demanded their pay and allowances, and joining the unceremonious servants, they made use of foul and abusive language, and laid their hands on everything they found. Fathers could do nothing to help their sons, nor sons for their fathers. Every man had enough to do in taking care of himself, and the scene was like the Day of Judgment."

It was a picture in miniature of the state of the whole empire for the next hundred years.

The usual civil war followed; then Zulfikar Khan, the paymaster, set up a puppet Emperor, in whose name he ruled for a few months until both were murdered. By this time Timur's descendants had become mere shadow-princes, incapable of power, delegating their authority into the hands of some "Mayor of the Palace." The next king-makers were two Sayyid brothers, whose wretched tool, the Emperor Farukh Siyar, struggled helplessly against their usurpations until blinded and murdered by their orders, after a reign of a few years, during which, we are told, "Muslims and Hindus united in prayers for the downfall of the government."

Of such little importance were the successors

of Aurangzib in death as in life, that not one has a mausoleum to mark his grave, and it is not known for certain where some of them were buried. "Deposed and blinded," "Deposed and murdered," "Deposed, blinded, and murdered," are the records opposite nearly all their names up to the time of Shah Alam, the most unhappy of all, who, blinded by Ghulam Kadir the Rohilla, remained a prisoner in the hands of Ghulam's conquerors, the Marathas, until rescued by Lord Lake in 1803. If there were any respite from revolt and invasion, it was generally occupied in fratricidal strife and intrigue. Every son of the Emperor knew that it must be "Takht" or "Takhta," "the Throne" or "the Bier," and seized any opportunity of getting rid of his brothers and near relations.

Two child kings, set up by the Sayyids in Farukh Siyar's stead, died—happily for themselves—of consumption; then came Mohammad Shah, the last Moghul to sit upon the Peacock Throne. Again there was a momentary pause on the road to ruin. Among the chief nobles was a truculent old Turkoman, son of one of Aurangzib's favourite officers, who figures in the chronicles of the time under the various names and titles of Mir-Kamr-ad-din, Chin Kilich Khan, Asaf Jah, and the Nizam. Hating the Sayyids, both as rivals and as

Shia heretics, he raised an army and went against them. Their power was broken, and when shortly afterwards one was assassinated and the other thrown into prison, there was space for strengthening the defences of what fragments of empire remained. The Nizam founded the "buffer state" of Hyderabad, to keep off the Marathas, and left his son to rule it while he directed affairs at Delhi as Grand Vezir.

The feeble, profligate Emperor, given over to debauchery and bad company, left his signet in the hands of his mistress, who used it as she pleased, and would not even show common civility to the one man who might have preserved the fragments of his empire for him. When Asaf Jah came to the durbar with the formal obeisance of the days when the Moghul Court was more than an empty splendour, the insolent boys who were Mohammad Shah's chosen companions would whisper unreproved to their master, "See how the Deccan monkeys dance!"

Weary of mockery and ingratitude, the old warrior made the excuse of a Maratha inroad to go back to the Deccan. There with a stout hand he put down foray and rebellion, so that at last the highways were free again for travellers and merchants. Even he, however, was not strong enough to refuse the *chauth*—a tax as disgraceful as the Danegeld of Ethelred the Unready. The utmost he could obtain was that his own officers should collect it from the people, and deliver it to the Marathas, who by this time were levying their blackmail not only in the Deccan but in Gujarat, in Malwa, in the very heart of the empire.

The leader among the wolf-pack by this time was no longer the Raja of Satara, the descendant of Sivaji, who was almost as little of an influence as the Emperor himself, but his Peshwa, or Prime Minister, Baji Rao. Unscrupulous as all former leaders, and of clearer sight than most of them, this man realised that the time had come for the Marathas to found the empire promised to Sivaji by the "Great Mother." "The Maratha flag shall fly from the Kistna to the Attock," he told the Raja, who, stirred to unwonted energy, replied, "Ay, you shall plant it beyond the Himalaya." "Let us strike at the withering tree," urged Baji Rao; "the branches must fall of themselves." And he acted upon his own counsel with such good effect that in a few years he led his horsemen to the gates of Delhi. Asaf Jah, hurrying to the Emperor's help, with power to call out all the resources of the state, could only muster thirty-four thousand men, and these were worsted by the usual Maratha tactics. The Nizam was obliged to make terms with the Peshwa, and to cede to him all the territories between the Narbada and the Chambal, including the whole of the province of Malva.

If Asaf Jah had hoped to win a breathing-space for the empire and himself by this surrender, he was soon undeceived; an enemy more terrible than any since the days when Timur the Lame had laid Delhi waste was coming upon Hindustan.

Nadir Shah, the Turkoman, had risen to the throne of Persia through the stages by which many Oriental kings have passed—first slave, then freebooter, then general under a king whose authority was only nominal, and lastly king in name as well as in fact. The rulers of Delhi had seen little reason to trouble themselves about him up to this time; if he chose to tear Kandahar from the Chilzais, it was many years since it had belonged to the Moghul Empire. They had forgotten how, in the day of their pride, Kandahar had been a stepping-stone to further conquest. When he seized Ghazni and Kabul, they solaced themselves with the thought that the wild tribes who infested the hills between Kabul and Peshawar might be trusted to bar the road to the south; they had forgotten that the subsidies formerly paid to the hillmen, like most of the payments due from Delhi, had fallen into arrears.

Then came the tidings, early in 1738, that Nadir

had crossed the Indus, and was on his way to Lahore.

"Notwithstanding all this, the careless Emperor and the ungrateful nobles, having covered their faces with the veil of gross negligence, were awaiting the approaching misfortune." Counsels were divided. Asaf Jah, the Nizam, objected to every proposal made by the Khan-Dauran or Captain-General of the Emperor's forces, and was also upon ill terms with Sa'adat Ali, the Viceroy of Oudh. The Emperor was not strong enough to put down their bickerings with a firm hand, and while they quarrelled the Persian army drew nearer and nearer. There was an action at Kurnal, a few miles north of Panipat—a miserable blunder from beginning to end, so far as the Moghuls were concerned; Sa'adat joined battle on his own account, hearing that Nadir's horsemen were plundering his camp and baggage, the Khan-Dauran followed him, "without due preparation" or waiting for orders, and the Nizam held stubbornly aloof. The Khan-Dauran was mortally wounded, and the Viceroy was taken prisoner, but their men fought so obstinately till the close of day that Nadir Shah, who, judging from the events of late years, had expected to meet with no resistance, was somewhat disconcerted, and began to consider whether it would

Mohammad Shah.

not be better to return to Persia, if he could obtain a sufficient indemnity before he departed. Some say at this point that the Emperor, who had lost what little courage he ever possessed at the Khan-Dauran's death, threw up the struggle; others that he was betrayed by Sa'adat Ali and Asaf Jah. Modern writers are inclined to think that these men have been maligned by partisan contemporaries. Be the fault whose it may, just when there was a hope of seeing the invaders depart, the wretched Mohammad caused himself to be carried to the Persian camp in his palanquin, a scanty retinue accompanying him.

Out to meet him came the Persian—a stoutly built man, over six feet high, burnt brown by exposure to all weathers. The Emperors sat side by side in the place of honour, and Nadir presented the ceremonial cup of coffee to his guest with his own hands, saying, "Since you have done me the honour to come here, you are my brother, and may you remain happy in the empire of Hindustan."

So much conventional courtesy demanded, then the real spirit of the man broke out: "What a ruler in Islam are you!" he cried in his rough, rude voice; "you not only pay tribute to those dirty Hindu savages in the south, but when an invader comes against you, as I have done, you give up the game without a single honest struggle!"

After this outbreak Nadir withdrew to another tent to arrange the terms of peace, while his servants spread the feast which Eastern hospitality and royal etiquette alike required of him. When he came back, Mohammad, surrounded by the Persian officers, was making as good a meal as Louis XVI. among the *sans-culottes.*

"What a man is this who can bear thus easily the loss of power and liberty!" scoffed the Persian, in angry contempt.

But Mohammad cared for nothing else so long as there should be peace in his days, and he readily agreed to all Nadir's conditions—which, indeed, he was in no position to refuse. The Persian army was to rest from its labours within the walls of Delhi, while Nadir collected an indemnity for the trouble and expense to which he had been put in coming thus far.

Side by side, the Persian on a horse, the Moghul on an elephant, the two Emperors entered Delhi, and were lodged in the red fort, Nadir making his headquarters in the Diwan-i-Khas, where Shah Jahan's inscription still mocked the fallen son of Timur: "If a Paradise be on the face of the earth, it is this, it is this, it is this." He was a stern disciplinarian, and for two days his

Nadir Shah.

army durst no more than eye the riches about them, and the quaking townsfolk went unmolested.

Then a false rumour flew that he had been murdered by command of the Moghul Emperor. It is said that the alarm was caused by a woman guard in the harem, who discharged her matchlock: whether this be true, or whether it be an instance of the almost invariable habit of the sons of Adam to put the blame for every disaster upon some woman, the citizens of Delhi rose out of sheer blind terror and fell upon the Persians. "About midnight the officers of Nadir Shah, frightened and trembling," told their master that three thousand of his men had been put to death. "The Shah, angry at being roused, said, 'The men of my army are maliciously accusing the people of Hindustan, so that I should kill a number of them, and give the signal for plunder.' But when this information was repeated over and over again to the Shah, he seized his sword, and he himself made that sword a standard, and issued the order for slaughter."

"From that night till five hours of the following day, man, woman, animal, and every living thing which came under the eyes of the Persians, was put to the sword, and from every house ran a stream of blood." The Chandni Chauk where the jewellers sat, the Dariba Bazaar, and the buildings round the Jama Masjid were set on fire; and through nine fearful hours of carnage and destruction Nadir watched from the little "Golden Mosque" overlooking the Bazaar—close to what is now the police station. There he sat, glowering, his protruding under-lip thrust forward, as Mohammad Shah and the nobles of Delhi came before him with downcast eyes. "What would you? Speak!" thundered the Persian. Mohammad answered with a burst of tears, and an entreaty for mercy upon his unhappy people.

So thoroughly did the terrible Nadir keep his men in hand that the massacre ceased instantly when he spoke the word. Many thousands (some say twenty, some a hundred thousand) lay dead amidst their burning homes. "For a long time the streets remained strewn with corpses, as the walks of a garden with dead flowers and leaves. The town was reduced to ashes, and had the appearance of a plain consumed with fire."

The soldiers having thus taken "the rest and refreshment" that they needed, their commander began to collect the indemnity. He seized upon all the royal jewels, "many of which were unrivalled in beauty by any in the world," and the contents of the treasury. "In short, the accumulated wealth of three hundred and forty-eight years changed masters in a moment." The great nobles were made to redeem their property by heavy fines, and contributions of elephants, jewels, and whatever else pleased the conqueror's fancy. Then a formal inventory of all the property in Delhi was taken, and each man was assessed according to his means. "Now commenced the work of spoliation, watered by the tears of the people." Many slew themselves to escape torture or disgrace. "Sleep and rest forsook the city. In every chamber and house was heard the cry of affliction."

Having wrung the uttermost farthing from the citizens, married his son to a daughter of the Emperor, and made a treaty whereby he was recognised as lord of all the country west of the Indus, Nadir Shah returned to Persia. Before he went, with his own hand he invested Mohammad with all the trappings of royalty, and bade the nobles of Delhi serve their Emperor loyally or expect punishment from himself. He carried off with him the most skilful workmen and artisans of Delhi, and other plunder to the value of eighty millions of pounds, besides what each man had been able to purvey for himself. "His

Majesty bestowed on Nadir Shah, with his own munificent hand, as a parting present, the Peacock Throne"—never again to be used by the House of Timur after the terrible day on which Emperor and Shah had sat side by side upon it and drunk coffee together after the massacre had ceased. Doubtless the Emperor felt that it was a small price to pay for seeing the last of his conqueror.

But though Nadir Shah came not again, he had shown the way to Delhi, and there were others ready to glean where he had reaped. Once again invaders came from Ghor and Ghazni, as in the days of Mahmud the Image-breaker. When Nadir was assassinated in his tent by his own followers in 1747, his empire fell asunder, and the southern portion yielded to an Afghan chief, Ahmad Shah Daurani, who in the following year marched down into the Punjab. Here he was met by a Moghul army, and to the surprise of all concerned suffered such a defeat that he was thankful to turn his back upon Hindustan for the time. During the campaign, the Nizam's cousin, the Vezir of Delhi, was killed by an Afghan round-shot while he prayed in his tent, and the loss broke the heart of the Emperor, whose insensibility in former years had amazed the Persians. "The staff of my old age is broken, is snapped: no such faithful servant can I find again." He fell dead among the cushions of his despoiled throne, an Emperor reduced to such mean estate that his coffin was an old clock-case, found in the palace, over which was flung a tattered cloth from the harem.

First one titular Emperor succeeded him, and then another—feeble creatures, who each reigned for a few years, and was then murdered by a too powerful subject. It was in the days of the first, Ahmad, that serious trouble arose with the Afghans of Rohilkhund, that race for whom Macaulay and Burke expressed a sympathy that would certainly have been chilled at the fountain-head if either politician had ever experienced their methods. These thieves and ruffians had risen to such a pitch of insolence that the Nawab of Oudh was fain to call the Marathas to his help. The empire was little the better for the change of spoilers; the new allies gave a temporary check to the Rohillas, but indemnified themselves for their trouble by levying *chauth* everywhere.

Ahmad Shah returned once more to India, and had to be bought off with the cession of the Punjab. This took effect merely for a short time; in 1756 he was in Delhi, where his troops repeated the horrors of Nadir Shah's sack, and removed anything of value that had escaped the notice of the Persians.

In 1759 he returned to India for the fourth time, and his approach was the signal for the murder of the Emperor Alamgir II. Delhi was sacked again, this time by Rohillas and Pathans in conjunction, who slaughtered and spoiled till they were driven from the ruins of the city by the stench of the decaying corpses.

The heir-apparent was a fugitive, the throne was empty,—who was to be master of the little tract of country round Delhi and Agra, the sole remainder of the empire of the Great Moghul? The withered trunk had fallen, and the twigs had begun an independent growth. The Deccan, like the empire, had broken into numerous little states, the chief of which was governed by the Nawab of Arcot; all were nominally vassal to the Nizam of Hyderabad, who sometimes found them more than he could control. The descendant of Sa'adat Ali was now the sovereign of Oudh and Allahabad, far greater and more powerful than the Emperor whose viceroy he was supposed to be. Afghans held the Punjab, Gujarat and Malwa had been seized by the Marathas. Of European powers, the day of Portugal was over and that of Holland drawing to its close. The French East India Company was paramount in Southern India, and both Hyderabad and Arcot made appeal to the Governor of Pondicherry in the case of disputed succession.

The English East India Company was of far less importance, though it had extended its influence since the days of Sir Thomas Roe. Bombay had been gained by the marriage of Charles II. with the Portuguese princess, who, abused on all sides for her religion or for her "beggarliness," brought a more valuable dowry to her husband's country than any queen-consort before or after her. Fort St George had been established in 1639, in the time of Shah Jahan. The Emperor Farukh Siyar's only claim to remembrance is that in 1715, at the request of the Scotch surgeon, William Hamilton, he granted to the English factory at Calcutta the possession of lands extending for ten miles along either bank of the Hugli. Hamilton, bidden to name his own reward for curing the Emperor of a tumour, had, like Gabriel Boughton, asked nothing for himself,

In the last agonies of the Moghul Empire, Bengal had drifted so far apart that what befell there seemed to concern Delhi not at all. It could be nothing to the Emperor, when the

Nawab of Bengal attacked Calcutta in 1756, and shut up his European prisoners in a space of twenty feet square, or when, in the following year, a tall, raw-boned youth, Robert Clive, avenged the victims of the "Black Hole" on the battlefield of Plassey.

It seemed a question whether the death-blow to the empire should come from Central India or from the north—from the Marathas or the Afghans. The Marathas were no longer ruled by one hand, whether the hand were that of the negligible Raja of Satara or that of his Peshwa, Balaji Rao, son of that Baji who had vowed to plant their banner at Attock; they had split up into many little states under various rulers, such as the Gaikwar of Baroda—Holkar who had possessed himself of half Malwa—and Sindhia of Gwalior, whose ancestor had carried the Peshwa's slippers. All for the moment were united—nominally for the faith of the Hindus, in reality with intent to take what they could from Delhi before other spoilers had stripped it bare. Their leader was the Peshwa's cousin and minister, Sadasheo Rao, commonly known by his title of "the Bhao," who came to war with silk-lined tents and richly caparisoned horses, and officers arrayed in cloth of gold, so that his army looked like that of the Moghuls in the hour of their glory. No longer depending on the light-armed irregular horsemen that had often scattered the troops of Delhi in flight, he also brought a park of artillery, and a force of drilled infantry under the command of an officer trained by Monsieur de Bussy, the French general. On their way northwards they were joined by Suraj Mal, leader of the Jat army.

Delhi was sacked again of what little remained to it; the flowered silver ceiling of the Audience Hall was torn down, and thrown into the melting-pot, while Ahmad Shah Daurani waited on the frontier of Oudh, unable to move in the heavy rains. It was not till October that he crossed the Jumna, and placed himself between Delhi and the army of the Marathas who were entrenched behind a ditch fifty feet wide and twelve feet deep, on the plain of Panipat. Their allies, the Jats and the Rajputs, had deserted them, but there were more left than Ahmad Shah would find it easy to tackle, even with the help of Najib, the chief of the Rohillas, and the Nawab of Oudh, who had joined him in this struggle of Mohammedan against Hindu.

The Afghan made no attempt to storm the position; with fewer foot than the Marathas, and only forty guns as against their two hundred, he knew that he must play a waiting game. So he encamped "at the distance of twice the range of a cannon-ball," and through the short winter days and long winter nights of the next two months watched from his red tent outside the defences.

The opposing hosts had changed characters; the Marathas sat within their entrenched position, protected by their artillery, while the Afghan horsemen hovered about the country cutting off supplies, and falling upon the detachments who sallied out to bring grass and forage, until none dared venture from the camp.

Though skirmishes took place daily, the Afghan officers pleaded in vain to be allowed to advance in force. Ahmad Shah knew that hunger and privation and close confinement were all fighting for him against the undisciplined Maratha hordes, and he waited, while the Bhao vainly attempted negotiation, offering to accept any conditions of peace that might please the Shah. All the Shah's allies were ready to make terms, with one exception—Najib the leader of the Rohillas. With brutal common-sense, he maintained that the Marathas would never be bound by agreements. "Oaths are not chains; they are only words,—things that will never bind the enemy when once he has escaped from danger. By one effort we can get this thorn out of our sides." Ahmad Shah, to whom he appealed, expressed a profound disbelief in Maratha penitence; now that there was a chance of making an end of these pests, he would not forego it.

It was the night of January 5, 1761, and the Maratha leaders, who had not tasted food for two days, were assembled in their great durbar tent, shivering with cold, and demanding, since death was inevitable, to be led forth to die sword in hand. With perfect composure the Bhao distributed the pan and betel which are the signal for dismissing an assembly, and all swore to make a sally an hour before daybreak and drive away the enemy, or perish where they stood. Together they consumed the last morsel of food left in the camp; they dyed faces and hands yellow with turmeric; they left one end of their turbans to hang loose, in token that they were ready for death.

An hour before the cold January dawn had broken they poured forth from the camp. Until noon the battle swayed to and fro, like all battles, "with confused noise and garments rolled in blood." The air was rent with shouts of "Har, Mahadeo!" and "Din! din!" and the dust from beneath the hoofs of the cavalry darkened the sky, so that no man could see the face of him who stood at his side. So fierce was the Maratha onslaught that Ahmad Shah sent word for the ladies of his household to mount swift steeds and be ready to gain "the verge of safety and the nook of security" if his men were borne down.

At the critical moment, when the battle was neither won nor lost, the Shah sent out his reserve to rally those who fled, and cut down those who refused to turn back. Still fortune wavered, and the Marathas were not yet overpowered, when Mulhar Rao Holkar, having received a message from the Bhao, turned and left the field; the Gaikwar followed him. Then the fight became a rout and the rout a grim butchery. The Bhao, who had been seen to descend from his elephant and mount his Arab charger just before Holkar's flight, disappeared in the eddy; his body was found afterwards beneath a heap of dead, so gashed and mangled that it was recognised only by three pearls that the spoilers had not stripped from it. Sindhia escaped by hard riding, with a wound that lamed him for life. Thousands were killed upon the field; the dead bodies lay strewn shoulder to shoulder all the way from Panipat to Delhi. Many prisoners were taken; the women and children were kept as slaves, the men ranged in line and given a few grains of parched corn and a few drops of water in the palms of their hands, after which their heads were cut off and piled in heaps outside the Afghan tents.

The Peshwa was moving down to the help of the Bhao, of whose plight he had heard, when, as he crossed the Nerbada in the middle of January, he met a runner who gave him a letter. He opened it and read the words, "Two pearls have been dissolved, twenty-seven gold mohurs lost, and of the silver and copper the total cannot be cast up."

Then he knew what had befallen the Bhao's army, and from that day he pined away until he died. The power of the Marathas was broken; not a family among them but mourned kinsmen missing or slain. The wolf-pack would rend and spoil and devour for many years to come, until a stronger hand than that of the Afghans curbed them; but yet never again would they be strong as when they met fate on the plain where the invaders of Hindustan have met it from the beginning.

Ahmad Shah returned to his own country; the Moghul Empire of Delhi had ceased to exist except in name.

EPILOGUE

ON THE ROAD TO DELHI

EPILOGUE.

ON THE ROAD TO DELHI.

THE Maratha power had been scotched but not killed, and a new and terrible adversary was rising in the south, where Hyder Ali had usurped the throne of Mysore.

There was a miserable period of chaos and anarchy. A Rohilla chief sacked Delhi and blinded the Emperor, Shah Alam II., perpetrating such hideous cruelties upon his family as cannot be written. Blind and helpless, the Great Moghul passed into the hands of the Marathas, who were overrunning all the country. Between war, famine, and robbery, Hindustan was gradually becoming depopulated at the close of the eighteenth century, and communication between the few villages that still existed was frequently cut off by the wild beasts that infested the highway. Save in Rajputana, scarcely any reigning family in India "could boast more than twenty-five years of independent and definite political existence."[1]

All over the land Hindu and Muslim looked with longing to the one power strong enough to quench all these disorders and give peace in their time.

"The goodness of the English is beyond all bounds," wrote a Muslim chronicler about the year 1764, "and it is on account of their own and their servants' honesty that they are so fortunate and wealthy.

"They are a wonderful nation, endowed with equity and justice," writes another, a few years latter. "May they be always happy and continue to administer justice."

"When will you take this country?" a faquir asked Mountstuart Elphinstone in 1801. "The country wants you. The Hindus are villains. When will you take the country?"

It was a question asked over and over again; but even when the battle of Buxar (1764) had settled the fate of Bengal, and the storming of Seringapatam (1799) had made it possible to effect the pacification of Southern India, and the treaty of Basain (1802) had decided that the Maratha Confederacy was no longer to spoil and ravage a distracted country, no new ruler was yet proclaimed in Delhi.

[1] Sir A. Lyall.

For in Delhi a poor old man, whom Lord Lake had rescued from the Marathas, sat beneath a tattered canopy and called himself by the titles of the bygone Emperors who had made Delhi great. At no time of his life had he been ruler of more than "from Delhi to Palam"[1]—as a popular couplet ran, but he was the representative of the Great Moghul.

Two more after him sat in the despoiled palace, in squalor and poverty, unable even to keep order within the red walls of the Fort. Then came the time when Englishmen, encamped along the rocky spur of the Aravali hills overlooking the city, chafed in impotence and wrath through long summer days, because it was still a far cry to Delhi.

It was in September 1857 that the Sappers and Miners opened the Kashmir Gate, and the last of the sons of Timur ceased to reign, even in name. It was in December 1911 that an English king showed himself to the crowds who thronged the city, upon the wall where the Moghul Emperors were wont to stand, and once more made Delhi the chief city of India as in the days of old.

[1] Palam is a village less than eleven miles from Delhi.